CHRISTIAN QUESTIONS

VOLUMES 1–3

VOLUME 1: WHAT IS PRAYER?
VOLUME 2: WHAT ARE THE SPIRITUAL GIFTS?
VOLUME 3: WHAT IS FAITH?

J. D. MYERS

CHRISTIAN QUESTIONS, VOLUMES 1-3
© 2019 by J. D. Myers

Published by Redeeming Press
Dallas, OR 97338
RedeemingPress.com

ISBN: 978-1-939992-69-7 (Paperback)
ISBN: 978-1-939992-70-3 (Mobi Kindle)
ISBN: 978-1-939992-71-0 (ePub)

Learn more about J. D. Myers by visiting RedeemingGod.com

All rights reserved. No part of this publication may be reproduced, stored in or introduced into a retrieval system, or transmitted, in any form, or by any means—electronic, mechanical, photocopying, recording, or otherwise—except for brief quotations, without the prior written permission of both the copyright owner and the publisher of this book.

Unless otherwise noted, all Scripture quotations are taken from the New King James Version˚. Copyright © 1982 by Thomas Nelson, Inc. Used by permission. All rights reserved.

Scripture quotations marked "NIV" are from The Holy Bible, New International Version˚, NIV˚ Copyright © 1973, 1978, 1984, 2011 by Biblica, Inc.˚ Used by permission. All rights reserved worldwide.

Scripture quotations marked "NASB" are taken from the New American Standard Bible˚, Copyright © 1960, 1962, 1963, 1968, 1971, 1972, 1973, 1975, 1977, 1995 by The Lockman Foundation. Used by permission. All rights reserved.

Cover Design by Taylor Myers
TaylorGraceGraphics.com

JOIN JEREMY MYERS AND LEARN MORE
Take Bible and theology courses by joining Jeremy at
RedeemingGod.com/join/

Receive updates about free books, discounted books,
and new books by joining Jeremy at
RedeemingGod.com/reader-group/

INTRODUCTION TO THE "CHRISTIAN QUESTIONS" BOOK SERIES

This "Christian Questions" book series provides down-to-earth answers to everyday questions. The series is based on questions that people have asked me over the years through my website, podcast, and online discipleship group at RedeemingGod.com. Since thousands of people visit the site every single day, I get scores of questions emailed in to me each month from readers around the world. Many of the questions tend to be around various "hot topic" issues like homosexuality, violence, and politics. Other questions, however, focus more on how to understand a particular Bible passage or theological issue. For example, I receive hundreds of questions a year about the unpardonable sin in Matthew 12.

I love receiving these questions, and I do my best to answer them. But after I answer the same question five or ten times, I realize that it might be better if I had a ready-made and easily-accessible resource I could invite people to read. This also provides the reader with a better explanation than I can give in a short email. For people who want the *full* experience, there are also online courses available for many of these questions at RedeemingGod.com/courses.

So the goal of this "Christian Questions" book series is to answer the questions that people send in to me. Below is the current list of books in the "Christian Questions" series. Most of these are not yet published, but I include the list to show you where the series is headed.

What is Prayer? (Now Available)
What are the Spiritual Gifts? (Now Available)
What is Faith? (Now Available)
What is Hell? (Now Available)
How Can I Study the Bible? (Coming in 2019)
Why is the world so messed up?
Can God forgive my sin?
What is the unforgivable sin?
What is baptism?
What is the church?
What is repentance?
How can I evangelize?
Can I lose eternal life?
Why did Jesus have to die?
Should Christians keep the Sabbath?
What is demon possession?
How can I gain freedom from sin?
What is election and predestination?
Does God love me?
Why did God give the law?
Does God really want blood sacrifices?
What is sin?
What is the best Bible translation?
Can I trust the Bible?

If you have a question about Scripture, theology, or Christian living that you would like answered, you may submit it through the contact form at RedeemingGod.com/about/ or join my online discipleship group at RedeemingGod.com/join/.

Other Books by Jeremy Myers
Nothing but the Blood of Jesus
The Atonement of God
The Re-Justification of God: A Study of Rom 9:10-24
Adventures in Fishing (for Men)
Christmas Redemption
Why You Have Not Committed the Unforgivable Sin
The Gospel According to Scripture (Forthcoming)
The Gospel Dictionary (Forthcoming)
Tough Texts on the Gospel (Forthcoming)
The Bible Mirror (Forthcoming)
The Grace Commentary on Jonah (Forthcoming)
Nin: A Novel (Forthcoming)
Studies on Genesis 1 (Forthcoming)
Studies on Genesis 2–4 (Forthcoming)
God's Blueprints for Church Growth (Forthcoming)
The Armor of God: Ephesians 6:10-20 (Forthcoming)

Books in the *Close Your Church for Good* Series
Preface: Skeleton Church
Vol. 1: The Death and Resurrection of the Church
Vol. 2: Put Service Back into the Church Service
Vol. 3: Church is More than Bodies, Bucks, & Bricks
Vol. 4: Dying to Religion and Empire
Vol. 5: Cruciform Pastoral Leadership (Forthcoming)

All books are available at Amazon.com
Learn about each title at the end of this book

TABLE OF CONTENTS

Intro to the "Christian Questions" Books 3

WHAT IS PRAYER?

Foreword 21
How to Talk with God 23
    What Prayer is Not 24
    What Prayer Is 26
    Praying Like Moses 28
    Just Talk to God 29
    Conclusion 30
What Should You Pray For? 33
    The Disciples' Prayer 35
    Our Father in heaven 36
    Hallowed be Your Name 37
    Your kingdom come, Your will be done 37
    Give us this day our daily bread 38
    And forgive us our debts, as we forgive our debtors ... 39
    Do not lead us into temptation, ... 40
    The Disciple's Prayer is Dangerous 41

How Did Jesus Pray? 43
The Lord's Prayer 44
The Structure of the Prayer 44
The Posture of Prayer 45
The Prayer Requests 47
Jesus Conversed with God 48

How to Receive Answers To Prayer 51
Pray According to the Will of God 52
Pray in Jesus' Name 53
How Prayer Works 55
How God Answers Prayer 58

10 Dangerous Prayers 63
1. Teach me Humility 64
2. Teach me Patience 64
3. Teach me How to Forgive 65
4. Teach me the Truth 65
5. Lead me Wherever You Want me to Go 67
6. Help me Understand the Plight of the Poor 68
7. Make me More Like Jesus 69
8. Give me More Faith 70
9. Give me Victory over Sin and Temptation 70
10. Please Help my Annoying Neighbor Come to Faith 71
Conclusion 71

Praying Powerful Prayers 73
The Posture of Prayer 74
The Person of Prayer 75
The Petitions of Prayer 75
To Do What Cannot Be Done 76

    To Know What Cannot Be Known 78

    To Be Filled With What You Cannot Be Filled 80

    Praying Impossible Prayers..81

    Can I Get an "Amen"?!..82

What About Unanswered Prayers? 85

    It is Not a Lack of Faith..86

    It is a Love for Freedom 87

    God Stays and Prays With Us 91

Other Questions About Prayer 93

    Can I pray when I'm angry at God? 93

    What about prayer for healing? 97

    What about praying in tongues?...98

    What about praying Scripture?...98

    How Does God talk to us in prayer? 99

    Do I need to say "Amen" at the end of my prayers?..............101

    Do I need to pray over my meals? 103

    Do I need to use words in my prayers? 104

Learn More about Prayer.. 107

    Take a Course on Prayer...107

    Receive Emails on Prayer 108

    Additional Resources on Prayer..108

    My Podcast on Jonah 2.. 108

    My Book and Course on the Armor of God 109

    My Book and Course on *Cruciform Pastoral Leadership*.......... 109

WHAT ARE THE SPIRITUAL GIFTS?

A Parable 115

Why Did God Give Spiritual Gifts? 119
- Edification of the Body 119
- Evangelism of the World 120
- Exaltation of God 121
- Conclusion 121

What Are the Spiritual Gifts? 123
- The Use of the Spiritual Gifts 124
- The List of Spiritual Gifts 126

How Can I Know My Spiritual Gift? 137
- Self-Analysis 137
- Seek the Input of Others 138
- Spiritual Void Analysis 139
- Spiritual Gift Analysis 140
- Serve and Experiment 141

Are Some Gifts Better Than Others? 143

The Dangers of the Spiritual Gifts 147
- Two General Dangers 147
- The Specific Dangers 150

Have Some of the Gifts Ceased? 161

What About Tongues? 165
- Tongues in the Old Testament 165
- Tongues are Human Languages 167
- Tongues as a Sign of the Kingdom 168
- Tongues and 1 Corinthians 14 170
- Are Tongues for Today? 170

Embrace Your Gifts 173
- The Frustration of Conformity 173

    Be Who You Are...177

    Embrace Your Insanity 178

Spiritual Gifts Inventory 181

WHAT IS FAITH?

Acknowledgements.. 225

Foreword 227

Author's Preface.. 231

Introduction 233

Defining Faith 237

    The Definition of "Faith" 239

    Faith in the Promises of God 244

    Faith is Reasonable Certainty...246

    How to Know You Believe...248

    How to Know You Have Eternal Life 250

    Believe in Jesus for Eternal Life 252

    Conclusion 254

How Faith Works 259

    The Giant Excel Spreadsheet 262

    The Spreadsheet at Work...267

    1. There are no Degrees of Faith.....................................270

    2. There are Countless Truths we Can Believe 271

    3. Some Things are Easy to Believe; Others are Hard............273

    4. We Cannot Choose to Believe Anything....................276

    5. When A Belief Changes, Other Beliefs Also Change 281

    Conclusion 285

Six Misconceptions About Faith 287

    Faith is Not a Blind Leap 288

    Faith is Not "All or Nothing" 291

    Faith is Not Hope 292

    Faith is Not Trust 294

    Faith is Not an Action 299

    Faith is Not a Gift 302

    Conclusion 310

Five Clarifications About Faith 311

    Faith Comes by Hearing 312

    Faith is Mental Assent 314

    Faith Like a Child 318

    Faith and "the Faith" 323

    Faith and Faithfulness 324

    Conclusion 328

Understanding Scriptures on Faith 329

    Genesis 12 and 15 329

    Matthew 6:30 336

    Matthew 8:10 (Matt 15:28; Luke 7:9) 344

    Matthew 17:20 (Luke 17:6) 347

    Luke 12:42-48 (Matt 24:45-51) 351

    John 3:16 354

    John 6:28-29 355

    John 11:25-26 357

    John 20:31 361

    Acts 6:7 362

    Acts 13:48 363

    Romans 3:21-26 365

    Romans 4:4-5 367

    Romans 10:17 367
    2 Corinthians 13:5..368
    Ephesians 2:8-9 370
    Colossians 1:23..372
    1 Timothy 5:8 373
    James 2:14-26...374
    Conclusion 382

Conclusion **383**

Afterword **385**

About J. D. Myers... **389**
    Join Jeremy Myers and Learn More 389

CHRISTIAN QUESTIONS
VOLUME 1

WHAT IS PRAYER?

HOW TO PRAY TO GOD THE WAY YOU TALK TO A FRIEND

J. D. MYERS

WHAT IS PRAYER?
How to Pray to God the Way You Talk to a Friend
© 2017 by J. D. Myers

Published by Redeeming Press
Dallas, OR 97338
RedeemingPress.com

ISBN: 978-1-939992-50-5 (Paperback)
ISBN: 978-1-939992-51-2 (Mobi Kindle)
ISBN: 978-1-939992-52-9 (ePub)

Learn more about J. D. Myers by visiting RedeemingGod.com

All rights reserved. No part of this publication may be reproduced, stored in or introduced into a retrieval system, or transmitted, in any form, or by any means—electronic, mechanical, photocopying, recording, or otherwise—except for brief quotations, without the prior written permission of both the copyright owner and the publisher of this book.

All Scripture quotations are taken from the New King James Version®. Copyright © 1982 by Thomas Nelson, Inc. Used by permission. All rights reserved.

Cover Design by Taylor Myers
TaylorGraceGraphics.com

JOIN JEREMY MYERS AND LEARN MORE
Take Bible and theology courses by joining Jeremy at
RedeemingGod.com/join/

Receive updates about free books, discounted books,
and new books by joining Jeremy at
RedeemingGod.com/reader-group/

TAKE THE ONLINE COURSE ABOUT PRAYER

There is an online course related to this book.
The audio lessons and downloads in the course
will help you learn more about prayer
and might also serve as a good small group Bible study.
Learn more at RedeemingGod.com/Courses/

The course is normally $197, but you can
take it for free by joining the Discipleship Group at
RedeemingGod.com/join/

*This book is dedicated to
a close friend who is always there
to listen when I am happy, angry, or sad,
a confidant who never breaks trust
no matter how dark the secret I share,
and a counselor who never judges
my deepest doubt, sin, or fear.*

This book is dedicated to God.

Thank you, Father, for listening, loving, and never leaving.

FOREWORD

I remember when I was new to the Christian faith. I was unable to wrap my head around the sacred practice of prayer. Others had God on speed-dial while God's number always seemed to be changing for me. Over the years, doubts and questions kept piling up.

I didn't understand why we had to be so loud. Is God deaf? Does God consider us more spiritual if we are passionate and yell our prayers to Him? I didn't understand why we repeated God's name over and over again as if we were going into a trance-like state. Or did God forget His name?

I didn't understand what posture I needed to take for God to accept my prayers. Would God hear me better if I were on my knees? Would God like my prayers more, or even be fonder of me as His child, if I raised my hands?

And why did friends' prayers for God to give them parking spots at malls and convenience stores get answered, but not mine for my ailing and addicted mother? Is God cruelly selective in answering prayer?

I had tons of questions. Those haunting questions kept me stuck, stagnant, and stale in my prayer life. Where was J. D. Myers' book *What is Prayer?* when I needed it?

I consider it an incredible privilege and honor to write a few words in support of this superbly written and enlightening book. J. D. Myers tackles the complexity and conundrum of prayer with a pastoral and prophetic heart, a brilliant and wise mind, and a courageous spirit obviously in touch and in tune with both God and God's people.

The good news is there is no conundrum in how to pray to God—at least not anymore. J. D. Myers sheds the religious and superstitious garb off of prayer and makes a simple, provocative, and liberating claim: Prayer is talking to God as you would talk to a friend.

I highly recommend this book not only to new Christians who want to learn how to pray but also to the experienced and inquisitive God-lover who still has many questions. Thank you, J. D., for such a gift to the Christian community!

Mark Karris
Author of *Divine Echoes: Reconciling Prayer with the Uncontrolling Love of God*
MarkGregoryKarris.com

CHAPTER 1

HOW TO TALK WITH GOD

Whether you pray or don't pray, whether you act or don't act, our relationship is still there—and ultimately that's all that counts. "But if you can manage it," God adds, "it will be a whole lot more fun if we can keep the conversation going."
—Robert Farrar Capon
Health, Money, & Love

A young pastor fresh out of seminary was leading his first service in his new church out in the country. Due to many years of studying Scripture and a head filled with theological knowledge, he viewed himself to be quite spiritual while the uneducated members of his congregation were somewhat backwards. So he decided that during his first service he would show the people what *real* prayer sounded like. He wanted to show them how spiritual he truly was. So after welcoming the congregation, he invited them all to bow their heads for the opening prayer. Then he launched into a long, eloquent, flowery prayer, full of big theological terms and allusions to Scripture. As this prayer went on and on, and as both children and adults started to fidget and look around at each other, one wee little woman in the choir decided to take the matter in hand. When the pastor paused to take a breath, she hollered out, "Jes' call 'im Father, an' ask 'im fer somethin'!"

This is a humorous story, but sadly, the pastor's prayer far too often reflects what goes on in Christian churches and Bible studies around the world. More tragically still, most churches don't have a brave little ol' lady in the choir to call out the pastor on his super-spiritual, self-righteous prayer. So people go through life not knowing how to pray.

Many Christians don't know what to say in prayer. They don't know how to address God, whether or not to use "King James English" with "Thee's" and "Thou's," how long the prayer should be, and what sort of prayer requests to include. When they hear the "professionals" pray, such as the pastors, priests, and seminary professors, they think to themselves, "There is no way I could ever sound like that when I pray!" And since they think they don't know how to pray, they just don't pray. Even among those who do pray, there are many bad habits which get picked up along the way.

WHAT PRAYER IS NOT

Most people learn to pray by listening to others pray. We learn how to pray, not by thinking about prayer or learning from Scripture about prayer, but by watching and listening to others pray. And frankly, we learn some very bad prayer practices this way.

For example, when some people pray, they seem to think that prayer requires a spiritual tone of voice, a new set of words, a sing-songy cadence and rhythm, with a repetition of certain words or phrases. So it is not uncommon to hear people pray this way:

Father God in heaven, holy art thou above all things, and thy name, Father God, is worthy to be praised, Father God. Hallelujah! Praise Your name, Jesus!

Oh, Father God, Lord God, Holy Jesus, we come before you today, as your children, Father God, to beseech you with our many needs, Father God. But before we do so, oh Holy Father in Heaven, Father God, we ask thee to forgive us for our many sins. We have failed thee in so many ways, Father God, so that as the prophet Isaiah says, all our righteous works are as filthy rags before thee, Father God!

> *And so we thank thee for sending thy holy Son, Jesus Christ, Father God, the Lord of the universe and the master of all, Father God, the Lamb who was slain before the foundation of the world, Father God, to die for our sins on that wretched cross, oh holy Father God. Hallelujah!—Praise Jesus—So that we might be forgiven of our many trespasses against you, Oh Holy Father God …*

And the prayer goes on this way for many minutes.

Is this prayer? Many seem to think so, since this type of praying is rather common in some Christian churches. This sort of cadence praying will differ from church to church and from person to person, so that there will be different rhythms that get followed and words that get repeated, but the basic approach is the same. I have heard some people start throwing in biblical Hebrew or Greek words, while others switch back and forth between English and speaking in tongues. But ask yourself: Would you ever talk to anyone else in such a fashion? If not, then why do we talk to God this way? Do we think this is what He expects or demands?

Occasionally, people will start talking to Satan during these prayers as well:

> *Father, we thank you for your presence here today, and for the fellowship of the saints we feel in this room, and Satan, we cast you out in the name of Jesus! Flee this place because we are washed in the blood of the Lamb! And God, may the words that we sing and the prayers of our hearts be holy unto you this day. Get thee behind, me, Satan! So we pray, God, for Pastor Tom as he brings the Word today …*

When I hear prayers like this, I often wonder who the person is praying to, God or Satan? I sometimes wonder if God gets frustrated as well that we are allowing Satan to butt into a conversation we are supposed to be having with God. God is probably saying, "Satan's gone! Now talk to Me; not him."

Sometimes the bad habits we have in prayer are not so much about the words we say, but about the proper posture of prayer. For example, it is not uncommon for churches to teach, especially to children, that the proper way to pray is with head bowed, eyes closed, and hands folded. This, of course, helps keep the children from fidgeting and talking during prayer, but we must ask what exactly we are telling children about God if we teach them that in order to talk to God, they have to sit and act a certain way.

There are numerous other types of bad habit prayers, and maybe none of the examples above match your own prayer patterns. But even if you do not pray the way I have written above, listen to yourself pray sometime, and ask yourself, "Where did I learn how to pray this way?" Why am I saying these certain words? Why am I changing my voice? Why am I bowing my head and folding my hands? Why do I pray to Jesus or to the Holy Spirit? Why do I repeat this certain phrase over and over?" Asking these sorts of questions will help you discover any bad prayer habits of your own.

The goal, of course, is not just to discover bad prayer habits, but to break these habits and learn to really pray as God wants and desires. Thankfully, learning to pray properly is quite simple. It all begins by simply understanding what prayer is.

WHAT PRAYER IS

When we come to understand prayer, we are able to almost instantly break most of our bad habits about prayer. When we truly understand how to pray, most of our questions and uncertainty about how to pray simply fade away. When we understand what prayer is, we lose our fear of praying and discover that we already know how to pray.

So what is prayer?

I am not even going to try to get technical and fancy with my explanation. Being a Bible scholar, I was tempted to break out the Greek and the Hebrew and pull out my big stack of books, but that would then defeat the purpose of showing you how simple prayer is, and how you can have confidence that you are praying the "right" way. So in trying to answer the question, "What is prayer?" the simplest and most practical answer is best.

So what is prayer? Prayer is simply talking to God as you would talk to anyone else. Prayer is having a conversation with God. If you know how to talk to people, then you also know how to talk to God. That's it! If you want to put the book down now, you can. If you know how to have a conversation, then you know how to pray. There is nothing magical or mysterious about prayer. Prayer is nothing more than talking to God as you would talk to a friend.

I suppose I should qualify that last statement. Although prayer is "nothing more" than talking to God, it is certainly nothing less! I don't want you to miss how shocking the gift of prayer actually is. Prayer allows you to talk to *God* as you would talk to a friend! You can talk to God more easily and more readily than you can talk to the President of the United States. Prayer allows you to start up a conversation with God, the creator and ruler of the universe. There is no idea more shocking. That God would be so friendly and make Himself so available to us is amazing.

I hope that this truth doesn't make you more nervous about prayer, but rather more amazed. God has made Himself available to you all the time about anything. You do not need a priestly mediator, or special words, or a holy language, or a spiritual frenzy in order for God to pay attention to you. All such things are *religious* trappings that do nothing but get in the way of actual communication with God.

Mark Karris has defined prayer similarly, and in his book on prayer, he writes this:

> Prayers are not magical incantations or secret coded messages wrapped in sacred energy. To pray simply means *to talk to God*. Try this thought experiment. Let's assume you have been praying for your ailing mom. Repeat this sentence out loud: "I have been *praying* that God heals my mom." Now say, "I have been *talking to* God about healing my mom." ... Simply substituting "praying" with "talking" has the potential to reduce thinking that views prayer as some magical incantation or other form of superstition while in-

creasing the relational component of prayer.[1]

PRAYING LIKE MOSES

It is quite common for Christians to be jealous of the relationship that Moses had with God. In Exodus 33:11, we are told that God spoke to Moses, as a man speaks to a friend. And we think, "Wow! Imagine having such a close relationship with God! It would be so nice to speak to God like I speak to one of my friends. I could tell Him anything. I could talk to Him at any time. I wouldn't have to worry about using the right words. How I long for this type of prayer!"

Guess what? You have it! The Bible doesn't tell us what kind of friendship Moses had with God so that we could be jealous of Moses, but instead to show us what kind of friendship all of us have with God, if we simply take advantage of it. This is exactly what the Apostle John writes in 1 John 1:3. After basically saying, "Hey, I know all of you reading this wish that you could have been an Apostle, seeing what Jesus did, hearing Jesus teach, and hanging out with Jesus over a meal. Well, Jesus is my friend, and I am writing this letter to tell you how you and I can be friends. This means that if you are my friend, and I am Jesus' friend, then you are friends with Jesus too. Let me show you how." And John goes on to give some really practical advice on how to remain in fellowship (friendship) with Jesus, with God, and with one another. John ends his letter talking about prayer, where he basically says, "So just boldly talk to God. When you talk to God, He hears you, because He's your friend" (1 John 5:14).

Earlier in his letter, John wrote that we can love God and love others because God first loved us (1 John 4:7-8). By writing about how to love and be loved, John reveals that God is our friend, that God loves us, and that God wants to be in a close friendship with us. The greatest proof of

---

[1] Mark Gregory Karris, *Divine Echoes: Reconciling Prayer with the Uncontrolling Love of God* (Orange, CA: Quoir, 2018), 24. This book is not yet available, but Mark Karris was gracious enough to send me a pre-release version. As a result, the page numbers will likely be different than those cited here.

this, John says, is that God sent Jesus into the world (1 John 4:9-10). This means that you are so important to God, He is dying (literally) to talk with you. You don't need to be scared of talking to God, or nervous about what to say. Just talk to God the way you talk to a friend who thinks only good things about you.

JUST TALK TO GOD

Do you want to learn how to pray? Do you want to know what to pray for? Do you want to know how long to pray and where to pray? The answers to all such questions are answered by simply asking the same questions about a friend. Do you know how to talk to a friend? Of course. It's easy. It's natural. It's normal. Do you worry about what to talk to your friend about? No. That's one reason they are a friend. It is not even uncomfortable to sit in silence with a good friend. Do you worry about how long you should talk to a friend? No. Sometimes the conversations are long; sometimes they are short. The length of the conversation doesn't matter when you're talking to a friend. Do you worry about where you are going to talk to your friend, or how you are going to sit, or what words you should say? No! These are not of any concern when you are talking to a friend.

One more beautiful thing about talking to God as a friend is that He is always with you. He is always paying attention and always there. He is with you throughout the day, going where you go, doing what you do, and hanging out with you as you eat, as you work, as you drive. Even as you sleep! But not in a creepy way.

The bottom line is that if you want to learn how to pray, all you need to do is talk to God as you would talk to a friend. Tell God what is going on in your life. Keep Him in the loop. Are you angry? Tell God. Are you sad? Let Him know! Did you see something beautiful or experience something joyful? Thank Him! Do you have needs and concerns? Ask Him for advice or help. Did you just sin? Well, He saw it, and He is not mad, but He does want to talk to you about it. He may even want to laugh with you about your sin. I know that this goes against the traditional Christian view of sin as being a terrible affront to God, but when I talk to God about my sin, I have often found that rather than scowling at me with stern eyes and folded arms, He tends to have a sparkle in His eyes and a half-smile on His lips. He chuckles and says, "I can't believe you fell for that *again*!" Then we talk about what happened and how to avoid it in the future.

Do you see how no matter what is going on in your life, God wants to be part of it and communicate with you about it?

But what if you are the silent type? What if you are a person of few words? What if you have trouble talking to anyone about anything, including your friends? That's okay too! God is absolutely fine with just sitting in your presence as you do whatever it is you're doing. You might say five or ten words to Him throughout the day, but He's fine with that, because it is who you are (and who He made you to be). Of course, if, on the other hand, you are a chatterbox and can talk to anyone about anything, that's great with God. Go ahead and include Him in your unending stream of words. (Don't take offense! You know who you are! Embrace it!) Whoever you are and whatever your conversation style, include God in the mix and just talk to Him as you would anyone else. Since your relationship with God already exists, and since you are already walking with God through life, you might as well make your journey more enjoyable by talking with God along the way.

One word of caution though. As you go about your day, talking to God whenever, wherever, and about whatever, you might want to keep your prayer life as an inner dialogue. Otherwise, if you talk out loud to God while you shop at the supermarket or work at your job, people will think you're crazy. The great thing about talking to God as a friend is that He knows your thoughts as well.

CONCLUSION

God wants to be real to us, and for that to happen, we need to be real with Him. He doesn't want fake religiosity, either in our lives or in our prayers. So be who you are and talk to God as you would talk to anyone else. Do not feel that you need a special prayer voice, special prayer words, or a special prayer posture. Feeling that you need such things will usually only get you in trouble.

I once sat through a church service that concluded with communion. A relatively inexperienced person was invited to offer the prayer for the communion. So he came to the front, picked up the communion bread and held it high in the air above his head. Then he began to pray. "Oh Lord!" he shouted. "We have gathered here in thy presence, and we thank thee for this holy bread, the fruit of thy loins ..." I did everything I could to not break out laughing. Needless to say, I did not partake of communion that day, for I could not remove from my head the image of bread coming from the loins of God. This man's prayer was genuine, but he also was trying to use words and terminology that he had heard elsewhere but didn't understand. And so he ended up thanking God for how we were going eat the fruit of His loins.

Another time, I was discipling a brand new Christian. He knew nothing about God, Jesus, Scripture, or church, and had never even heard anyone pray except for me. After our discussion one day, I asked him if he wanted to pray. He had heard me pray, and so knew that it was just like talking to anyone else, and so he agreed. Being the rough character that he was, this is what he said in his prayer:

> Hey God, you know I've f***** up a lot in life. Thanks for Jeremy helping me learn all this s*** from the Bible about Jesus and how you love and forgive me. Help me to remember what I'm learning and not f*** up anymore. Thanks ... Amen.

After he finished praying, he looked at me and said, "How was that?" I smiled at him and said, "It was perfect. And God loved it too." And I am certain God did. It was honest. It was real. Best of all, it was exactly how this man talked to his friends. As this man matured in his faith, I knew that God would eventually go to work on his language, but for now, God just enjoyed that this new child of His was talking to Him as a friend.

So what is prayer? It is simply talking to God in a normal way, just as we talk to anybody else. Since this is the case, this means that you don't really need to read books on prayer. Not even the rest of this one. You don't need to be taught *how* to pray. You don't need to attend prayer training seminars. You don't need to learn a prayer language. You don't need to memorize lots of Scripture in order to pray. You don't need to learn Hebrew. If you know how to talk, you can pray! All you need to do is just imagine God sitting next to you, and talk to Him as you would talk to anyone else.

Do you want to pray? Aside from the fact that you are talking to *God*, prayer is nothing special. "Jes' call 'im Father, an' ask 'im fer somethin'!" Talk to Him as you would talk to anyone else, and your prayers will be just fine.

But what is it you should ask God for? This is the question we consider next.

CHAPTER 2

WHAT SHOULD YOU PRAY FOR?

It is one thing to know what prayer is. It is quite another knowing what to pray for. We all, of course, want to "pray according to the will of God," so that our prayers can be heard and answered. And so lots of people have developed various systems and suggestions over the years for teaching Christians what to pray for. These range from prayer cards and prayer lists to praying through acronyms such as ACTS: Adoration, Confession, Thanksgiving, and Supplication. Many people also recommend praying through Scripture.

I am not opposed to any of these ideas and suggestions. If they work for you, use them. I would, however, propose that all such prayer systems run the risk of taking you away from what we learned in the previous chapter, that prayer is nothing more than simply communicating with God. If prayer is simply communicating with God, then you don't need cards, lists, acronyms, or memorized passages to talk with God any more than you need such things to talk to your spouse, your children, your neighbor, or a coworker. I do not know anyone who maintains a "conversation topic list" for what they want to say when they talk to other people. So why would you use such things to talk to God? If such a list would make conversation with people unnatural, then it also makes conversation with God unnatural.

I do actually know of one person who used a "topic list" to talk to another person. It was me. I was in Junior High and there was a girl in our church's youth group that I really liked. But I was terrible at talking with girls, so I decided that if I was going to talk to her, I needed to come up with a list of topics beforehand to help me through a conversation. So I wrote up a list of about ten items on a 5x7 notecard. Then I sneakily put the notecard in a see-through pocket of my Bible so that if I started talking to her at church, I could glance at the notecard in the pocket of my Bible without her knowing that I was getting cues from my card.

The next Sunday I got the opportunity to use my card. She was standing around after the service, so I went up and launched into my "conversation." Much to my dismay, she was much less interested in my ten conversation topics than I was, and I blew through all ten in about two minutes. Then I had nothing left to talk about. So I stood there awkwardly for another few seconds, and then said, "Well, okay. Bye!" and walked off. I sometimes wonder if she still remembers that conversation as being the strangest conversation she has ever had in her life. More likely than not, she forgot all about it five minutes later.

The point is that cue cards and topic lists are only marginally helpful in having a conversation with someone else, and might actually be more detrimental than beneficial. This is not only true when you engage people in conversation, but also when you engage God in conversation. Just as conversation lists and cue cards are unnatural in normal conversations, so also, they can be detrimental to your conversations with God. When prayer becomes natural and normal, you discover that like any other conversation, you can carry it out all day long.

Nevertheless, it is true that initially, it is awkward to talk with God. We are afraid of saying the wrong thing or don't know what to talk to Him about. But once again, this is exactly how it is when you first start developing a friendship with anyone else. Initial conversations are nearly always awkward as you both struggle to find areas of common interests and topics that both of you are knowledgeable and passionate about. Of course, with God, He knows all things and is passionate about all things, and so He is happy to talk about whatever is on your mind or whatever interests you. But still, for the person who is just starting out, it is helpful to have some conversation starters. Some ice breakers are helpful in any conversation, especially when it's a conversation with God.

So in this chapter, we are going to briefly look at what many call "The Lord's Prayer" in Matthew 6:9-13 and Luke 11:2-4. This prayer is not actually "The Lord's Prayer" because Jesus is not actually praying. Instead, He is simply giving His disciples some suggestions on what to pray for when they communicate with God the Father. So for this reason, it is better to call this "The Disciples' Prayer" or "The Model Prayer." It provides a model, or framework, for disciples of Jesus to follow when they communicate with God. Let us look at what Jesus tells His disciples about communicating with God.

THE DISCIPLES' PRAYER

The most surprising thing about the suggested "prayer requests" that Jesus provides to His disciples is that every single one of these requests has the potential to turn your life upside down. There are no mundane prayer requests in the prayer that Jesus instructs His disciples to pray. Each line of this prayer is designed to invite God to overthrow, upend, and destroy your life. When you talk to God about the items in this model prayer, God enters your life like a bull in a china shop and tears everything down.

Afterwards, of course, God takes the shards of crystal glass scattered all over the ground and, from these shards, makes the most beautiful mosaic you have ever seen. This truth is taught all over the Scripture. If you want God to work in your life through prayer, the beginning stages of God's work will feel an awful lot like destruction. But if you bear with Him through the demolition, He will raise your life up from the ashes and rubble into something far better than you could ever ask or even imagine. The truth we see in the prayers of Jesus and the pages of Scripture is that death precedes resurrection. This is something to be aware of as you listen to Jesus about how to pray.

Before we look at His instructions, though, note that this model prayer from Jesus is not a prayer to be memorized and recited. You have not prayed the Disciple's Prayer if you mindlessly recite the words of this prayer once or twice a day. I once stayed overnight with a family where the children had been taught to recite this prayer before bed. As the children climbed into bed, their father said, "Don't forget to say your prayers!" The children knelt at their beds and said this:

*OurFatherwhoartinheavenhallowedbythyname
thykingdomcomethywillbedoneonearthasitisinheaven
giveusthisdayourdailybreadandforgiveusourtresspasses
asweforgivethosewhotresspassagainstus
leadusnotintotemptationbutdeliverusfromevil
forthineisthekingdomandthepowerandthegloryforeveramen.*

It took them all of ten seconds. Then they climbed into bed having said their "prayers." But this is not why Jesus gave us this prayer. It is not simply a set of words to memorize so that you know exactly what to say when you pray, and the quicker you get it over, the better. No, Jesus taught this prayer to show the sorts of things you can say to God when you are in a conversation with Him. The Disciple's Prayer provides a few conversation topics to get you started. But these are not the only topics you can talk to God about. Since prayer is a conversation with God, you can talk to Him about anything that is on your heart and mind.

Below is a quick summary of how each line in the Disciple's Prayer will upend, overturn, and destroy your life as you know it. I am using the prayer found in Matthew (Matt 6:9-13) because it is familiar to most people.

Our Father in heaven

Praying to God as our Father is revolutionary in itself. Many people view God as a Ruler or King who sits on His throne and stares down at us as we grovel at His feet. But Jesus invites us to think of God as our Father, and to speak to Him as a loving, caring Father. Don't think of God as a high and lofty Judge, staring at you with a scowling face. Instead, think of God as a strong, kind, and caring man who loves to chat with you about life and share His wisdom as the two of you take a walk in the country, go for a drive into the city, or watch the football game. He is the man who wants to hear about your day and is genuinely interested in everything you say.

As a side note, many people pray to Jesus or to the Holy Spirit. This is not necessarily wrong, since prayer is simply a conversation, and we can have conversations with Jesus and with the Holy Spirit. Nevertheless, don't neglect your ongoing conversation with God, your Father, for when Jesus told us what to pray for, He instructed us to direct our prayers to God, our Father.

Hallowed be Your Name

This is a declaration that we want God's name to be glorified. When you pray, tell God that you want to let people know how amazing He is. The danger in this is that when we pray for God to be glorified, and for His name to be praised among the people, what we often subconsciously mean is that we want *our* name to be praised and glorified among people. Oh sure, when this happens, we imagine how we will stand in front of the adoring crowds and point our finger to heaven saying, "Give God the glory!" while we bask in the glory for ourselves. Yes, we want God to be gloried, but we often want to ride His coattails to some glory of our own.

But Jesus doesn't say this will happen. This first prayer item is for God's name to be glorified; not ours. And if Scripture is any guide, God often chooses the strangest ways to glorify His name. He uses shepherds, children, and donkeys more than the rich, powerful, and popular. So while it is okay to expect that God will glorify His name through you, just know that God's movement toward glory might involve a lot of downward momentum for yourself. When you follow God toward glory, you are more likely to be led toward obscurity and poverty than toward riches and fame.

Your kingdom come, Your will be done, on earth as it is in heaven

To pray for God's kingdom to come means to pray for God's will to be done. The concepts are one and the same. The Kingdom of God is the rule and reign of God, and so when God is ruling and reigning, His will is being done. This means that when you talk to God, make it plain that you want to be involved in helping Him carry out His plans and desires on this earth. This is what it means to pray for His will to be done. And this is something we all want, right? Some people even include the phrase "Not my will, but Yours be done" in their prayers (following the example of Jesus in Luke 22:42).

But again, this is a dangerous thing to say to God, for while you might be fine with God carrying out His will on earth, it is quite another thing when God steps into your life and starts trying to change your plans, your goals, and your dreams. We are usually fine with God carrying out His will in the lives of other people, as long as He doesn't mess up *our* life. If you are like me, when it comes to our own life, we want our own will to be done; not God's. Why? Because God's will for our life usually looks much less enjoyable than our own plans for our life. Following God's will for our life will lead us into death, slavery, obscurity, and suffering, rather than into riches, fame, honor, and glory.

But have courage and faith. God's plan truly is better, though it may not initially appear to be so. Note that the final statements of this prayer in verse 13 contain the same sort of ideas that Jesus states here. The Kingdom of God is God's rule and reign on earth, and it arrives by His power and is for His glory.

Give us this day our daily bread

Don't read more into this prayer item than is here. This is a request for God to provide for your daily needs. This is encouraging, because it once again shows that God wants you to talk to Him about what you have on your heart. Or in this case, God wants you to talk to Him about what you do *not* have in your stomach. So yes, you can talk to God about your need for food. Though it is not just about food, but also about our other physical, social, medical, financial, and psychological needs. You can talk to God about anything that concerns you.

So how is this a dangerous prayer? Well, note that Jesus only mentions *daily* bread. Daily bread means "enough for today." This is not a prayer for a full fridge and a growing retirement account. It is not a prayer for job security or financial freedom. For most of us, this is a terrifying prospect. If you are like me, you trust God for today and you trust God for tomorrow, but for your own peace of mind, you would like tomorrow's provision today. So if that is how you feel, go ahead and talk to God about it. If it is a concern you have today, He wants to hear about it.

And forgive us our debts, as we forgive our debtors

There is some question here about whether Jesus is talking about sins or financial debts. The word Jesus uses in Matthew 6:12 is not the typical word for sin (*hamartia*), but is the word that typically refers to some sort of financial debt or burden (*opheilēma*). However, in the parallel version of Luke 11:4, Jesus does use the normal word for sin, but then switches to the same word for debt that Matthew uses. So is Jesus referring to sin or debts? The answer is both. Jesus is referring to anything that you might have against someone else, or which they might have against you, being either a fault committed or finances owed.

When you talk to God, ask Him for release from all your burdens, whether they are moral or financial. Again, if it is something weighing on your heart and mind, then it is fair game for your conversation with God. This might sound nice when it is directed toward you, but Jesus also invites you to release other people from the faults they have done to you or the finances they owe. This is much harder to talk to God about, and is not something that most people want to do.

By the way, it is worth mentioning that the word Jesus uses for "forgive" here (*aphesis*) does not mean to simply erase. There are two words for "forgiveness" in the Bible, and the one Jesus uses here means something closer to "release." Very often, there are conditions attached to this form of forgiveness, so that you will not experience it unless you first fulfill the conditions. (See the volume in this "Christian Questions" book series about forgiveness which explains this in more detail.) In this case, when you talk to God about being released from your addiction to sin or your burden of debt, He is not just going to wave a heavenly magic wand and do away with your addictions to sin or your burdens of debt. Instead, in communication with Him, you and He will come up with a plan of action to break free from sin and pay off your debt. The same can be true with how you interact with those who owe you money or who have wronged you.

So again, when you talk to God about these things, He does not just come into your life and erase your past and do away with your debts, as much as you might like Him to do that. He first invites you to consider how you might release other people who have wronged you, and then He provides input and advice so you can also be freed from your own sin and debt. There are no easy fixes here, but it is something that God wants to talk with you about, and walk with you through.

Do not lead us into temptation, but deliver us from the evil one

God doesn't actually lead anyone into temptation (Jas 1:13), so this phrase probably means something closer to "Help us resist temptation when it comes." At a more basic level, this is an invitation by Jesus for you to talk to God about your areas of struggle. Since God wants to talk to you about everything and anything, He definitely wants to talk to you about any areas in which you face temptation.

This might be awkward for you, because maybe you think that God is so holy He doesn't want to hear about your secret thoughts, hidden behaviors, and impure desires. But if that is what you think, you are wrong. One of the main reasons Jesus became human is because God wanted to show humans that He loves us so much, He will step right into our sinful condition with us so that He can love us there and lead us out of the mess we find ourselves in. So go ahead; talk to God about your sin. It is only when you invite God into your sin with you that He will be able to begin delivering you from it.

When I try to deal with temptation by myself, I almost always fail. But I experience the most victory over temptation when I swallow my pride and realize that God is not going to be offended by what I am struggling with. When tempted, I invite God into the temptation with me to talk to Him about it. I might say, "Hey God, do you see what I'm dealing with here? What do you think? Should I do it? I really, really want to, You know." Then we talk about it, the pros and cons of doing what I am tempted to do, and usually, He persuades me to resist.

Yet even when I fall to temptation, rather than wallow in guilt and shame for days on end (the way I used to), I try to immediately invite God back into the mess I've caused. I have a sheepish laugh with Him about it, saying, "God, look at this mess. What was I thinking? I don't know why I did that … again. And just like every time before, it wasn't as fun as I thought it would be." Then we discuss what happened to cause me to fall into the sin, and how I can avoid these temptations in the future.

Be aware, however, that once we invite God into the sinful areas of our life, He doesn't stop with the one area in which we asked Him for help. After He helps us sweep one room clean, He usually points to a locked closet and says, "Now what's in there? Anything you need help with?" God is in perpetual "spring cleaning" mode, and once He gets going, there is no stopping Him. Along with locked closets, He might find some cobwebs in the corner and trash which we shoved under our bed hoping He wouldn't find. But He will.

This is why talking to God about our sin is so dangerous. There might be certain sinful areas of our life that we are rather attached to. It becomes somewhat painful when God turns on the light in those dimly-lit rooms and cobweb-filled basements, and starts to open up dusty boxes to see what's inside. But if we listen to His input, get His advice, and talk to God as we go, the process will be more liberating than painful. And though God never gives up, He also is not too pushy, but gently leads to the next area He wants to clean.

THE DISCIPLE'S PRAYER IS DANGEROUS

So the Disciple's Prayer can be quite dangerous. Later in this book we will consider ten dangerous prayers (see Chapter 5), but as we have seen here, the prayer that Jesus instructed His disciples to model is also full of life-changing and world-changing requests. So be careful about talking to God about the topics in this prayer. I am not saying you should not talk to God about them, but that you should be aware of the consequences that might come into your life as a result. Prayer is a powerful gift from God, and every phrase in the Disciple's Prayer is a minefield just waiting to turn your life upside down ... but in a good way. Never forget that God is a loving Father who only wants what is best for His children. That means He only wants what is best for you. His plans for your life may seem scary at first, but they are always bigger and better than any plan you may have.

Imagine what your life would look like if you truly believed that God was your loving Father who only wanted what was best for your life, and so you sought to do everything possible to bring praise and glory to Him through your words and actions? What would your life look like if you sought after the Kingdom of God rather than the kingdoms of men? How would you function if you only had enough for today, and didn't know how God would provide for tomorrow? What might happen in your life if you worked to release people from their bondage to sin and debt as God works to release you from the same things? How might your life be different if you truly saw sin the way God sees it and didn't engage in the pet sins we think we cannot live without? Yes, this prayer that Jesus instructs His disciples to pray is revolutionary, life-changing, and dangerous.

Now although this is the prayer that Jesus taught His disciples to pray, it is not the only way to pray. We see this by comparing the "Disciple's Prayer" with the way Jesus Himself prayed in John 17. Though there are many similarities, there are also significant differences. This is what we will see in the next chapter, where we consider the true "Lord's Prayer."

CHAPTER 3

HOW DID JESUS PRAY?

There are numerous instances in the Gospel accounts of Jesus praying. Sometimes He prayed all night (Luke 6:12), though He also got up early to pray (Mark 1:35). Sometimes His prayers were long; sometimes they were short (John 12:28). What we can learn from this is that even with Jesus, there was no set way to pray. For Jesus, it seems that prayer was not so much a time that He set aside to specifically talk with God, but was closer to just picking up with an ongoing conversation with God.

The same can be true with you. If you always have the lines of communication open with God, then there really is no such thing as a long or short prayer, but just re-engaging with God in a conversation that has been going on for some time. This is why special postures or places for prayer, while occasionally helpful, can also be detrimental to your prayer life. The same goes for saying "Amen" at the end of your prayer. I still say "Amen" when I pray publicly, but this is just to indicate to others that I am now talking directly to them instead of to God. But if prayer is an ongoing conversation with God, then it never really stops. You might temporarily stop talking about one particular issue or request, but the line of communication with God remains open and active, ready to be picked up at any time. This is partly what Paul meant when he wrote about praying without ceasing (1 Thess 5:16).

This is also how Jesus prayed. As you look at the various prayers of Jesus in the Gospels, it becomes obvious that the prayer life of Jesus was simply part of an ongoing conversation He had with God. He was always aware of God's presence, and always kept focused on what God was doing through Him and around Him, and when Jesus sought to have a direct conversation with God, it was not as though He started and stopped His prayers, but rather just picked up where He left off before, or turned to God (who was already there) and simply started talking to Him about what was currently going on. Similarly, the "end" of the prayer is not the end of praying, but just a temporary lapse or pause in the discussion that would be picked up again at a later time.

Let us look at the true Lord's Prayer in John 17 to see this in more detail, and also to learn what we can from how Jesus prayed.

THE LORD'S PRAYER

John 17 records the prayer that Jesus prayed in the Upper Room with His disciples at the conclusion of their last supper together. Though the Gospels frequently record Jesus going off by Himself to pray, this is the only recorded prayer of Jesus of any length which provides an indication of the sort of things Jesus might have said when He prayed. So if you want to learn how to pray like Jesus, there is no better prayer in Scripture to study. In the sections below, you will see how Jesus structured His prayer, the posture He used, His prayer requests, and also a few insights into how Jesus did *not* pray. It is important to note that even though these provide insights into how Jesus prayed, this does not mean that you must follow the exact same structure, outline, or posture, or even that you should pray for the same things that Jesus prayed for. This prayer in Scripture is not provided so that we might copy it, but so that we might learn more about the heart of Jesus and how He communicated with God.

The Structure of the Prayer

The prayer is divided into three basic sections. First, Jesus prays for Himself (17:1-5), then for His disciples (17:6-19), and finally for all who would believe in Him (17:20-26). The prayer of Jesus has a "concentric circle" approach to ministry, where Jesus' relationship with God is at the center, and Jesus works His way out from there to the disciples and then to all who will believe in Jesus, which includes us today. While not all prayers must follow this pattern or structure, it is nevertheless helpful to note that Jesus does begin by praying for Himself and His relationship with God.

If you are like most people, you have found that it is nearly impossible to pray if you are not in right fellowship with God. After all, if you are not on "speaking terms" with God, how do you expect to speak with Him? So although this prayer of Jesus does not provide a universal pattern for all prayer at all times, it is nevertheless helpful to remember that since prayer is a conversation with God, it is important to make sure that you are in a good relationship with God. How can you talk to Him if you don't want to be near Him or with Him?

So while on the one hand, you must make sure that your prayers are not self-centered and that you only pray for yourself and your needs, it is nevertheless true that the starting place for prayer is your own relationship with God. When sin, disobedience, or rebellion get in the way of your communication with God, your prayers should include some confession and repentance. Even when your relationship with God is wonderful, it is still a good idea to include some relationship building conversation in your prayers.

Again, never forget that prayer is just like communicating with anyone else, such as a spouse or friend. In any relationship, it is wise to frequently check the pulse of the relationship, and take care of any issues that are between you so that the friendship and communication can continue. If you would do this with a friend, spouse, or coworker, how much more should you do this with God?

The Posture of Prayer

If you have ever seen an artistic rendering of what Jesus looked like during His prayers (such as the prayer in the Garden of Gethsemane in Matt 26:36-56), you will likely remember that the portraits depict Jesus as kneeling before a rock, with this hands clasped in front of Him on the rock, and His eyes turned upward toward the sky. As a result of pictures like this, some believe that this is the proper posture of prayer.

Yet note that nothing much is said in John 17 (or anywhere else, for that matter), about the posture of Jesus during His prayers. The text does not tell us if Jesus was sitting, standing, or reclining. Since Jesus and His disciples are still indoors at this point, and since reclining on the floor was the typical way of eating meals in first century Middle Eastern culture, it is possible that Jesus was still on the floor while praying. Or maybe He stood up. We just don't know. One thing is for sure though: Jesus definitely was not folding His hands, bowing His head, and closing His eyes. To the contrary, the text says He "lifted up His eyes to heaven" (17:1), which indicates that His eyes were open and His head was raised.

But even this posture is not the "God-approved" posture for prayer. It is not as if such things as kneeling or standing, arms up or arms down, eyes open or eyes closed make any difference in whether or not God hears and answers our prayers. If God is concerned about any sort of posture in our prayers, it is the posture of our hearts, which no one can see but Him alone. So when you pray, don't be overly concerned about what your hands, your head, or your eyelids are doing. The only thing that matters to God is what is going on in your heart. As long as you are having a conversation with Him, your hands can be busy at work and your eyes can be alertly watching your surroundings (I often pray while I drive).

Just like with any other conversation with any other person, there is no "one right way" to sit or stand. The posture of prayer has nothing to do with who you are talking to, but everything to do with what the two of you are doing while you talk. God is happy to talk with you wherever you are and whatever you are doing. So whether you are vacuuming, driving, mowing the lawn, walking the dog, performing your duties at work, watching TV, laying on your bed, or reading this book, you can be in conversation with God.

The Prayer Requests

The previous chapter looked at the "Disciple's Prayer" and some of the things you can pray for when you communicate with God. Here in the "Lord's Prayer," we see that Jesus prayed for some of these same things. For example, Jesus prayed that God's name would be glorified through His own life and ministry (17:1-5). In praying for His disciples that they would carry on the work that Jesus started (17:16-19), Jesus was essentially praying that the Kingdom of God, or the rule and reign of God, would continue to spread upon the earth. He does not pray for daily sustenance or the forgiveness of debts, but He does ask that God protect His disciples from the evil one (17:11, 15).

One of the main requests in Jesus' prayer is that those who believe in Him will live in unity with each other, just as Jesus lives in unity with God (17:11, 21, 23). I find it sadly ironic that although this is the primary prayer request of Jesus for His church, the one thing that the church is most known for is our lack of unity. When the world thinks of Christians, they often think of people who are divided. And they are not wrong. There are thousands of denominations in the world, and we are all divided over some of the silliest things. Yes, some of the divisions are necessary and important, like whether or not Jesus was truly God, but when we divide over the mode of baptism, whether women can be pastors, music styles, or church governance structure, such divisions bring great sadness to Jesus. In reality, there are relatively few things we must all agree on. A few such items might be that eternal life is by faith alone in Jesus Christ, that Jesus is the Lord and Master of the church, and that we are to love all people in His name. Beyond these, there should be nothing that divides us.

I sometimes think that if the church truly wants to rise up and bring glory to God as Jesus prays here in John 17, the best thing we could do is to stop praying for Aunt Mabel's bunion, our neighbor's lost dog, and how the rent is overdue, and instead seek to create unity in the church as an answer to Jesus' prayer. This is not to say that you cannot talk to God about health issues, lost pets, and financial difficulties. You can and you should. Since God loves you, He wants to hear about such things. But at the same time, do not allow these relatively minor issues to cloud your vision for the unity that Jesus prayed for. In your prayer life and daily life, work to develop a broader vision for prayer than how we can use it to tell God about our aches, pains, and bills. Work toward what Jesus worked for, which is to glorify God through carrying out His will on earth, which is primarily accomplished through living with one another in love and unity. When you pray for this, you can know with certainty that you are praying according to the will of God.

JESUS CONVERSED WITH GOD

As you read through the prayer of Jesus, the one thing you might notice is that it is very conversational. Though there are some patterns and requests which align with the "Disciple's Prayer" from Matthew 6, Jesus also departs from that model prayer, and simply talks with God about what is on His heart. Since Jesus knows that He is about to be arrested and crucified, His concern is that God's work on earth will be continued, that His disciples will be cared for and protected, and that all who come to follow Jesus will be part of God's unified plan for the work He is doing in the world. And since these issues are on the mind of Jesus, this is what Jesus talks to God about.

Notice that Jesus does not engage in needless repetition of the name of God. Nor does He try to ward off the devil. Jesus is not concerned with including any flowery or fancy language to impress those who are present with His advanced holiness. Truthfully, if you compare the prayer of Jesus in John 17 with any of the other passages in John where Jesus is talking to humans, there is almost nothing that sets this prayer apart from any other conversation. The conversation Jesus has with God sounds pretty much just like a conversation He might have with Peter, or Matthew, or John. For Jesus, communicating with God was just like communicating with others.

Note as well that this prayer seems to be a continuation of a much longer conversation Jesus has been having with God. Because this prayer is part of a longer, ongoing conversation, Jesus does not have the need to fit everything in, follow a prayer outline, remember any prayer requests, or even begin and end the prayer with a flowery introduction and conclusion. In fact, between John 16:33 where Jesus stops talking to His disciples and John 17:2 where He starts talking to God, the only real transition is that Jesus looks heavenward. It is so casual, it is as if Jesus had been talking to the disciples and then turned His head to start talking to God. His tone and language and posture and even the content of what He is saying does not really change. For Jesus, prayer is just continuing a conversation with God.

When understood this way, prayer becomes much less of a mystery about how to pray, what to pray for, who can pray, or where to pray, and much more like a conversation you have in everyday life. If you can talk with a friend, you can talk to God. This is how Jesus prayed, and how you can pray too.

CHAPTER 4

HOW TO RECEIVE ANSWERS TO PRAYER

Earlier in this book I said that prayer is nothing special. Though this is true in a sense, it is not so true in another sense. Prayer may be the most special thing ever. Think about it. Prayer gets you face time with God. Prayer is one-on-one with the creator of the universe. Most amazingly, prayer allows you to give your input into what God is doing in the world. Through prayer, you get some say in how God runs the universe. Imagine that! Furthermore, I am convinced that there may be some things which God wants to do in the world, but He won't do except through prayer. That is, there are aspects of God's will which are contingent upon people asking Him for them. There are some things God won't do unless people ask Him to do it.

Yet if this is so, why is it that so many of our prayers go unanswered? Yes, I know that there is no such thing as an unanswered prayer. I know that God saying "No," is just as much of an answer as God saying "Yes." So maybe a better way of asking the question is, "Why does prayer seem so ineffective?" If prayer gets you face time with God, if prayer grants you some say in how God runs the universe, then why does it seem that most of your prayers don't actually affect much change?

If this is your frustration with prayer, there are three basic answers for you to consider. First, maybe you are not praying according to the will of God, or what it means to pray in Jesus' name. Second, maybe you don't understand how prayer works. Finally, maybe you don't quite understand how to receive answers to your prayers. This chapter provides input on these three areas.

PRAY ACCORDING TO THE WILL OF GOD

One of the benefits to approaching prayer as a conversation with God is that prayer no longer becomes a way to get stuff from God, but instead becomes primarily a way to grow in your relationship with God. When prayer is an ongoing conversation with God, you learn that prayer is not about presenting your wish list to a Santa Claus in the sky, but is instead about getting to know the heart, desires, and goals of a person who loves you very much.

As you get to know the heart, desires, and goals of God for your life and for this world, you come to better understand the sorts of things God wants you to ask Him for. And when you ask for the things that God wants you to ask Him for, He will always say "Yes," because these requests are according to His will. So the key to seeing God answer your prayers is to learn what is important to God and what He wants to accomplish in this world, and then pray for those things.

As you do this, you will also discover that the things God wants are also the things you want. Though you may think you want a mansion with a fancy car, when you grow in your relationship with God, you discover that such material possessions are not what your heart really longs for. Your heart actually longs for the things God longs for. God wants you to live in fellowship and unity with Him and with others, and be at peace with all people. God wants you to be generous, kind, gracious, patient, and merciful, just as He is with you. So when you ask God to help build these things into your life, He is more than happy to bring them to pass.

When Psalm 37:4 says that if you delight in the Lord, He will give you the desires of your heart, this does not mean that God will give you whatever it is you want. It means that when you enjoy being in God's presence, and when you enjoy talking with God and learning about what is important to Him, He places His desires into your own heart, so that your desires come from His desires. He gives you the right things to desire, and then He works to help fulfill those desires. This is what it means to ask according to the will of God (1 John 5:14).

Praying according to God's will then, is not so much when we ask God for the things we want, but when we first seek God's heart and will on various matters, and then ask Him for these things. Proper prayer occurs when we speak God's heart back to Him, asking how we can get actively involved in what He is already doing in the world. Prayer is when we verbalize to God our desire to join Him in accomplishing His will that He has whispered to our hearts.

PRAY IN JESUS' NAME

A similar concept to praying according to the will of God is praying in Jesus' name. Many people seem to think that to "pray in Jesus' name" simply means to tack the words "… in Jesus' name, Amen" at the end of their prayer. This is not what it means at all. To pray "in Jesus' name" means to pray as if Jesus Himself was praying our prayers.

When an ambassador visits another country "in the name of the king" (or president), it is as if his king (or president) is speaking the words that the ambassador speaks. The leaders of these other countries are to assume that whatever the ambassador says, it is as if the king (or president) himself said them. The ambassador speaks "in the name of the king."

Since this is so, the ambassador must be certain that what he says is exactly what the king himself would say. If an ambassador says something foolish or insulting, he could easily start a war, ruin a trade agreement, or destroy a treaty. To be a good ambassador, the ambassador needs to know the mind and heart and will of his king so intimately that the two minds are nearly one.

This is what it means to pray "in Jesus' name." These three words are not a magical incantation that you can tack on to the end of your prayers to get whatever you want. Instead, to pray in Jesus' name means to develop a mind frame in which you know you are speaking for Jesus. You are approaching the throne of God as if Jesus Himself was speaking through you. This means that, like an ambassador, you must so intimately know the mind, heart, and will of Jesus in whatever situation you are praying about, that the words you speak are the same exact words Jesus would speak if He Himself were the one making the petition to God.

In John 14:13-14, Jesus instructs His disciples to pray in His name. His words can be expanded and paraphrased as follows:

> But when you pray, spend time thinking about what I value, what I instructed you to know, how I lived my life, the kind of example I provided, the people I hung out with, the goals I sought to achieve, and the relationship I have with God. Take careful notice of what I taught and what I prayed for. Then, offer your requests to God in light of these things. And when you do, make these requests boldly, knowing that the words you speak are the same words I am speaking. When you pray this way, know that your prayers will be answered.

So when you are praying something which you know with absolute certainty is the will of God, and which Jesus Himself would pray, this is when you can pray "in Jesus' name," as if He Himself were praying your prayers. You can know you are praying according to the will of God when you pray the things Jesus prayed for, or when you pray for the things which God has revealed in Scripture.

But what about when you are not quite as certain? What about when you want to pray for something, but you are not sure whether or not your request is the will of God or your own will? Does this mean you cannot and should not pray for such things? No. You can and should. But rather than pray for such things "in Jesus' name," this is when it is best to tell God, "… yet not my will, but yours be done." In other words, tell God what is on your heart and mind, but also let Him know that you understand that you are unsure about His will in this situation, and although you have presented your requests to Him, you will submit to whatever He decides to do. Unless you are praying the clear commands and instructions of Scripture, it is likely that most of your prayers will be of this second sort, where you recognize that your heart can be deceived and your mind darkened, and so you leave the decision up to God.

So to pray in Jesus' name does not mean that you will get whatever you ask for if you simply tack on some magic words at the end of your prayer. To receive what you ask for in prayer requires you to pray according to the things God wants you to pray for, or to pray for the things that Jesus Himself prays for. When you pray "in Jesus' name," this means that you should pray as if it is Jesus Himself praying through you. When you pray, if you cannot imagine Jesus praying for it, you probably shouldn't pray for it yourself. Can you imagine Jesus praying for a Lamborghini and a mansion? No? Then you shouldn't pray for such things either.

But when you do pray for the things Jesus would pray for, when you do pray for the things that are according to the will of God—and especially His revealed will in Scripture—this is when God steps in to act boldly and mightily in response to your prayers. This is why the prayers of a righteous person accomplish much (Jas 5:16). It is not because the person is so righteous and holy, but because such a person better understands the heart of God than others, and so when they pray, they are praying according to the will, desires, and goals of God. When you pray this way too, your prayers will also accomplish much.

HOW PRAYER WORKS

Another reason you sometimes don't see God working in response to your prayers is because you might not understand how prayer works. Or maybe it is better to say that you might not understand that prayer *is* work. This truth is something I learned from C. S. Lewis in his essays "Work and Prayer" in the book, *God in the Dock,* and "The Efficacy of Prayer" in the book, *The World's Last Night.*

Essentially, the argument of C. S. Lewis is that any responsibility in this world which God can pass on to human beings, He does pass on to human beings. He prefers not to do something if a human can do it. This is because we are His ambassadors on earth. As the image of God in this world, we carry out the work of God. Toward this end, God has provided two means by which we can accomplish these God-given tasks:

work and prayer. And just as we view work as a way of getting things done in the world, we must begin to view prayer similarly.

Here are some excerpts from Lewis' essay, "Work and Prayer" which explain this point:

> Everyone who believes in God must therefore admit (quite apart from the question of prayer) that God has not chosen to write the whole history with His own hand. Most of the events that go on in the universe are indeed out of our control, but not all. It is like a play in which the scene and the general outline of the story is fixed by the author, but certain minor details are left for the actors to improvise. It may be a mystery why He should have allowed us to cause real events at all, but it is no odder that He should allow us to cause them by praying than by any other method.

> Pascal says that God "instituted prayer in order to allow His creatures the dignity of causality." It would perhaps be truer to say that He invented both prayer and physical action for that purpose. He gave us small creatures the dignity of being able to contribute to the course of events in two different ways. He made the matter of the universe such that we can (in those limits) do things to it; that is why we can wash our own hands and feed or murder our fellow creatures. Similarly, He made His own plan or plot of history such that it admits a certain amount of free play and can be modified in response to our prayers. If it is foolish and impudent to ask for victory in war (on the ground that God might be expected to know best), it would be equally foolish and impudent to put on a [raincoat]—does not God know best whether you ought to be wet or dry?

> The two methods by which we are allowed to produce events may be called work and prayer. Both are alike in this respect—that in both we try to produce a state of affairs which God has not (or at any rate not yet) seen fit to provide "on His own." And from this point of view the old maxim *laborare est orare* (work is prayer) takes on a new meaning. What we do when we weed a field is not quite different from what we do when we pray for a good harvest. But there is an important difference all the same.

> You cannot be sure of a good harvest whatever you do to a field. But you

can be sure that if you pull up one weed that one weed will no longer be there. You can be sure that if you drink more than a certain amount of alcohol you will ruin your health or that if you go on for a few centuries more wasting the resources of the planet on wars and luxuries you will shorten the life of the whole human race. The kind of causality we exercise by work is, so to speak, divinely guaranteed, and therefore ruthless. By it we are free to do ourselves as much harm as we please. But the kind which we exercise by prayer is not like that; God has left Himself discretionary power. Had He not done so, prayer would be an activity too dangerous for man and should have the horrible state of things envisaged by Juvenal: "Enormous prayers which Heaven in anger grants."

Prayers are not always—in the crude, factual sense of the word—"granted." This is not because prayer is a weaker kind of causality, but because it is a stronger kind. When it "works" at all it works unlimited by space and time. That is why God has retained a discretionary power of granting or refusing it; except on that condition prayer would destroy us. It is not unreasonable for a headmaster to say, "Such and such things you may do according to the fixed rules of this school. But such and such other things are too dangerous to be left to general rules. If you want to do them you must come and make a request and talk over the whole matter with me in my study. And then—we'll see."

I love how Lewis concludes his essay by talking about prayer as if it were a conversation you had with a headmaster of a school in his study. This is right in line with what we have been learning in this book about prayer. More importantly, though, Lewis shows the close connection between work and prayer as a means of accomplishing God's will in the world. This explanation by Lewis shows how important prayer is, and also how to go about accomplishing God's will in this world.

Prayer is not a lesser form of work, but a greater and more powerful form. This is why God leaves Himself some discretionary power to say "No." God is willing to talk to you about everything and anything, but since He alone knows everything, He allows Himself the freedom to say "No" to the things you ask for which run contrary to His will, goals, and purposes for this world. This understanding of prayer as a form of work brings us to the third truth which will help you understand how God answers your prayers.

HOW GOD ANSWERS PRAYER

One of the primary ways God wants to answer your prayers is to have you answer them yourself. As you grow in your relationship with God through prayer, God places His desires into your heart so that you know how to pray according to His will. But God doesn't just place His desires into your heart so that you can pray for them. No, God gives you these desires so that you can actually go do something about them. Very often, the burdens God places on your heart and mind regarding the needs or issues of other people is not simply so that you can pray about them, but so that you can do something about them.

It is not uncommon in the church, and especially in church prayer meetings, for people to gather together and share the prayer requests that lay heavy on their hearts. Then, after they share these requests, they sit in a circle and pray about them. They might pray for the neighbor lady whose husband is in the hospital, for the coworker who just got laid off, for the homeless people to find work, and for more people to start showing up for church. These are all valid prayer requests, and all of them, I believe, are within the will of God. However, I do not believe that God wants us to do nothing but pray about these requests. I think God sometimes makes needs known to us, not so that we can pray about them, but so that we can do something about them.

I once saw a comic strip where a guy was praying, and he said, "God, why aren't you answering any of my prayers?" God's reply was, "I was about to ask you the same thing." Praying for needs is important, but one way God wants to answer our prayers is by us going out to be the answer to our own prayers. Sometimes we fail to see answers to prayers, not because God doesn't care or doesn't want to answer, but because God is saying to us, "Answer your own prayer! Why do you think I laid that burden on your heart?" He lays needs upon our minds so that we can both pray and do something about these needs.

Proper petitionary prayer is when we speak God's heart back to Him, asking how we can get actively involved in what He is already doing in our lives and in the world. Prayer requests are not primarily those petitions we present to God, but are instead the verbal requests we make to Him which mirror the requests He has whispered to our own hearts. In a sense, we could almost say that God prays to us so that we can pray His prayers back to Him. God lays on our hearts and minds the things He wants done in the world, and then as we become aware of these issues and needs, we pray these requests to God, asking how we can collaborate with Him in the work He is doing.

This is exactly the point of James 2. For centuries, the church has argued about James 2:14-26 and what it teaches regarding the connection between faith and works. This is tragic, for such a debate only shows that those who engage in it don't understand what James is talking about at all. The passage is not about how to determine whether or not our faith is genuine. The passage is about how to see God work in response to our faith. We could say that James 2 is about how to see God work in response to our prayers.

In the church that James was writing to, there was one group of people who had need of food and daily clothes. There were others within the church who could meet those needs by providing food and clothes. But rather than providing for the needs of others, this second group instead said to the first, "I have faith that God will provide for you." In modern church lingo, we say, "I'll pray for you."

James blasts this sort of thinking. He says, "What good is that? Faith isn't going to help in this situation! Faith isn't going to put food on their table or clothes on their backs! The reason God made those needs known to you is because you have the means to help. Don't believe in God to provide for the needs of others; you provide for them. Don't ask God to give them food; you give them food. Don't pray for God to give them clothes; you give them some clothes."

The point of James is that while faith is wonderful and prayer is good, talking about your faith and how you will pray for God's provision is worthless when it comes to actually helping these other people. Yes, it is true that God can provide for their needs, but the way God wants to provide for their needs is through you! Faith is not sitting back and waiting for God to act while we do nothing. Faith is when we recognize that God is pointing out the needs to us because we have the means to meet the needs. While faith alone is genuine and good, faith alone does nothing to help those in need.

So yes, faith can exist by itself. But what's the point? Yes, you can pray for the needs of those around you, but if you do nothing to actually meet those needs, why pray? Faith, by itself, is worthless. Prayer alone accomplishes nothing. For faith to truly be energized, for faith to truly move mountains, for faith to accomplish much, you must join your faith with your actions, and seek to meet the needs for which you pray.

Though there are some things only God can do, there are many things that God cannot do except through us. Prayer is not so much us asking God to do things for us, but us asking how we can do things with Him. Most of the things you pray for can be accomplished by inviting God to work through you to meet the need you pray for, and then stepping out in faith to actually meet the need. We could say that God prays to us before we pray to Him, and so our prayers to Him are nothing more than a recognition of what He has been inviting us to do in this world. When we see a need and we pray for it, it is only because God has revealed that need to us and has invited us to get involved with Him in meeting it. In some sense then, when we wonder if God hears and answers our prayers, what we should really be wondering is if we hear and answer His.

When we pray, "Lord, reach our community with the gospel!" God says, "Yes! I want to send you to reach your community with the gospel. Are you ready to love and serve them like Jesus? Let's go!" When we pray, "Lord, help that homeless man find a job," God says, "Okay. I will do that if you take some time to go help him find a job." When we pray for

God to end violence, stop wars, rescue victims, feed the hungry, clothe the poor, and help the sick, God is asking us to do the same things with Him. Indeed, God cannot do these things unless we participate with Him. Sometimes prayer is not so much a question of whether God hears our prayers, but whether we hear His.

As a pastor, I participated in the Wednesday night prayer meetings of our church. One week, one of the elders shared a prayer request about a retired pastor who was moving into town the following Wednesday. He asked that we pray for this man's transition, that he would safely arrive in town and get unpacked and settled in without problems. So the next Wednesday, when everybody gathered for our weekly prayer meeting, I began by announcing that God had heard our prayer and answered. I said that a whole group of people from the church had shown up to help this retired pastor unpack his moving van and get settled into his new house with his wife. The people were ecstatic to hear that God had answered our prayer in such a tangible way and that He did so through some of the people in our own church. Then they asked who these people were, for none of them had heard that this was happening. I smiled and said, "It's us. Let's go." And we went. There was some grumbling later on that the pastor had cancelled the prayer meeting to go move boxes, but overall, I think people got the point.

I hope you do too. If you want to see God answer your prayers, the first place to look for answers might be in your very own life. God does want to answer your prayers, and He probably wants to answer them through you.

CHAPTER 5

10 DANGEROUS PRAYERS

Although prayer is simply talking to God as you would talk to a friend, prayer is not something to take lightly. As indicated previously in this book, through prayer, God gives His children divine "say so." Prayer gives us a seat at God's council table, where He hears our input and bases some of His decisions on what we say. For this reason, prayer can be quite dangerous. But this is also why God sometimes answers our prayers with a "No." Ultimately, as C. S. Lewis pointed out, God gives Himself discretion on whether or not to grant our requests, because without this discretion, the power of prayer would destroy us.

Nevertheless, in my experience, there are some prayers that God always grants, and these prayers are quite dangerous to you and to your life. The reason God always grants these prayer requests is because they are within His will for our lives. In praying them, however, we often fail to realize how devastating these requests will be to our lives once they are granted. So in this chapter I want to share with you the ten most dangerous prayers you can pray. Although these prayers are dangerous, I still recommend that you pray them, for while they may seem to destroy your life at first, they will ultimately allow you to partner with God in extraordinary ways.

I share these dangerous prayer requests with you from personal experience. I have prayed all the dangerous prayers below ... and suffered the consequences as a result. But I reaped the rewards of these prayers as well. Though they ruined my life, they also saved my life.

I had my life all figured out, and it was all going according to my perfect plan. Then I started praying the prayers below, and before long, all my hopes and dreams lay shattered around my feet. I was publicly shamed and humiliated. I was without work and without money. I didn't know who I was or what I was supposed to do. I often tried to pick up the pieces of my life and glue them back together, but God would come through with His baseball bat and smash it all to hell (almost literally ... all of my plans and dreams deserved nothing more).

So I know the danger of these prayers, but also their importance and their power. When you pray these prayers, God will start to do work in your life as you never before imagined. Yes, it will be painful and scary, but God will take the pieces of your life and reconstruct them into a beautiful mosaic that reflects His light and love to a watching world. When you pray these prayers, watch out, for your life is about to change!

1. TEACH ME HUMILITY

After you pray this Christian prayer for humility, be ready for people to badmouth you, slander you, and drag your name through the mud. If you pray for humility, be ready for false accusations, for that "skeleton in the closet" to be revealed, or for people to belittle you and talk down to you as if you were inferior. Praying for humility is a dangerous prayer, because the only way to learn humility is to be placed in humbling situations. So if you pray for humility, be ready.

2. TEACH ME PATIENCE

Much like the prayer for humility, a prayer for patience is dangerous because the only way to learn patience is to be put in situations where your patience is tested and tried. If you pray for patience, you will soon be surrounded by the most annoying people you have ever met. Your car will break down when you are late for an appointment. Your children will go bonkers in the waiting room at the doctor's office. Your other prayers will go unanswered. When you pray for patience, get ready for setbacks, roadblocks, and pitfalls. So if you pray for patience, take a deep breath and hold on to your seat; you are in for a wild ride that will seem to last forever.

3. TEACH ME HOW TO FORGIVE

If you ask God to teach you how to forgive, He is going to do two things. He will first point out to you your many sins. He does this, not to shame you, but to show you how much you have been forgiven by God. We learn to forgive only when we come to understand how much we have been forgiven. After you have seen how much God has forgiven you, God will then bring people into your life who badmouth you, cheat you, sin against you, and do all kinds of horrible things to you. The only way to learn how to forgive others is to have people in your life whom you must forgive. So when you pray to learn how to forgive, watch out! For you are about to be hurt, slandered, maligned, mistreated, and abused. But when you finally learn the great ability to forgive, life will seem better, because you won't be bogged down with anger and bitterness.

As a side note, please note that forgiveness is not the same as forgetting. If you are being mistreated and abused, forgiveness does not require you to stay in that situation. Forgiveness does not require you to trust those who hurt and abused you. If you are being hurt, abused, or mistreated, you can forgive, but you must also get out. (I write more about this in my book on forgiveness in this Christian Question series.)

4. TEACH ME THE TRUTH

This prayer seems pretty innocent. What could be dangerous about truth? Don't we all want truth? Don't we want to know what God is really like, and what Scripture really says? Don't we want to know where we are wrong in our thinking and in our theology? The truth is that most Christians do not actually want to know where they are wrong. Most Christians don't *really* want to understand Scripture better. What they want is to have Scripture support their own beliefs and ideas. They want to remain safe and secure in their theological beliefs. They don't want to have their theological boat rocked.

This is why a prayer for truth is so dangerous. When you pray for truth, God is going to come into your life and start questioning some of your central beliefs about Him. The Holy Spirit will start raising dangerous questions about your understanding of certain biblical texts. Jesus will gently nudge you to rethink how you follow Him into the world. When you pray for truth, you will soon discover that some of your most cherished doctrines might be wrong. You may soon discover that the God you worship might not actually be the God revealed in Scripture. You may find that the way you are comfortable "doing church" is not actually found in the Bible.

When these sorts of truth bombs explode in your life, it feels like the bottom has fallen away. It feels like there is nothing firm to stand on, that you have nothing left but questions and doubts. It feels like you are tumbling down the theological rabbit hole. For a time, you will not know up from down, in from out, or even right from wrong. Such theological vertigo is extremely disconcerting for most people, but it is what often happens when you pray for God to help you better understand Scripture and to show you where you are wrong in your thinking about Him and His ways.

The prayer for truth is a dangerous prayer. If you are comfortable in your theology and believe you are right in almost everything you believe about God and the Bible, do not pray this dangerous prayer. But if you do pray this prayer and are willing to see it through, the world God opens to you is one you will never want to leave. You will discover such freedom in thinking for yourself. When your eyes are opened to the truth, you will love how clearly you see things and will never want to return to the way you viewed things before.

5. LEAD ME WHEREVER YOU WANT ME TO GO

One way this Christian prayer is often prayed is with the words, "Here I am, Lord, send me." If you are like me, when you have prayed this prayer, you imagine that God is going to send you into a high-profile ministry with a big church and lots of prominence in the community. You imagine that maybe you will become an advisor to the President, or the CEO of an international Christian relief organization. And to hear many Christian leaders talk, this "upward ministry trend" does indeed seem to be the way God leads many people. This is why you will almost never hear Christian leaders say that God is leading them downward into insignificance and poverty. No, when most Christian leaders talk about how they were led by God, it is almost always to bigger churches, with more prominent ministries, where there will be larger salaries, and greater power.

While I do not deny that God sometimes leads people in these directions, I think that more often than not, when we follow Jesus wherever He leads, He actually leads us downward, but we refuse to go. Jesus leads us to the gutter. He leads us to the gates of hell. He leads us where lives are broken, where sin is blackest, and where Satan's chains are strongest. This is why the prayer to follow Jesus wherever He leads is so dangerous.

If you want to do great things for God in His Kingdom, you must understand that greatness in God's Kingdom does not look like greatness in the kingdoms of this world. It usually looks like the exact opposite. God's path to greatness usually does not mirror what you have in mind. God's path to greatness usually leads to prison, death, and the gates of hell. I once heard Francis Schaeffer say in an interview that if given the choice between two ministry positions, we should choose the one with less fame and glory, as this is likely where God is actually leading.

This dangerous prayer usually goes hand-in-hand with the prayer for humility. In my experience, choices in ministry usually come in pairs. There is often one path that leads to greatness and glory, and another path that leads to obscurity and insignificance. Though the temptation is to choose glory and honor, Jesus might actually be calling you to follow Him downward into humility. So be sure you really mean it when you tell Jesus you will follow Him wherever He leads.

But then sit back and enjoy the ride, for there is nothing as wonderful as being right where God wants you to be. You will start using your God-given gifts and talents in ways that are exhilarating and liberating. You will discover that you no longer feel like an outsider who is looking in to where all the action is taking place, but will instead find yourself in the middle of the action of God's expanding Kingdom work in this world. The joy of working with God in this world while using your gifts to expand the Kingdom is the most indescribable experience you can have in this life.

6. HELP ME UNDERSTAND THE PLIGHT OF THE POOR

The poor and the needy are all around us, and since Scripture so often invites us to consider the plight of the poor, it is normal and natural to pray for God to help you understand their situation, and to do what you can to help. But this is also a dangerous prayer.

One way God might help you understand the poor is by causing you to become poor yourself. Or maybe you will lose your job and struggle to find a new one. Until you have faced the difficulty of putting food on the table, of finding work to provide for your family, or of putting a roof over one's head, you cannot understand the plight of the poor. So if you like your nice house, your two cars, your steak dinners, and your Caribbean vacations, don't ask God to help you understand the plight of the poor. If you long to have compassion for others and empathy to understand the plight of the poor so that you can better help and care for them, this is the prayer for you.

7. MAKE ME MORE LIKE JESUS

Praying to be more like Jesus is a very common prayer in Christianity, yet I advise you to think twice the next time you pray this prayer. Jesus was beaten and bruised, scorned and mocked, despised and rejected. Are you sure you really want to be like Jesus? It's good if you want to be like Jesus in His abilities to teach, love, serve, and heal, but these abilities also led Jesus to be crucified and killed. I do not think it is possible in this world to have one without the other.

When you pray to be like Jesus, other people will do everything they can to stop you. And I'm not talking about the world. People of the world were actually quite open to Jesus. He was the friend to prostitutes, tax-collectors, and sinners. The main opposition to Jesus came from religious people. Similarly, when you seek to be more like Jesus, you will likely find that your pastor and your church-going friends might be the most upset. The reason is that Jesus often challenges the *status quo*, and especially the *status quo* that claims to represent God.

But when you pray to be more like Jesus, trouble will also come directly from God. God will always work to make you more like Jesus, and so when you invite Him to do this work in your life, He steps in and starts to break down, burn away, and slough off anything and everything that does not look like Jesus. God may purify your life with His refining fire, but it still burns.

Soon enough, however, you will have people saying that you are like a breath of fresh air to be around. People will sense the presence of Jesus in you, and will feel comfortable telling you things they cannot tell anyone else. They will desire to be with you and around you for reasons they cannot explain. People will feel loved and accepted in your presence, just as people felt accepted in the presence of Jesus. When we become more like Jesus, we allow others the joy of being themselves, free from judgment and open to God's love.

8. GIVE ME MORE FAITH

Christians like our beliefs in nice, neat packages. But life is not like that, and neither is life with God. When you pray for God to give you more faith, you are likely to enter into some of the most difficult and doubt-filled times of your life. You will begin to question everything you have ever known and everything you have ever believed. You may even begin to doubt God's goodness. You might begin to wonder if God even exists.

This is not bad. Embrace the doubts. Understand that if what you believe is true, it can stand up against all questions. Truth does not fear a challenge. There is no other way for your faith to grow unless your faith is tested, and faith is only tested by questions that challenge your faith. So don't be afraid of questions. Don't be afraid of doubt.

When you pray for faith, you will initially gain more questions than faith. But don't be alarmed. As you learn to live with doubt, God will make Himself known to you in new and exciting ways, and both your knowledge and your faith will grow.

9. GIVE ME VICTORY OVER SIN AND TEMPTATION

Praying for victory over sin is like praying for victory over a great enemy. It is wonderful to pray for, but how do you think this victory will be achieved? It will only be achieved by facing it in battle. David could have prayed all he wanted for victory over Goliath, but he never would have been victorious over Goliath if he had not faced the giant in battle.

It is the same with you and your sin. Yes, pray for victory over sin and temptation, but know that when you pray for this, the onslaught of sin and temptation will only get worse. The battle will intensify. The giants will come forth and will mock you and your puny sticks and stones with which you intend to do battle.

Just remember, of course, that when such temptations come in response to your prayer, God is not the one sending the temptation. God does not tempt; nor does He allow you to be tempted above what you can bear. So when you face your giant, or even a whole army of giants, do not fear, for God is on your side, and if you are facing heavy temptation, know that God is standing by your side ready to help no matter what your challenge might be. God will never abandon you in the fight, no matter how large the enemy.

So if you pray this Christian prayer, be ready for an onslaught of all the wiles of the devil, but also be ready for God to battle with you at your side. And as God battles at your side, you will become a better, stronger, and more able soldier in the ongoing fight.

10. PLEASE HELP MY ANNOYING NEIGHBOR OR COWORKER COME TO FAITH

This is a great Christian prayer. Does God want to reach your annoying neighbor or your rude coworker with the gospel? Of course He does! But in light of what you learned in the previous chapter, do you know how God is going to reach your annoying neighbor or coworker with the gospel? That's right. He's going to use you.

I once heard a story of a Bible study group who decided to make a prayer list of all the people they "disliked" the most, and then pray for these people every week as part of the Bible study. Over the course of the next ten years, all but one of the people on that list became believers. Furthermore, almost all of them became Christians because the members of that Bible study showed grace, love, mercy, and forgiveness to these "annoying" people in their lives.

If you are going to pray for someone, be prepared to answer your own prayers. When you pray for God to reach someone with the gospel, God is likely going to send you.

CONCLUSION

When you are going through difficult times in life, it is normal to ask,

"Why me? Why is God allowing these things to happen to me?" When you are surrounded by devastation and difficulties and you find yourself asking, "What did I do to deserve this?" don't be surprised if the answer you receive back from God is, "You asked for it!" When you face difficulties in life, don't assume that God is punishing you, for the opposite is actually true. God does not punish.

Instead, when you face trials and troubles in life, it is more than likely that God is simply answering your prayers. God molds, forms, and shapes you in response to your prayers for Him to do so. But more often than not, in order for God to teach you humility or patience, to give you compassion for the poor, or to help you understand Him and His ways more clearly, He must first break you down so that He can then build you up and form you into what He wants you to be. The prayers suggested in this chapter will accomplish this reconstruction by God. These prayers are dangerous, but they are also essential, as we learn to follow Jesus wherever He leads.

CHAPTER 6

PRAYING POWERFUL PRAYERS

During the presidency of Lyndon B. Johnson, the Baptist minister Bill Moyers was asked to be the Presidential Cabinet's press secretary. At one of the meetings, President Johnson asked Bill Moyers to open the meeting with prayer. As Moyers began to pray, the President said, "Speak up, Bill, I can't hear you."

"I wasn't speaking to you, Mr. President," Moyers responded.

Imagine the audacity! And yet, this is exactly what we have been seeing in this book about prayer. Prayer is not fancy. Prayer is not for other people. Prayer is just talking to God. As we saw earlier in this book, prayer is when we "Jes' call 'im Father, an' ask 'im fer somethin'."

God doesn't need big words and long prayers. He doesn't need fancy or flowery language. He just wants us to come to Him as His child and talk to Him. That's the way all the saints in the Bible prayed. Every person in Scripture who is known for their great faith in God is also known for their simple and straightforward prayer life with God. Abraham, Moses, David, Elijah, Elisha, and Daniel were all men of great faith and simple prayers. It was also this way with Jesus.

And so it is not surprising that the prayers of the Apostle Paul are also simple and straightforward. Paul writes about prayer multiple times in his letter to the Ephesians (cf. Eph 1:15-21; 3:14-21; 6:18-20), but let us look at the description of his prayers in Ephesians 3:14-21 as an example of how Paul prayed and what he prayed for.

THE POSTURE OF PRAYER

For this reason I bow my knees ... (Eph 3:14a).

In Ephesians 3:14, Paul writes that when he prays, he bows his knees to God the Father. The term "bow my knees" is an idiom for kneeling. But does this mean that Paul knelt when he prayed? Maybe. But maybe not. While it might be true that Paul physically knelt on his knees when he prayed, Paul might also be using a figure of speech to describe the posture of his heart when he approached God in prayer.

The phrase "I bow the knees" comes from Isaiah 45:23. Isaiah 45 is a prophecy about the rule and reign of the Messiah. It is about how He alone will deliver Israel, and bring all her enemies to destruction. It is a lesson to the world in how He alone is Ruler and King. Isaiah writes that "Every knee will bow, every tongue confess" the Lordship of the Messiah (cf. Rom 11:4; Php 2:10). Isaiah is saying that the Messiah deserves proper honor and respect, and that this can be symbolized by kneeling before Him. Yet even here, what matters more than the position of one's legs is the posture of one's heart. Despite what Paul writes here, one does not need to physically kneel in order to pray.

In fact, Paul himself might not have actually knelt when he prayed. Jewish prayers were often said while standing up (Matt 6:5). Jesus, of course, condemns the practice of praying in a way to be seen and heard by men, and so maybe Paul preferred to pray kneeling. But we just don't know. And that is exactly the point. God doesn't care about the position of your body as much as He cares about the posture of your heart. There is no "one right way" to position your body when you pray, just as there is no "one right way" to position your body when you talk to anybody else. Just as you can talk to anyone while you are doing anything, so also, you can talk to God while you are walking your dog, driving your car, mowing your lawn, doing the dishes, lying in your bed, or sitting on your back porch. Yes, you can even pray while kneeling, if you so desire. But regardless of your position, come with the respectful posture of a kneeling heart, submitting your life and your desires to God.

THE PERSON OF PRAYER

... to the Father of our Lord Jesus Christ (Eph 3:14b).

Note as well that, just like Jesus instructed, Paul directs his prayers to God the Father. He says he prays to the Father of our Lord Jesus Christ. Once again, this brings to mind the intimacy of prayer. It is like a little child coming to ask something from his daddy.

I read a story a while back about a man who was in the army who got promoted to the honorable rank of Brigadier General. When he received the news, he excitedly called his wife at home to inform her. But when she informed their young son, he became a little sad. When she asked the little boy why he was sad, he said, "Can I still call him daddy?"

Many people are like this little boy. They hear that the person to whom we pray is "God Almighty, Creator of Heaven and Earth, the Lord, Master, and Sovereign Ruler of the Universe," and while they are happy to pray to a God with such honorable titles, they are afraid to simply call Him "Father" and ask Him for something. But that is exactly what Paul does in Ephesians 3. He prays to the Father.

So while it is true that our Heavenly Father is King, Ruler, Judge, Lord, and Master, and therefore worthy of all honor and respect, it is also true that He is our Father, and wants us to simply address Him as such, coming before Him like a child to his daddy. I hear some people refer to God as Daddy or Abba, which is also fine. Again, the point is not to get too caught up with the right words, but to simply speak to God in a way that is comfortable and personable.

THE PETITIONS OF PRAYER

The most instructive elements about Paul's prayer in Ephesians 3:14-21 are his requests. By looking at what Paul prayed for, we can learn what sorts of petitions we can ask for in prayer as well. And the most striking thing about Paul's prayer requests is their audacity. Paul is not content to pray about toe bunions and the weather. He enters boldly before the throne of grace and tosses down the most daring requests. Paul does not pray for the mundane and commonplace; he prays for the impossible.

Do you ever get bored with prayer? If so, it might be because your prayers lack boldness. You know you're supposed to pray, but it sometimes seems that God doesn't hear or answer your prayers, or that you pray the same old thing over and over and over. When this happens, prayer becomes more of a habit you mindlessly perform than the powerful force in your life that it is supposed to be. But when you pray the way Paul prays, you will never get bored with prayer because you are asking for the impossible. When you pray the way Paul prays, your prayers will be anything but ordinary.

Paul prays for three things in his prayer. Clearly, these three petitions are not the only things Paul prays for when he prays (for he lists other prayer requests in Eph 1:15-21), but these three items provide some good ideas on what Paul prayed for and how you also can pray.

To Do What Cannot Be Done

> *That He would grant you, ... to be strengthened with might through His Spirit in the inner man, ... that you, being rooted and grounded in love (Eph 3:16-17).*

The first impossible prayer request of Paul is that God will enable the Ephesian Christians to do what cannot be done. In Ephesians 3:16-17, Paul prays that God will give them the power ... to be rooted and grounded in love. Initially, this may seem like just another ho-hum request from Paul. But when you read this request in the context of everything Paul has written in Ephesians 2–3, you see that one of the main problems in the Ephesian church was a failure to love each other.

Paul spent two chapters talking about how Jews and Gentiles are one in Jesus Christ, and how they are to get along. For some, this might seem like an impossible task. Some Gentiles would be thinking, "You mean I have to love that annoying Jewish neighbor of mine? There's no way! He's always judging me by his standards of living and acting 'holier than thou.' I can't love him. I can't fellowship with him!"

Some of the Jews, on the other hand, were likely thinking, "You mean I have to go over to that Gentile's house when he invites me over for dinner? I can't do that! He might serve meat sacrificed to idols! He might not be following the strict cleanliness laws. I might become ceremonially unclean! Paul can't be serious. There's no way I can get along with them!"

Many people today fail to grasp the deep divide that existed between Jews and Gentiles in Paul's day. If you were to take all the divisions that exist today—cultural, political, racial, economic, and religious—and lump them all together, this is similar to the strife that existed between Jews and Gentiles. And in Ephesians 2–3, Paul instructed them to get along and live in unity with each other. Here in Ephesians 3:17, he tells them that he is praying for them to be rooted and grounded in love for each other.

As I write this, every day includes news about how the world is being ripped apart by political divisions, racial strife, economic disparity, theological disagreement, and a wide variety of similar issues. The various political parties strongly disagree about critical issues such as healthcare, global climate change, gay rights, gun rights, open borders, and taxes. Regardless of where you stand on these issues, how easy will it be for you to love and befriend a person who holds opposite views? You might say, "There's no way. I can never be in the same room with such a person, let alone love and like them!"

Yet this is exactly what Paul is instructing the Ephesian Christians to do, and is exactly what he prays about in Ephesians 3:17. He wants people to love each other who, in every other walk of life, hate and despise each other. In other words, Paul is praying for the impossible. He is praying for two groups who hate each other to turn their hate into love.

Of course, the only way that Christians can do this is to understand that we are all loved by God, regardless of our political, economic, racial, social, cultural, or theological backgrounds. Once you see that God loves "them" as much as God loves you, you then begin to realize that He wants you to love "them" as well, regardless of whether or not they ever change their views. This is what Paul means then he talks about being "rooted and grounded" in love. We can only love others with the love of God when we know that we are loved and that the love of God which He extends unconditionally to us is also extended unconditionally to others.

So the first prayer request is an impossible prayer request. It is a request to do what cannot be done, to love those you would rather hate. Paul says, "I know you cannot love these people by your own power. So I am praying that God will give you His power to do what He asks, to love the unlovable." Do you want to spice up your prayer life? Start asking God to show you the people you hate, and then to transform your hate into love. Then step back and watch out, for you are about to encounter more Trump voters (or Hillary voters) than you ever knew existed. And it may not just be people with political or cultural differences, but people with theological differences as well. There are all sorts of issues that divide Christians, and Paul prays the impossible prayer for us to live with each other in love.

To Know What Cannot Be Known

> *That you ... may be able to comprehend with all the saints what is the width and length and depth and height—to know the love of Christ which passes knowledge (Eph 3:18-19a)*

Paul turns from praying for the Ephesian Christians to do what cannot be done, and asks God to let them know what cannot be known. The second prayer request in Ephesians 3:18-19 is a prayer for knowledge. Paul wants them to comprehend the width and length and depth and height of the love of Christ which passes knowledge. Once again, this is an impossible prayer.

Imagine a third grade teacher giving her class a test on quantum physics. They can't know quantum physics! Most educated adults can't grasp quantum physics. It would even be absurd to try to teach quantum physics to third graders. They don't have the right mathematical foundation or brain power to grasp even the elementary principles of quantum physics, let alone comprehend it.

This is similar to what Paul prays for here. He is praying that the Ephesian Christians would know the love of Christ, which passes knowledge. Paul prays for them to know what cannot be known. And unlike quantum physics which can be understood and grasped by some people, Paul's description of the love of Christ indicates that nobody fully understands or comprehends this vast subject. Paul writes about its width, length, depth, and height, indicating that the love of Christ is eternal, or infinite. It is without beginning or end. It cannot be measured or contained. It is wider than the universe, farther than the east is from the west, and deeper than the ocean. God's love is so vast, it cannot be understood or comprehended. Yet Paul prays that the Ephesian Christians will come to know it anyway.

This is another impossible prayer.

Nevertheless, it is a prayer which God works to answer. Though you will never come to fully understand, grasp, or comprehend the length, width, breadth, or height of God's love for you in Jesus Christ, you can come to learn a little more about it each and every day. This is what Paul hopes will happen with the Ephesian Christians, and which you can pray for yourself as well. Imagine how your life will change if each and every day you became more and more convinced of how much Jesus loves you? Imagine how much excitement each day would hold if you knew that somehow, in some way, Jesus was going to show you that He loves you.

Many Christians live with so much fear in their life. Fear of the future. Fear of the unknown. Fear of sickness and death. Fear of sin. Yet since perfect love casts out fear (1 John 4:18), as you come to know how much God loves you, your fear of all these things fades away as well. You come to know that you are safe and secure in the loving arms of God. You come to realize that even though you may face sickness, trial, danger, or sword, God will never leave you nor forsake you. If this sounds like what you want, then begin to pray for the impossible. Pray that you will come to know that which cannot be known. Pray that you will comprehend the love of Christ which surpasses knowledge.

To Be Filled With What You Cannot Be Filled

That you may be filled with all the fullness of God (Eph 3:19b).

The third prayer request of Paul in Ephesians 3 follows the same pattern of the previous two. Paul continues to pray for the impossible. He prayed that the Ephesians would do what cannot be done and know what cannot be known. This third petition is that the Ephesian Christians would be filled with what they cannot be filled. The last half of Ephesians 3:19 contains Paul's prayer that the Ephesian Christians be filled with all the fullness of God.

How big is God? If you know some theology, you know that God is omnipresent. This means that He is everywhere. God is fully present everywhere, and He even exists where nothing else exists beyond the limits of space and time. How great is God? How powerful is He? Again, in theological terms, He is omnipotent. He is all powerful. With a mere thought, He could obliterate the universe. With another mere thought, He could recreate it. He can do whatever He wants, wherever He wants, whenever He wants, however He wants. (Thank goodness He's a loving and merciful God—this kind of power would be terrible in the hands of a tyrant).

So with God's omnipresence and omnipotence in mind, think of what Paul is praying for in Ephesians 3:19. He prays that you, as a teeny, tiny speck of flesh and bones, made from dust, dying, decaying, sinful, insignificant piece of the vast universe, with life that is but a breath, that you may be filled with all the fullness of God. This is an impossible prayer request from Paul.

It wouldn't even matter if the structure of our body was much larger. When King Solomon built the first temple, he prayed a prayer on the day the temple was dedicated (cf. 1 Kings 8). He said, "But will God indeed dwell on the earth? Behold, heaven and the heaven of heavens cannot contain You. How much less this temple which I have built!" (1 Kings 8:27). Solomon, the wisest man who has ever lived saw the truth that God could not be contained in any sort of building or structure.

Yet Paul prays that the Ephesian Christians will be filled with all the fullness of God. This also is an impossible prayer request. If God could not fill the temple, how can God fill a Christian? The solution, I believe, lies in how God answers the previous two impossible prayer requests from Paul. The fullness of God in the world is best seen in how Christians know they are infinitely and unconditionally loved by God and then learn to show this same love to others. The fullness of God in our lives is seen and experienced through the love that comes to us from God and the love that we show toward others. Just as Jesus is the fullness of God, we, as the body of Christ on earth, reveal the fullness of God to the world in the same way that Jesus did. We are filled with God the way Jesus was filled, as we show God's love to the world. So even this third and final impossible prayer request is answerable by God, and is answered as we show love to one another.

PRAYING IMPOSSIBLE PRAYERS

We have seen three impossible prayer requests from Paul. He prayed that the Ephesians would do what cannot be done, know what cannot be known, and be filled with what they cannot be filled.

Have you ever thought of praying for the impossible? How does your prayer life compare to Paul's? Paul prays for the impossible; what do you pray for? If your prayer life is boring, maybe it is because your prayer requests are boring. When you start praying for the impossible, you will quickly discover that prayer becomes exciting, thrilling, and even a bit terrifying. Rather than try to think up more things to pray about, you begin to wonder about the wisdom of praying for certain things. I mean, if you asked God to help you get along with that annoying neighbor, you might discover that God will start having you spend more time with that neighbor. Is that really what you want? If you pray for God to save the co-worker who intentionally blasphemes God when you're around, don't be surprised if you get assigned to work on a project with him. God wants you to ask Him to do the impossible, but only if you are willing to let Him do the impossible through you.

And when God starts to work in response to impossible prayers, He will do more than we can even ask or imagine. Paul writes in Ephesians 3:20 that God is able to do exceedingly abundantly above all we ask or imagine. What is impossible with men is possible with God. When we think something is impossible, God can run circles around it with His eyes closed and one hand tied behind His back. Nothing is impossible for Him.

So what is your impossible situation? Keep it in your mind and ask God to take care of it, knowing that He will likely take care of it through you. And don't worry about coming up with solutions for impossible problems. You don't have to make suggestions to God about how to handle impossible situations. All you have to do is present your requests to God and let Him take care of it. All you have to do is say, "God, here it is. I don't see a way out. It's yours." Ask God for the impossible.

CAN I GET AN "AMEN"?!

The last word of Paul's prayer in Ephesians 3 is the word "Amen." Based on this, as well as some other places in Scripture where the word "Amen" is used (cf. Deut 27:15-26; 1 Chr 16:36; Neh 5:13; 8:6), some Christians think that every prayer should be concluded with the word "Amen." But the word "Amen" actually means "Truly, so be it, let it be." When you pray impossible prayers, you are simply asking God to let it be as you have prayed. And when you pray according to His will, know that He will do what you have asked.

God does the impossible because this is how His name is glorified as stories of what God has done are shared from generation to generation.

The story of Hannah in the book of 1 Samuel is a great example. Hannah was unable to have children, and so she prayed to God. She asked for the impossible. God heard her prayer and opened her womb, and within one year she gave birth to Samuel. We are still telling that story today.

Consider the account of Elijah in 1 Kings 18. He held a contest between God in heaven and the false god Baal. Elijah and the prophets of Baal built altars and each called on their own God to light the fire. God answered Elijah's prayer and rained down fire from heaven.

We could go on and on through Scripture. In response to Joshua's prayer, God halted the sun in the sky for a full day. In response to prayer, Peter was set free from prison. In a way, the Bible could be viewed as one long account of how God acts on behalf of those who pray impossible prayers.

And don't let the fact that they are Bible stories make you think that something similar could not happen with you. In November of 1835, George Mueller set out to prove that God hears and answers prayer. In looking for ways to prove this, he wrote:

> It needed to be something which could be seen, even by the natural eye. Now, if I, a poor man, simply by prayer and faith, obtained without asking any individual, the means for establishing and carrying on an Orphan-House, there would be something which, with the Lord's blessing, might be instrumental in strengthening the faith of the children of God, and being a testimony to the consciences of the unconverted, of the reality of the things of God. …When I was asking the petition, I was fully aware what I was doing. I was asking for something which I had no natural prospect of obtaining, but which was not too much for the Lord to grant.

By the time George Mueller died, the Orphan House founded and funded by prayer was able to house 1000 children at a time.

If you have spent much time praying for the impossible, you might have similar stories yourself. I once prayed a man out of a life-sentence in prison. From a judicial point of view, prison is probably where he belonged. But under mercy and grace, I was convinced that prison was not at all where God wanted him. So I prayed. On the night before his trial we went down to a local lake. It was March and the ice had just melted. He sat there on the shore, staring at the mountains thinking he would never see them again. Then he stripped off his shirt and pants and went swimming in the ice cold water, thinking he would never again feel lake water on his skin. The next day, he received a "Not Guilty" verdict. Why? Because of one thing—praying for the impossible. The man is now married, has a child or two, and is serving God with all his strength.

Does God answer prayers for the impossible? Of course He does. He is able to do exceedingly abundantly above all that you ask or imagine. If you want the impossible done in your life, pray for the impossible. Then let God work.

But what if you have prayed impossible prayers that were according to the will of God, and yet God never answered and never stepped in to work in impossible ways? What happens when you pray for God to work, but God doesn't seem to hear, listen, or respond? This question is considered in the next chapter.

CHAPTER 7

WHAT ABOUT UNANSWERED PRAYERS?

The most frustrating thing about prayer is how so many prayers seem to go unanswered. Yet many common Christian responses to unanswered prayer are less than helpful. When prayers go unanswered, it is never wise to quote Bible verses about needing more faith or that we should view our trials as an opportunity to prepare for even greater trials in the future. It is also unhelpful to spout the old Christian cliché that there is no such thing as unanswered prayer. We all know that sometimes God says "No" or "Wait" to our prayers, especially when we pray for things out of ignorance that might actually damage ourselves or others.

These sorts of responses to unanswered prayer are cruel and insensitive when said to the barren mother who prays for God to open her womb, the parents who pray fervently for God to heal a child with terminal cancer, the single person who is lonely and wants a spouse, or to the father who needs work so that he can feed and clothe his family. Are not all such requests within God's will? Of course they are! Are many of them impossible prayers? Yes! Then why does God seem to do nothing in response to such prayers?

The truth is that I don't really know. And neither does anyone else. So don't believe any pastor or theologian who says they do have the answer. Nevertheless, there are several things we do know about how God works through prayer and in our lives, and once we come to understand these truths, we begin to understand why there are so many unanswered prayers.

IT IS NOT A LACK OF FAITH

When we fail to see God respond to requests that we know are within His will, we must never think that the reason God did not respond positively is because we didn't have enough faith. Tragically, this is often what some Christians say and teach to others. "If you just had more faith," they tell the parents at a child's funeral, "God would have healed your child." This may be the most damaging lie ever told about prayer.

The reason many people say such things is because there are numerous passages in the Bible which seem to indicate that we must have "enough faith" before God answers our prayers (cf. Matt 13:58; 21:22; Mark 11:24; Luke 7:9, 50; 18:42; Jas 5:15-16). Yet the reason that modern Christianity has a twisted understanding of these passages is because we fail to grasp the nature of faith.

I teach a lot more about faith in my "Gospel Dictionary" online course, but briefly, it is critical to understand that faith does not come in "quantities." You cannot have 50% faith, or even 99% faith. Faith is more like a light switch that is either On or Off. Yet at the same time, faith is not an "all or nothing" proposition. That is, there are countless truths we can either believe or disbelieve, and they do not all stand or fall together. Some truths you will believe (the switch is On), and some truth you will not believe (the switch is Off). Some of these truths are hard to believe, while others are quite easy. Furthermore, you cannot choose to believe anything. You must be persuaded to believe, based on the evidence of facts which you already believe. Sometimes, when we come to believe something that we previously did not, this new belief has a cascading effect through numerous other beliefs—like a complex Excel spreadsheet. But they do not all stand or fall together like a house of cards.

When these truths about faith are taken into consideration, all of the passages from the New Testament about people's "lack of faith" take on entirely new meanings. It is not that people didn't quite have enough faith; it is that they simply didn't believe certain things. But even this truth about faith could be abused when talking to mothers who pray for sick children or fathers who pray for a job. So it is best to never question anybody's faith.

It is true that faith is a factor in our prayers. It is true that we must believe that God can do what we ask of Him. But faith as small as a mustard seed is able to move mountains (Matt 17:20). So the smallest amount of faith will do. Every person I have ever talked to or prayed with who has agonized in prayer over some desperate situation has more than enough faith for God.

Can we really believe that God is so petty that although He wants to heal a sick and dying child, He won't do so until the "faith meter" of the parents rises to a certain level? Does God sit idly by, watching our faith like a thermostat until it rises to 80%, but if we only get to 79%, He says, "Oh! So close! I'm going to have to let your child suffer and die." Is that what God is like? Of course not! This sort of god is a satanic lie.

So if the lack of "enough" faith is not the reason some prayers go unanswered by God, what is the reason? The answer is found in one of the things we humans value the most: our freedom.

IT IS A LOVE FOR FREEDOM

We humans love freedom. But we love freedom because God loves it more. Our love for freedom is a poor reflection of His love for freedom. And He doesn't just love His freedom, but ours. God wants us to have a relationship with Him, and created us for this very purpose. But in order for a true relationship to exist, there must be the freedom to reject that relationship. God desires that we love Him, but for love to be real, it must be free. And since He freely loves us, He gave us a degree of genuine freedom so that we might (or might not) love Him in return.[1]

This means that God is not in absolute control of all things. I know that this is a shocking thought to some, but it is the requirement for love.

---

[1] For an excellent discussion and defense of this idea, see Thomas Jay Oord, *The Uncontrolling Love of God* (Downers Grove, IL: IVP, 2015).

If God was in absolute control of all things, there could be no such thing as love, for love, by definition, does not seek to control.[2] On the one hand, if humans have a degree of freedom, but God forced His will upon people because He is stronger and more powerful, then this would not be love, but spiritual and psychological rape. On the other hand, if God did not give us a degree of freedom, and simply programmed us to do what He wants, then we would not be human, but would instead be robots, which cannot show genuine love. For love to truly be love, the object of love must be free to not love in return.

Since God does not control all things, but gives humans a degree of genuine freedom, this means that humans can use this freedom to do things that are contrary to God's will. In other words, we can sin. This explains why this world is full of sin. Sin happens because humans use our God-given freedom in a way that God does not want. And because freedom is genuinely free, God cannot simply take it back or turn it off when we seek to use our freedom in ways that are damaging and hurtful to ourselves and others.[3] Sinful human activity such as theft, rape, murder, and war are all contrary to God's will, but they happen because God provided freedom to humans, and some humans use this freedom in hurtful and harmful ways.

But it is not just sin. There are also natural disasters. Could not God stop natural disasters without violating anyone's free will? Well, the truth of the matter is that there are a nearly infinite number of factors that go into any single natural disaster, and a good many of these factors involve free human decisions.[4] Hurricanes and floods don't just come out of nowhere. Weather patterns, rain clouds, and rising sea levels are all influenced in various ways by the behaviors and actions of human beings. In a world where sinful or selfish actions have far-reaching effects, natural disasters cannot be magically averted if the forces of cause-and-effect are

---

[2] Ibid., 181.
[3] Ibid., 168.
[4] Cf. the discussion in Gregory A. Boyd, *Satan and the Problem of Evil* (Downers Grove, IL: IVP, 2001), 218, and Gregory A. Boyd, *Is God to Blame?* (Downers Grove, IL: IVP, 2003).

to remain in place.[5]

Due to creaturely freedom, many aspects of the world are simply broken, and God cannot unilaterally fix everything that has gone wrong. While God does everything He can to protect us from the pain, there are some things God just cannot do without violating His gift of freedom, and therefore, violating love. As Greg Boyd writes:

> God's ultimate goal is to have creatures eternally participate in his triune love. The integrity with which he gives the risky gift of freedom is what makes this love possible and renders this freedom irrevocable. But this freedom is also what makes nightmares possible. God cannot avoid the possibility of these nightmares without also canceling out the possibility of love.[6]

However, this does not mean God is powerless or without resources to fix what is wrong with the world. Quite to the contrary, God's loving grace and wisdom are taking effect every day in our lives, and especially through our lives. As indicated earlier in this book, often when we pray to God to fix something that is wrong with the world, He agrees with our prayer and then asks us to fix it with Him.

It is for good reason that the New Testament speaks of the church as the "body of Christ." Just as Jesus was the incarnation of God on earth, the church is now the incarnation of God on earth. We are God's hands, feet, and mouth to a sick, lost, and hurting world, and there are many things that God wants to do in this world which He can only do in collaboration with us.

> God desires and needs human collaboration to accomplish his will. How can a struggling friend pay rent unless someone gives them money? How can racism be rooted out of the crevices of human hearts and minds unless someone teaches love and peace? How can child trafficking come to an end unless people stand up and rescue children? How can environmental pollution be reduced unless individuals and corporations take practical steps?

---

[5] Oord, *Uncontrolling Love*, 175.
[6] Boyd, *Satan and the Problem of Evil*, 215.

The answer to all of these questions is, "They can't."[7]

Since God often works to answer prayer in collaboration with human partners, this means that answers to prayer often take time to appear. This is especially true when the answers to prayer require advances in the scientific fields of medicine, psychology, and sociology. Though many in these occupations do not recognize it, they are being guided by God to help the world go in the direction God desires.

But again, since God does not override human free will, such changes take time. And tragically, many people live (or have lived) in times when medicine has not yet solved the problem of cancer or barren wombs, when sociology and government have not solved the problem of homelessness and poverty, and when psychology has not yet solved the problem of mental illness or psychotic breakdowns. But God is at work, and all who wish to work with God in these areas should do as much as they are able to coordinate their work with God's work so that millions of prayers are answered.

So the reason many prayers do not get accomplished is not because they are outside of God's will, or even because God says "No" to them. To the contrary, He may very well be saying "Yes," but other factors and considerations are keeping His "Yes" from becoming a reality.

Sometimes these other factors include sin. Sometimes in order for God to say "Yes" to us, He would have to restrict or limit the freedom of someone else, which He is not always able to do. Sometimes God simply cannot do what we have asked, even though He would like to. Sometimes, God wants to do what we ask, but He wants to do it *with* us, and if we are unwilling to join Him in answering our own prayers, then God cannot do it on His own. Sometimes both we and God are doing everything possible to bring answers to our prayers to fruition, but a myriad of other factors keep it from occurring.

Nevertheless, when our prayers go unanswered, this is not the time to despair. We may not always know why certain prayers go unanswered,

---

[7] Karris, *Divine Echoes*, 147.

but we can know with certainty that unanswered prayers do not indicate a lack of care on the part of God. Even in unanswered prayer, God is there with us.

GOD STAYS AND PRAYS WITH US

When a woman prays for God to give her a child, God is right there with her, hugging and holding her, and crying with her about her emptiness. When a mother prays for her dying child to get healed, God is right there with her, grieving over a broken world where such things happen to innocent children. When a father cries out to God for employment, God is there providing input and advice to lead the man to a job.

Due to the problems that arise in this world of sickness and death, wombs do not always function the way God intended, medicine does not always work, and economies do not always provide work for all who need it. God is not a magician who can wave His magic wand to make everything better, but He is a Friend and Father who walks with us through the pain, stays with us in the darkest night, and leads us in the direction He wants us to go, even when things do not go the way He wants.

When your prayers go unanswered, know that this is not because God does not hear or does not want you to receive what you have asked of Him. Quite the opposite is true. When your prayers go unanswered, know that God is there with you in your pain and suffering, praying along with you for wisdom, insight, and direction, so that together, you might face and overcome all that this world throws your way. God will never leave you, forsake you, or abandon you. He will not withdraw from you to face the troubles of this world alone. When your prayers go unanswered, these are the times to turn toward Him for His care and prayer for you.

CHAPTER 8

OTHER QUESTIONS ABOUT PRAYER

I hope you have found this book helpful. If so, would you please leave a review on Amazon and tell others about the book as well? Thank you.

Nevertheless, you probably still have several questions about prayer. Since this is a short book on prayer, I imagine that not all of your questions were answered. Let me address a few of these possible questions here. If your question is not answered below, feel free to submit your questions about prayer (or any other subject), by joining my online discipleship group at RedeemingGod.com/join/. After you join, I will send you a few welcome emails and you can reply to any one of them to ask your question directly to me. You will also have the opportunity to take my online course on prayer (which is based on the content of this book) and receive further training about prayer by email. See you there!

CAN I PRAY WHEN I'M ANGRY AT GOD?

Many people wonder if they should pray to God when they are angry at Him. Life causes much pain and hardship in our lives, and these situations can create feelings of anger and resentment at God for not protecting us from them. Also, we sometimes feel that even though we try our hardest to serve and honor God with our lives, He does not do much to reward or recognize our efforts, and it is easy to feel neglected and overlooked. In such situations, we might become angry at God. When people get angry, they tend to turn away from God and stop praying

But this is exactly the wrong thing to do when you are angry at God.

Rather than cease praying when we're angry, we should start praying even more, and then pray honestly to God, telling Him how angry we are and what we are angry about. In the experience of many, it is in our angry prayers where we often experience the greatest spiritual breakthrough with God. Why? Because it is only when we are angry that we finally let our guard down and tell God what is really going on in our hearts.

When we are not angry at God, we feel that we must hide our true emotions, thoughts, and feelings from God, and come to Him with pious words and "religious" language. But all such ideas disappear when we are angry. It is only when we are angry that we let go of our religious attempts to not "shock" God with our emotions of fear, frustration, confusion, and doubt. It is only when we are angry at God that we are honest enough with God to tell Him what we really think with words that really represent what is in our heart. God does not want us to be alone in our pain and anger. He prefers to be with us in whatever we face, especially if we think He is the one who caused it.

God loves your honesty and will often meet you there. It is often only in the angry prayer where the honest requests of our heart are revealed. God is not offended when we get angry at Him. He is not shocked or outraged when the frustrations of this life finally get the best of us and we lash out at Him with a burst of emotion, and even foul language. Instead, it is here, I am convinced, that God lets out a loving sigh and says, "Finally! I was wondering when you were going to tell Me what was *really* going on. I know what has been eating at you, but until you were ready to talk to Me about it, I wasn't going to force the issue. But now that we're talking … well, I'm talking, and you're shouting … we can finally start to communicate. So let it all out. Trust Me, I can take it. There is nothing you can say to Me that I haven't heard a million times before."

Remember, God is your friend, and He wants you to talk to Him like a friend. When you are angry at a good friend, you often shout it out with them, knowing that they will remain your friend no matter what you say. Honesty is always the best policy in friendship, even when it is honesty about anger and when the friend is God. So praying when you're angry might be one of the best times to talk to God.

In fact, yelling at God actually reveals your love for Him. When you go to God in your anger, it is usually because you know He can be trusted with your raw emotions. Therefore, going to God in anger is not a sign of hate, but love. Going to God when you are angry and frustrated is an indication of your love for Him, because you are taking your biggest problems to Him.

Children often get angry at their parents for not giving them something they really wanted (like candy before dinner), or taking something away that they had (like a sharp knife). The parents, if they are good parents, do this because the parent sees the bigger picture and knows what is best. So while no parent enjoys having their children upset at them in such situations, the good parent can handle the child's anger because they know they did what was best.

Similarly, since God is our Father, He sees the big picture and knows what is best for us. But like any children, we may get angry and upset at Him when life does not go as we hoped, dreamed, or planned. Often, genuinely bad things truly do happen, and if we think God is someone who always protects us from bad things, we might feel like He has betrayed us. But the worst thing we can do in such situations is fail to go to Him with our feelings of anger and betrayal. He wants us to come to Him and tell Him what we are thinking and feeling. Such feelings are not sinful or carnal, but come from ignorance about the situation or about the true nature and character of God. It is only when we come to God in honest anger that we keep the lines of dialogue open so He can start to reveal to us the truth about Himself and how life really works.

In other words, God would rather have you come to Him in anger than run from Him in anger. When you are angry at God but try to hide it, this doesn't please God, for this is just a form of pious dishonesty. Therefore, if you feel like yelling at God, don't hold back. Tell God what is wrong. Tell Him what you think. Lash out at Him in anger, for there is no tongue lashing that is worse than the actual lashing He already received on the cross. In both cases, He accepts the pain out of His great love for us.

Recently, one of my daughters was angry at me, and I couldn't figure out why. As I tried to figure out what had happened, I gently probed her with questions. But rather than answer my questions, she just kept saying "Nothing!" No matter what I asked, that was her answer. This is how we act toward God when we don't vent our anger at Him, and instead just clam up about what we're feeling.

So yelling at God is a healthy spiritual and relational practice. The Psalmists all understood this, and in the Psalms, we encounter some of the angriest writing in all of Scripture and much of it is directed at God. The Psalmists had raw emotions and were not afraid to vent at God. If you ever feel like yelling at God, read some of the Psalms and yell at God along with the Psalmists.

So are you angry at God? Are you angry about something He allowed to happen in your life? Go ahead. Yell at God. Curse if you have to. There is nothing you can say that God hasn't heard already... It's not like God has virgin ears. Tell God your blasphemous thoughts. You have permission to be honest with God about your thoughts and your feelings. God always prefers angry honesty over the sullen silent treatment. So yell away.

In my own experience, the times where I have heard God's voice the most clearly are the times when I have just finished lashing out at Him in visceral anger and outrage at how He failed me, my family, or this world. It is after I have used God as a punching bag that I feel His arms wrap around me and say, "Well done. I'm glad you finally got that out into the open. You've been hiding it away, and now that you've brought it out, we can talk about it. Oh, and by the way, before we do talk about it, I want you to know that I love you. Nothing you just said could ever get in the way of My love for you."

And then we talk.

WHAT ABOUT PRAYER FOR HEALING?

I believe God can and does heal. But we cannot demand healing, and more often than not, God does not heal without the help of doctors and modern medicine. The vast majority of "divine healing" occurs in coordination with the divinely-guided medical practices of our day.[1] This is, in fact, what James is referring to when he writes about the effectiveness of anointing oil for healing. There is no "magical" healing power to anointing oil. Instead, rubbing, or anointing, with oil was a common medical practice in New Testament times. To learn more about this idea, read the following post: RedeemingGod.com/anoint-with-oil-for-healing/

But regardless of whether or not healing occurs, you must not think that the absence of healing means that God is punishing you, has abandoned you, or is just waiting until you have "more faith." Quite to the contrary, when you are sick and injured, God is right there with you, walking through the pain and suffering by your side.

It is so tragic when pastors and preachers tell people who are sick that they were not healed because they didn't have enough faith or that God is punishing them for some sin. Remember that even Paul was not healed by God when he prayed to have the thorn in his flesh removed (2 Cor 12:8).

When you are sick, or when you pray for someone else who is sick, feel free to pray for healing. But if the healing does not come, know God is always with you, that He is not punishing you for sin, and that while He wants you to be healed, various unknown circumstances or factors are keeping the healing from occurring. God hates sickness, but a myriad of causes may be stopping God from sending the healing that both He and you want. In such situations, recognize that God is with you, by your side, walking through the pain and suffering, so that your experience can also be used to touch the lives of others who face similar challenges. In this way, while you may not be healed of your disease or sickness, it will

[1] Oord, *Uncontrolling Love,* 191-216.

be redeemed for God's good purposes.

WHAT ABOUT PRAYING IN TONGUES?

I suppose this is another topic that will require a full book in this Christian Question series. My basic answer, however, goes back to the basic idea I have presented in this book about prayer. When I talk to a friend, I am only going to speak in a way that both of us can understand. If someone is speaking in tongues, then even though God can understand it, the person speaking cannot, let alone anyone else who happens to be listening. So I would say that anyone who desires to speak in tongues should do so only in private settings where they are having a private conversation with God, and even then, it is best to use words that you understand as well. A longer explanation will have to wait for another book.

WHAT ABOUT PRAYING SCRIPTURE?

I am a big fan of praying with Scripture. This is when you take passages from the Bible and turn them into prayers. I am especially fond of praying the Psalms. Praying the Scriptures in this way allows us to know that we are praying according to the will of God (if we have properly understood the particular text), and also teaches us how biblical authors thought and prayed. You can read something I previously wrote about praying the Psalms here: RedeemingGod.com/praying-the-psalms/

There is a drawback to praying the Scriptures, however. Once again, it all comes back to the idea that prayer is talking to God as you would talk to any other person. If a man wants to speak in romantic ways to his wife, he might be wise to begin by memorizing and reciting some romantic poems to her. But if this is all he ever does, then the romantic poems lose all romance, and they actually will harm the relationship rather than help it.

So also with any other conversation. If you want to talk about sports with a buddy from work, it might be helpful to read a paragraph out of the sports section of the newspaper as a way to get the conversation started, but if all you ever do is read quotes from sports columns, you are not likely to have many meaningful conversations with this other man.

It's the same with praying the Scriptures. Such a practice can be helpful, especially as a way to start a conversation, but if your prayer life consists only (or mostly) of just reading Scriptures to God, your prayer life will never grow or develop, and neither will your relationship with God. Use the Scriptures as prayer training wheels or conversation starters, but don't depend on them to keep the conversation going.

HOW DOES GOD TALK TO US IN PRAYER?

I believe that since prayer is a form of communication with God, this means that God also communicates with us. The problem is that God does not seem to communicate with us the way we communicate with Him. But maybe some of this is because we have not trained ourselves to listen.

So I encourage you to spend more time listening when you pray. You are not listening for an audible voice or anything like that, but for God to impress upon you the things He wants you to do. This might come to you through feelings in your heart, thoughts in your head, or even with something like images, visions, or a still small voice. The difficulty, however, is discerning when such things come from God and when they come from the imaginations of our own heart. Furthermore, this difference is often only realized in hindsight.

Of course, if you want to hear God speak with a little more certainty, the best way is to read Scripture. Since Scripture is God's inspired Word (2 Tim 3:16), this means that Scripture is God breathed, or God spoken, and so God has spoken to you through Scripture, and can even enlighten your mind and encourage your heart through the text of the Bible. While I often find that speaking to God with Scripture is helpful, I find that it is even more helpful to allow God to speak to me through the Scriptures.

But let me issue one warning. Regardless of how you hear the voice of God, never go up to someone else and say, "God told me ..." Just don't do it. Make it a rule to live by. If you are right, and God truly did say to you what you want to share, then it will still be true regardless of whether or not you tack on the words, "God told me ..."

Furthermore, these three words are little more than spiritual boasting. They are often used by people who want to prove how spiritual they are, or who want to use God's name as a trump card to get people to do what they say. In this latter case, such a use of the words "God told me ..." might be taking the Lord's name in vain. If you claim that God is behind something you say, when in fact it is only something that came from your own heart and mind, then you are attaching God's name to something He had nothing to do with in an attempt to give your idea or teachings more credibility. This is a very dangerous practice to follow. So whether God truly did reveal something to you or not, you don't need to tell people about it.

Ultimately, hearing the voice of God is an important topic, but one which likely cannot be taught. But one thing is certain. If you think you hear God's voice, it will always lead you to act in loving, encouraging, and reconciling ways toward others. It will never be mean or judgmental. If you want to say something mean or judgmental to someone else, don't blame it on God. God's only activity toward humans is to love, heal, and restore, and so when He speaks to us, it will be in ways that encourage us to love, heal, and restore others as well.

Never forget that since God is a God of love, He very often does not tell us what to do, but instead asks us what we want to do. God is not a controlling God. He has given free will to humans, and part of God's journey with humanity is to go with us wherever we go. So the next time you pray, "God, what should I do?" recognize that He might be saying back, "I don't know. What do *you* want to do?" This then creates an opportunity to have a conversation with God about the various available options. Often, God is not as concerned with *what* you do, as much as keeping the lines of communication open with Him *as you do it*.

Here are several blog posts that are related to this topic:
RedeemingGod.com/how-does-god-talk-to-humans/
RedeemingGod.com/how-to-hear-the-voice-of-the-spirit/
RedeemingGod.com/let-me-pray-on-that/
RedeemingGod.com/taking-the-lords-name-in-vain/

DO I NEED TO SAY "AMEN" AT THE END OF MY PRAYERS?

I have a friend who was asked by his pastor to pray over a fellowship meal at church. My friend had not prayed publicly before and was a bit nervous. But he got through the prayer just fine by thanking God for the food and bringing a few requests before Him. Near the end of his prayer, however, he forgot how to "properly conclude" a prayer, and so just said what came natural to him. He said, "Well ... goodbye Jesus." Everybody laughed, and he felt a bit ashamed afterwards, but I congratulated him and told him that God probably preferred "Goodbye Jesus" to the traditional ending of "Amen." His concluding words were genuine, and showed that he was talking to God the way he would talk to anyone else. This is exactly what God wants and desires for our prayers.

Many people end their prayers by saying, "Amen." While there is some biblical justification for this practice, the primary reason most follow this practice is because it is tradition. They hear others say "Amen" at the end of their prayers, and so they think that this is how a prayer is supposed to end. Yet I encourage you to stop saying "Amen" at the end of your prayers. I say this for three reasons.

First, it was primarily used in corporate prayer situations, and was primarily spoken by those listening to the prayer, not by those doing the praying. In several of the passages that encourage this practice (cf. Deut 27:15-26; 1 Chr 16:36; Neh 5:13; 8:6), it is not the person praying who says "Amen," but the people listening to the prayer. The practice of saying "Amen" seems to be a practice that was done during corporate prayer rather than private prayer, and was a way for the people to respond to what they were hearing.

But they weren't saying "Amen" just because it was a spiritual thing to say. They had a reason for saying it. This leads to the second reason we can stop saying "Amen" at the end of our prayers. The word "Amen" means "Truly" or "So let it be." When the people in Scripture said "Amen" as part of the corporate prayer, they were simply stating their agreement with what was said. Quite often in prayer meetings, I might find myself nodding my head in agreement or quietly saying the words "Yes" or "Yes, Lord" to what someone else is saying. This is similar to what the people were doing in Scripture when they said "Amen."

Third, saying "Amen" at the "end" of a prayer causes you to think that your prayer is over. I find that when I say "Amen" at the end of a prayer, I subconsciously think that I am done praying. By saying "Amen," I compartmentalize prayer and communication with God into an event that only occurs in specific places at specific times using specific words. But as we have seen in this book, just as an ongoing conversation with a friend or spouse is never over, so also, prayer conversations with God are never over. When you refuse to conclude your prayers with an "Amen," this is a little reminder that your communication with God is ongoing and does not have a beginning or an end.

Nevertheless, despite these three reasons to not say "Amen," there might be one instance where an "Amen" is helpful. This is when you are saying a prayer in front of other people, such as in a church service, a Bible study, or before a meal (but see the question below). In such situations, saying "Amen" is more for them than for God. It helps them know that you are turning from talking to God to talking to them. On the other hand, normal human conversations typically don't provide these sorts of verbal cues to tell others when you are done talking to someone. You just finish your sentence, then turn to the next person you are going to talk to. With a little training, I believe that pastors and Bible study leaders can do the same thing in their prayers. Talk to God with your eyes open, and then simply start talking to the people who are there. I have seen this done in churches and Bible studies from time to time, and I find it quite refreshing. God is treated like another person in the room, and when He is viewed this way, the person teaching the sermon or leading the Bible study then feels the freedom to turn to God again at any time during the service or study to continue the ongoing conversation with Him. In this way, the leader is not only teaching others about Scripture, but is also teaching others about prayer.

Such teaching about prayer through modeling prayer is also something that can be done at home with our children. One great way to do this is during our meals.

DO I NEED TO PRAY OVER MY MEALS?

There are some Scriptures which seem to form the background for the tradition of praying over a meal (Deut 8:10; 1 Tim 4:5; 1 Cor 10:31; Acts 27:35; Matt 14:19-21). But none of these texts specifically command or require that we pray over our meals. God does want us to be mindful of Him when we eat, and to thank Him and give glory to Him for the food He provides to us, but is a perfunctory prayer before we eat really the best way to do this? I am not so sure.

I clearly remember the time when I first began to have second thoughts about the practice of praying over a meal. I was probably about nine or ten and was at a church "Pot-Luck" with my family. My father was one of the pastors and he asked a church elder to say the prayer over the meal. After asking us all to fold our hands, bow our heads, and close our eyes, he said, "God, ... thank you for this food. Amen." Then he raised his head and said, "Let's eat!" I remember being a little startled at such a short prayer. I looked around nervously at the adults and saw some of them glancing at each other with looks that said, "Did that count?" But nobody said anything, and we all started eating. That prayer stuck with me, and it was one of the first times I started questioning why we do what we do in the church, and that there might be a different way to pray than how I had been taught.

Today, my family no longer prays over our meals. I know that this may seem strange to people who grew up with the practice of "Saying Grace" before a meal, but I found that this practice had taught me some bad habits about prayer and I did not want to teach these things to my own children.

Prayers over meals are usually quite formal, repetitive, and perfunctory. Everybody bows their head, folds their hands, closes their eyes, and then one person says some words to God about food and a few other requests, and then closes the prayer with an "Amen" and everybody then promptly forgets about God and moves on with eating the food that is before them. I think it is better to not pray at all over your food than to treat God this way, or to teach others that this is how prayer works.

If you feel that you must pray over your meal, I invite you to keep your head up and your eyes open as you thank God for your food, and then don't say "Amen" at the end of your prayer. Just turn from talking to God to talking to someone else at the table. This helps others see that communication with God is like communication with anyone else.

DO I NEED TO USE WORDS IN MY PRAYERS?

God knows your thoughts, so you do not need to actually verbalize your prayers. You don't need to say them out loud. In fact, you don't really even need to think the words themselves. Many people think that praying is only happening when we say or think words, but since there are numerous forms of communication, I do not believe that words are the only way we can communicate with God.

One form of prayer I have often found to be helpful is what I call picture prayer, or imaging prayer. Though I have used this type of prayer for decades, I recently heard Greg Boyd refer to a similar practice he follows which (if I remember correctly) he referred to as "Imagining Prayer." This form of prayer uses images and pictures in your mind instead of words. When I am praying for a certain situation or person, I find it very helpful to play a little movie in my head or draw a little picture of what I would like to see happen with the situation or person I am praying about. If I had a fight with my wife, rather than ask God for the ability to say I'm sorry, I imagine myself saying "I'm sorry" to my wife, and then hugging and kissing her. When I paint this picture in my head, I am also showing it to God, saying, "This is what I would like to see happen."

I find this approach to prayer to be fun and enjoyable. We all like watching movies, and this form of prayer can be like a movie that you direct in your head. This is especially helpful for people who do not think they are very good "talkers," or who tend to be more creative in their approach to life.

LEARN MORE ABOUT PRAYER

Thank you for reading this book on prayer. If you want to learn more about prayer and how you can grow in your relationship with God by communicating with Him as you would talk to a friend, there are more resources available on my website, RedeemingGod.com

TAKE A COURSE ON PRAYER

If you join my online discipleship group, you can take a course on prayer. The course has seven lessons and is based on the content of this book. There are audio files you can download as well as PDF transcripts, quizzes, and additional recommended resources. Scores of other people have taken this course, which allows you to interact with them in the comment sections of each lesson. I also try to respond to comments in the course lessons, so if you have questions about this book, the comment area might be a good way to connect with me (as well as others who are taking the course).

By taking this course on prayer, the practices and ideas in this book will be further solidified in your heart and mind, and you will begin to see your relationship with God grow as you learn to speak to Him as you speak to one of your closest friends. Go to RedeemingGod.com/join/ to sign up today. Note that to take this course on prayer, you need to join the Faith, Hope, or Love discipleship levels.

RECEIVE EMAILS ON PRAYER

When you join my online discipleship group, you can also opt in to receive a series of emails on prayer. There are over 20 of these emails, which you will receive weekly. Opt in to receive them by joining any of the four discipleship levels at RedeemingGod.com/join/ (Grace, Faith, Hope, or Love) and then updating your subscription preferences to receive these emails on prayer.

While some of the content of those emails is drawn from this book, there are several emails that contain information not covered by this book or in the course. And as I write more about prayer in the future, I will add it to the content in that email series. So once again, these emails will provide ongoing training, instruction, and encouragement to rethink everything you know about prayer and to put these ideas into practice. Also, if you ever have questions or comments about something you read in these emails, you can simply reply to any of these emails to reach me directly.

ADDITIONAL RESOURCES ON PRAYER

Along with all of the links in the previous chapter, here are some additional online resources which will help you grow in your practice of prayer and your relationship with God.

My Podcast on Jonah 2

I publish a weekly podcast in which we study through books of the Bible. Several episodes of this podcast were devoted to studying the prayer of Jonah in Jonah 2 and his other prayer in Jonah 4. These podcast episodes will be beneficial to you as you consider how (and how not) to pray. Go here to learn more about this podcast and how to subscribe: The One Verse Podcast.

If you want a brief synopsis of what I teach in the podcast, you can read a summary here: The Prayer of Jonah 2.

My Book and Course on the Armor of God

Though it is not yet published, I have written a book on the Armor of God in Ephesians 6:10-20, and will also produce an online course based on this book. As you may know, one major element of the armor of God is the power of prayer (Eph 6:18-20). In fact, prayer is the only "offensive" weapon provided by God for spiritual warfare. The sword of the Spirit is primarily defensive.

If you want to learn more about this book and this course, you can check my booklist or my course list. These lists will both be updated when the book and course are available. Those who are part of my online discipleship group at RedeemingGod.com/join/ will also be notified when these resources are available.

My Book and Course on Cruciform Pastoral Leadership

I have a chapter on prayer in my book, *Cruciform Pastoral Leadership*. As with my other books, I will be producing a course that goes along with this book. The chapter specifically focuses on the role and function of prayer within the life of the church body. It talks about prayer meetings, pastoral prayers, and the prayer life of regular Christians like you and me. There is a bit of overlap between that chapter and this book, but *Cruciform Pastoral Leadership* also contains numerous other suggestions for how pastors and churches can transform their church to better follow Jesus into the world. This book will be part of the "Close Your Church for Good" book series, so while you wait for it to be published you could begin by reading some of the other books that are already available. Start with Volume 1: *The Skeleton Church*.

If you want to learn more about these books and the courses that go with them, you can check my booklist or my course list. All members of my online discipleship group at RedeemingGod.com/join/ can take the course on *The Skeleton Church* for free, and those who join the Faith, Hope, or Love discipleship levels can take all the courses at no additional charge.

CHRISTIAN QUESTIONS
VOLUME 2

WHAT ARE THE SPIRITUAL GIFTS?

DISCOVER YOUR SPIRITUAL GIFTS
AND HOW TO USE THEM

J. D. MYERS

WHAT ARE THE SPIRITUAL GIFTS?
Discover Your Spiritual Gifts and How to Use Them
© 2018 by J. D. Myers

Published by Redeeming Press
Dallas, OR 97338
RedeemingPress.com

978-1-939992-57-4 (Paperback)
978-1-939992-58-1 (Mobi)
978-1-939992-59-8 (ePub)

Learn more about J. D. Myers by visiting RedeemingGod.com

All rights reserved. No part of this publication may be reproduced, stored in or introduced into a retrieval system, or transmitted, in any form, or by any means—electronic, mechanical, photocopying, recording, or otherwise—except for brief quotations, without the prior written permission of both the copyright owner and the publisher of this book.

All Scripture quotations are taken from the New King James Version˚. Copyright © 1982 by Thomas Nelson, Inc. Used by permission. All rights reserved.

Cover Design by Taylor Myers
TaylorGraceGraphics.com

JOIN JEREMY MYERS AND LEARN MORE
Take Bible and theology courses by joining Jeremy at
RedeemingGod.com/join/

Receive updates about free books, discounted books,
and new books by joining Jeremy at
RedeemingGod.com/reader-group/

TAKE THE ONLINE COURSE ABOUT SPIRITUAL GIFTS

There is an online course related to this book. The audio lessons and downloads in the course will help you learn more about your spiritual gifts and might also serve as a good small group Bible study. Learn more at RedeemingGod.com/Courses/

The course is normally $197, but you can take it for free by joining the Discipleship Group at RedeemingGod.com/join/

A PARABLE

Once upon a time, a CEO of a Fortune 500 company decided to send all of his managers an expensive gift for their loyalty and service over the years. He was an expert in working with people, so he carefully considered the strengths and abilities of each manager, while also taking into consideration their interests and hobbies. Then, based on what he knew about each person, he carefully researched and selected individual gifts for each manager. These gifts would not only delight and amaze them, but would also give them a sense of value, worth, purpose, and significance in life and at their job. Furthermore, each gift would also help them do their job with greater effectiveness and enjoyment. Each gift was perfect for each manager.

After the gifts arrived, the CEO had each one wrapped with beautiful paper and a large bow. Then he had the gifts hand delivered to each of his managers. Over the next several days, various managers started showing up in his office to thank him profusely for his gift. Many of them left notes of praise and adoration for his wonderful gift, and some even left a small gift themselves as a way of showing gratitude. The CEO also noticed over the next few weeks and months that many of the managers seemed happier and more content at work, and their output levels increased significantly. Their work became increasingly effective at helping the business accomplish its projects and achieve its goals.

Nevertheless, the CEO noticed that the work outcomes of four managers did not change significantly. Instead, their work production and quality actually decreased. This was troubling to the CEO, because he had spent so much time researching, planning, and purchasing these gifts for his managers. He began to wonder if he had made a mistake in getting the wrong gift for some managers, or if maybe they received the wrong gift. Since he deeply cared about each of his mangers, he decided to stroll down to the office of these four ineffective managers to see what the problem might be.

When he arrived in the office of the first manager, the CEO was shocked to discover that the gift had not been unwrapped. It sat on the manager's desk, glittering and beautiful with its wrapping paper and shiny bow.

"Why haven't you opened my gift and started using it?" the CEO asked.

The manager explained that the wrapping paper and bow were both so beautiful, and they matched the décor of her office so well, she thought it would be a shame to open the gift and ruin the paper, the bow, and how it brightened up her office. The CEO had a little chat with the manager, and encouraged her by saying that if she thought the paper and bow were beautiful, she would definitely love the gift inside, and it would be better than the package by itself. When she opened it, she discovered that the CEO was exactly right. Its appearance caused the paper and bow to pale in comparison, and it magnified the office decorations, and she immediately saw how it would also help her with her job.

Then the CEO went to the office of the second manager. Like the first manager, he was shocked to discover that the gift sat unopened on the desk. This manager was very business-oriented, and so the CEO had wrapped the gift in paper and a bow that was much more drab and business-oriented than the previous manager's gift. Therefore, he doubted that this manager cared much about the appearance of the gift, or how it matched the décor of his office (because there was none).

So he said, "Why haven't you opened my gift?"

The manager explained that he wanted to open it, and was planning on opening it soon, but he was so busy with all of his work, he had not yet found the time to open it. But after some encouragement, he opened the gift and discovered that it was the perfect gift to help him create more time in his job, and get more done in less time so that he could better enjoy his job and get home to spend more time with his family.

The CEO then walked down the hall to the office of the third manager. And while he expected to find the gift sitting on the desk still wrapped with its's box and bow intact, he instead discovered that this manager had indeed opened the gift, for it was sitting on his desk in all of its glory.

"I see you've opened my gift," the CEO said. "How do you like it and is it working?"

The manager sheepishly explained that while he loved the gift, and thought that it was the perfect gift for him, he hadn't yet started to use it because he wanted to read the manual first to make sure he was using it properly. The CEO encouraged him to start using the gift anyway, even before he had read the manual. He showed the manager that the gift was pretty intuitive, and didn't require many instructions. "You learn to use it simply by using it," he said. As he walked away, he saw the man pick up the gift and start to look it over.

The fourth manager was different than the other three. When the CEO walked into this man's office, he saw no sign or evidence of the gift at all. He didn't see a wrapped box on the man's desk, or the gift sitting anywhere in the office. So after a bit of small talk, the CEO inquired about the gift.

"How are you enjoying the gift?" he asked.

The man explained that while he was thankful for the gift, and saw how it might be helpful for his job, he thought his job performance was perfectly fine without the gift. So he had put it in the lower drawer of his desk.

The CEO invited the man to take it out of his drawer and try using it for a week or two. "If you still don't like using it after a few weeks, you can always put it back," he said. Then he left the office, knowing that the gift would never be put back into the lower drawer.

As you have probably figured out, this little parable is pure fiction. But it represents the way many Christians treat the gifts that God has given them, specifically, the spiritual gifts that they received from Jesus through the Holy Spirit when they became a new believer.

Some don't really even know they have the gift, and prefer to just look at the wrapping paper it came in, which is the enjoyment of Bible study and the church services they attend. Others know they have been given a gift by God, but they don't have time to figure out what it might be. They figure they are too busy with life and ministry to actually discover their spiritual gift. A third group has discovered what their gift is, but has not tried to use it. The gift looks scary because it invites them to step out in faith, or possibly make a fool of themselves in front of other people. Then there is the fourth group of people who feel they are doing just fine without their spiritual gift. They know what they are doing in life and ministry, and they are content with what they are doing, and feel that they don't need to put their spiritual gift to use.

To all these groups of people, God is saying "I gave you an amazing gift that is just for you. Nobody else has the unique gift which I planned, prepared, and freely provided just for you. Won't you discover what it is? Won't you learn how to use it? Won't you start putting it into practice? If you do, your life will change for the better. You will find greater significance, joy, and purpose in life. Your ministry will become more effective. Discover your gift and put it into practice. I promise you will not be disappointed."

Since you are a manager in God's business, what is your response?

The following chapters about spiritual gifts will help you unwrap your gift and start using it in your life. Let us begin by learning why God gave spiritual gifts.

CHAPTER 2

WHY DID GOD GIVE SPIRITUAL GIFTS?

Asking why God gave spiritual gifts to Christians is a bit like asking why God gave to you the various parts of your body. Why do you have a hand, a foot, or a mouth? The answer is that the various body parts are all necessary for the body to function the way God designed and intended it to function. So also with spiritual gifts and the church as the Body of Christ. God gave spiritual gifts to the church so that the church can function the way God designed and intended it to function.

Just as the various parts of our physical body allow us to live, exist, and function within this world, so also, our spiritual gifts allow the church to live, move, and have our being within this world. This church existence occurs in three general directions: toward one another, toward those in the world, and toward God Himself. We could also say that spiritual gifts have an inward, outward, and upward focus. Inward toward the church, outward toward the world, and upward toward God. Let us look at all three directions.

EDIFICATION OF THE BODY

The first reason God gave spiritual gifts was so that each individual believer could work for the edification and encouragement of all other believers. God gave spiritual gifts so that we might help one another within the Body of Christ. This is the inward focus or direction. Paul points out in 1 Corinthians 12 that just as each part of the physical body is given for the benefit of the rest of the body, so also, each spiritual gift is given for the benefit of the rest of the church. If you have the gift of teaching, you should teach. If you have the gift of service, you should serve. All parts are necessary and important, and each part should fulfill its role for their own joy and that of others. Only in this way will the whole body remain healthy, live in unity, and grow into maturity.

EVANGELISM OF THE WORLD

But spiritual gifts are not only for the encouragement and edification of the body, but also for the evangelism of the world which leads to the expansion of the Kingdom of God on earth. This is the outward focus of spiritual gifts. One of the main reasons the church exists in the world is to show the world what it looks like when people follow God's instructions, and live like Jesus with love for others. Spiritual gifts of service and mercy, for example, are not only so that we might help and serve other members of the church, but so that we also love and serve those who are outside the church. As we live and love in this way, people are drawn to the church and into the full experience of the Kingdom of God.

This understanding of spiritual gifts as having an outward focus toward the world is critically important for the health and vitality of the church. Many believe that evangelism best occurs through big events, large group gatherings, splashy programs, and expensive mass evangelism campaigns. But God designed His church to work on a much smaller scale and in a more relational way. Evangelism works best when each individual Christian uses their spiritual gifts to love and serve the people God brings into their life. Truly effective evangelism is based on relationship building and interpersonal connections, and spiritual gifts are partly given for this purpose.

EXALTATION OF GOD

The final purpose for spiritual gifts is the exaltation of God. This is the upward direction of spiritual gifts. Some Christians seem to think that God is only exalted when they sing worship songs to Him in a Sunday service or offer praise to Him through prayer. While both of these do exalt the name of God, individual Christians primarily exalt God through how they live their day-to-day lives. And how we live our lives is guided by our spiritual gifts. As we use our spiritual gifts to teach, serve, love, and help others, God is exalted through our words and actions.

Furthermore, the diversity of spiritual gifts reflects the glorious creativity of God. As each person lives their lives in unique ways, God is glorified through the beauty of diversity. God is also glorified and exalted as each unique person works together with other unique people to achieve common goals. The diverse gifts working together in unity reveals the inter-relatedness of God. Since God is relational within the Trinity and within His connections to humans, the interaction of spiritual gifts in relational settings also reveals the nature and character of God.

CONCLUSION

So as Christians practice and implement their spiritual gifts, the church itself grows in strength and maturity, expands over the face of the earth into the lives of others, and brings honor and glory to God. Since these three tasks are the purpose and goal of the church itself, we can see that spiritual gifts are central to God's work through the church in this world. Without spiritual gifts, the church could not exist or function, nor could God's work be done in the lives of others. It is critical, therefore, to discover your spiritual gift and start putting it into practice.

The first step in this process is to understand what spiritual gifts God has provided to the church. Only after you know what spiritual gifts are available can you begin to understand the spiritual gifts God has given you.

CHAPTER 3

WHAT ARE THE SPIRITUAL GIFTS?

There is some debate among Christians about how many spiritual gifts there are. Some people, for example, think that the Bible includes an exhaustive list of spiritual gifts, while others think that the gift lists are only a small sample of a much larger number of gifts, most of which are not mentioned in the Bible. Along with this, some people divide the gifts up into various categories, such as ministry gifts and miraculous gifts, or into three categories, such as teaching, service, and sign gifts. Furthermore, some argue that certain spiritual gifts are no longer in use.

This final question about whether certain gifts have ceased to exist or not will be addressed later. This chapter will address the questions of what the gifts are and how they can be categorized. Let us begin with discovering which spiritual gifts are mentioned in Scripture.

My belief is that the Bible does contain all the spiritual gifts. There are twenty-six of them. When people feel like they might have a spiritual gift that is not listed in Scripture, it is more likely that what they think of as a "spiritual gift" is instead a skill, hobby, talent, or ability. But these too work with spiritual gifts to help a person discover who God made them to be and what He wants them to do.

For example, some people are really good at math, but "Math" is not listed in Scripture as a spiritual gift. So a person who loves and enjoys math should seek to also discover their spiritual gifts so that they can partner their love of math with their spiritual gift as a way to discover the perfect ministry God has for them. In this way, while math is not a spiritual gift, it is part of their overall "SHAPE," as discussed in Chapter 8 of my book, *God's Blueprints for Church Growth*. Other talents and abilities are important considerations for the type of ministry you will perform, but these talents, interests, skills, and abilities are not spiritual gifts themselves, but work together with the spiritual gifts as listed in Scripture.

Before we consider the various spiritual gifts listed in Scripture, it is critical to first understand how and where the gifts are to be used.

THE USE OF THE SPIRITUAL GIFTS

Most books and teachings about spiritual gifts will correctly point out that spiritual gifts are given by God for the edification of the church. In other words, God gives spiritual gifts to Christians so that they can use these gifts to build up the church, the body of Christ. This is exactly what we learned in the previous chapter.

However, most of these other books and teachings think of "church" as the place that people go on Sunday morning to sit in a pew or a padded chair where they will sing songs, pray, and listen to a sermon. This mindset about "church" causes people to then think that spiritual gifts need to be used within this setting. Spiritual gifts, therefore, are often explained as abilities or talents to help add more people to the Sunday morning church service, or help make disciples of the people who show up in the church building on Sunday morning.

Many pastors and church leaders will also hasten to add that spiritual gifts can also be used on days other than Sunday, but usually only at church-sponsored functions, programs, and activities. So pastors and church leaders will invite church members to not only use their spiritual gifts on Sunday morning, but also find ways to plug these gifts into the Tuesday night women's tea and Bible study, the Wednesday night children and youth programs, the Thursday night homeless outreach, or the Saturday morning men's prayer breakfast.

The church is none of these things. In fact, it is possible for all of these activities to take place without any involvement of the church. This is because the church is not a building, a place, or a set of programs. As I point out in my book, *Skeleton Church*, the church consists of the people of God who follow Jesus into the world.[10] The church is made up of people. People do not go to church; rather, the church goes with people. Wherever there are people who are seeking to follow Jesus, there is the church. This is true even if there is no building, pastor, budget, programs, doctrinal statement, prayer meetings, songs, or sermons.[11]

If Jesus leads a woman to stay at home so she can love and raise her children, she is functioning as the church, whether or not she and her children ever set foot in the "church" building down the street. If a man obeys Jesus in working hard at his job, loving his wife, and providing for his children, he is serving in the church, even if he never attends a "church" service, a Bible study, or a men's prayer breakfast.

Do you see? Since the church is the people of God who follow Jesus into the world, then whenever these people use their spiritual gifts in their day-to-day lives with the people God places before them, then these people *are* edifying and building up the church. They do not have to "go to church" to use their spiritual gifts, for they *are* the church, and can use their spiritual gifts wherever they are.

This is what the following book tries to point out regarding the use of spiritual gifts. Your spiritual gifts can be used anywhere at any time with anyone. And while "church" will be mentioned frequently in the pages that follow, do not make the mistake of thinking that "church" consists of the four brick walls and the white steeple on the corner of Main Street, or even the programs and activities that many Christians get involved in to purportedly "serve the church." Thinking this way about "church" will only lead to shame and guilt when you try to use your spiritual gifts.

Instead, recognize that you *are* the church, and you can use your spiritual gifts wherever you already are and in whatever you are already do-

---

[10] Jeremy Myers, *Skeleton Church* (Dallas, OR: Redeeming Press, 2018).
[11] See my "Close Your Church for Good" series of books for a detailed explanation of why the church can more easily exist *without* all such things.

ing. If you ever start to feel guilty about how you are using (or not using) your spiritual gifts, "You're doing it wrong." Realizing what the church is (and is not) will help you gain the liberty, joy, satisfaction, and freedom that God intended you to experience in the use of your spiritual gifts. The spiritual gifts are not just for helping out at the building with the stained glass windows across town, but are to help you live and love like Jesus wherever you are, in whatever you are doing, with whoever is in front of you right now.

THE LIST OF SPIRITUAL GIFTS

Below is the list of spiritual gifts mentioned in Scripture. The brief list is then followed by an alphabetically arranged list, which includes an explanation of each gift.

Romans 12	1 Corinthians 12
Exhortation	Administration
Giving	Apostleship
Leadership	Discernment
Mercy	Faith
Prophecy	Healing
Service	Helping
Teaching	Knowledge
	Miracles
	Prophecy
	Teaching
	Tongues
	Interpretation
	Wisdom

Ephesians 4	Misc. Passages
Apostleship	Celibacy (1 Cor 7:7-8)
Evangelism	Hospitality (1 Pet 4:9-10)

Pastor-Teacher
Prophecy
	Martyrdom (1 Cor 13:1-3)
	Voluntary poverty
	  (1 Cor 13:1-3)
	Craftsmanship (Exod 31:3-5)
	Creative communication
	  (Acts 16:25; 1 Cor
	  14:26; Eph 5:19)

Administration: To steer a group toward the accomplishment of God-given goals and directives by planning, organizing and supervising others (1 Cor 12:28; cf. Acts 15:12-21). It is based on the Greek word, *kubernēsis*, which means "to steer, guide" and can be used in reference to the helmsman of a ship. Those with this gift understand the goals of the group, and the steps needed to achieve those goals. The group could consist of anything from a country or multi-national business to a local outreach ministry or a family. Politicians, CEOs, and mothers often have the gift of administration.

Apostleship (Missionary): To be sent forth to new frontiers with the gospel, providing leadership over church bodies and maintaining authority over spiritual matters pertaining to the church (Eph 4:11; 1 Cor 12:28; cf. 1 Cor 9:19-23; cf. Acts 12:1-5; 14:21-23). The word is based on the Greek word *apostolos*, which means "one sent forth." While the office of "Apostle" is no longer in use today, the gift of apostleship is still given by God in the form of missionaries who take the gospel to unreached people groups (See Chapter 7 in my book, *God's Blueprints for Church Growth*).

Craftsmanship: To make, construct, or build things (Exod 28:3-4; 31:3-5). Those with the gift of craftsmanship will often be skilled at using tools to help and inspire others through artistic, creative means. Those with this gift will also be good at making or fixing things, and will often find themselves drawn toward jobs such as architecture, engineering, construction, creative design, and culinary arts.

Creative Communication: To teach and share biblical and spiritual truths in creative ways that rely less on words and books and more on art, music, poetry, plays, photography, dance, and other similar outlets (Mark 14:26; Acts 16:25; 1 Cor 14:26; Eph 5:19). Nearly all artists, designers, actors, and musicians have the gift of creative communication. As people who capture God's creative beauty and wonder through the experience of the five senses, they use their gift to create beauty and inspire change in others.

Celibacy: To voluntarily remain single without regret and with the ability to maintain controlled sexual impulses so as to serve the Lord without distraction (1 Cor 7:7-8). Those with the gift of celibacy often devote their lives to a single cause, task, or mission, so that all of their time and energy can be devoted to this purpose, without the risk of neglecting a spouse and children. Just because someone is unmarried this does not mean they have the gift of celibacy. Those who desire to get married can and should do so. However, while looking and praying for the spouse that God has for them, they can use their time of singleness to focus on serving God and others.

Discernment: To clearly distinguish truth from error by judging whether a certain behavior or teaching has a divine, satanic, or human origin (1 Cor 12:10; cf. Acts 5:3-6; 16:16-18). Those with the gift of discernment also tend to be helpful in helping others know and understand their own spiritual giftedness. People with the gift of discernment often work as life coaches, counselors, and mentors.

Evangelism: To be a messenger of the good news of the gospel with their words, lives, and actions (Eph 4:11; cf. Acts 8:26-40). The Greek word, *euangelistēs*, means "preacher of the gospel" but since the gospel includes instructions for all of life and theology, the evangelist will not only preach the gospel, but will live out the truths of the gospel in a way that inspires others to do the same (See Chapter 7 in my book, *God's Blueprints for Church Growth*). Their life serves as a guiding light to others in this dark world. The evangelist is also proficient at discipleship, as they walk alongside others to help them practice the gospel in their lives. They will often live a transparent life, showing their failures and weaknesses to others, so that others can learn about God's grace, love, and forgiveness through them.

Exhortation (Encouragement): To come along side of someone with words of encouragement, comfort, consolation, and counsel to help them be all God wants them to be (Rom 12:8; cf. Acts 11:23-24; 14:21-22). The Greek word, *paraklēsis*, means "calling to one's side," and is related to the work of the Holy Spirit as our Paraclete, our Comforter or Encourager (John 14:16, 26). Just as there are people who serve with their hands, these people serve and encourage with their words. Those with the gift of encouragement include coaches and teachers who see the potential in others, and cheer them on to rise to this potential.

Faith: To be firmly persuaded of God's power and promises to accomplish His will and purpose and to display such a confidence in Him and His Word which cannot be shaken by circumstances or obstacles (1 Cor 12:8-10; cf. Heb 11). Those with the gift of faith know what they believe and why they believe it, and are able to inspire action in others based on their beliefs. They are often called upon to encourage others to step out in faith and follow God to accomplish seemingly impossible tasks. Other people are drawn to those with the gift of faith because they find hope and strength in their presence. Those with the gift of faith often find themselves in positions of visionary leadership.

Giving: To share what material resources you have with liberality and cheerfulness without thought of return (Rom 12:8; cf. Acts 4:36-37; 2 Cor 8:1-5). They give without ulterior motive or conditions attached to how the money should be spent. Some believe that when God gives the gift of giving, He also gives the gift of making lots of money so that the giver can financially support multiple ministries and missionaries around the world. Givers often give away the vast majority of their substantial income, sometimes up to 90% or more. In ancient Roman society, those with the gift of giving would be called Patrons.

Healing: To be used as a means through which God makes people whole and restores health to the sick, whether they are physically, emotionally, mentally, or spiritually ill (1 Cor 12:9, 28, 30; cf. Luke 9:1-2; Jas 5:13-16). Note that healing is not just miraculous healing, but the ability to use modern medicine and science to bring about healing in someone's mind or body. As a result, those with the gift of healing often find themselves in the fields of medicine and psychology.

Helping: To render support or assistance to others so as to free them for other work (1 Cor 12:28; cf. Acts 6:2-4). They bear the burdens of others to help them accomplish their work more effectively. Those with the gift of helping find great satisfaction in doing menial jobs behind the scenes so that others can be freed up to do other tasks. While those with the gift of helping rarely receive much recognition or praise, the truth is that without their gifts, the people who often receive recognition and praise would not have the time or energy to do what they do. Therefore, the gift of helping actually allows the other more "flashy" gifts to function. People such as janitors, custodians, nurses, parents, classroom aids, assistant coaches, secretaries, and all other "behind the scenes" staff likely have the gift of helping.

Hospitality: To warmly welcome people, even strangers, into one's home as a means of serving people who need food or lodging (1 Pet 4:9-10; cf. Gen 18:1-15). They cheerfully open their homes to care for other people. True hospitality is not standing behind a counter at the "Hospitality Center" that exists in some church buildings, but requires you to open your own home to other people so they can share your food and enjoy a roof over their heads. The Greek word, *philoxenos*, means "love of strangers." Note that in biblical times, these "strangers" were usually Christians who were traveling from town to town and came with letters of introduction, but it does not have to limited to only Christians. Non-Christians can (and should) be welcomed into your home as well. However, wisdom dictates that you should know something about the people you invite into your home, for it is always unwise to welcome *complete* strangers into one's home.

Interpretation of Tongues: To translate the message of someone who has spoken in another language for those who do not understand what was said (1 Cor 12:10; 14:27-28). As will be discussed briefly below, the gift of tongues is speaking in an actual foreign language. Therefore, in order for what is said to make sense to other people, it must be interpreted. Those with the gift of interpretation are sometimes able to understand what foreigners are saying, even if they have never learned the other language. Some who have the gift of interpreting tongues also find that they can quickly and easily learn foreign languages.

Knowledge: To seek to learn as much about a particular subject as possible through the gathering of information and the analysis of that data (1 Cor 12:8; cf. Eph 3:14-19). Those with the gift of knowledge enjoy reading and studying, and find that they are able to easily learn, retain, and recall facts. Those with the gift of knowledge are also able to synthesize various streams of learning to develop new ideas and insightful ways of looking at difficult topics. People with the gift of knowledge find themselves in the fields of science, mathematics, literature, history, and theology.

Leadership: To live in front of people in such a way as to motivate others to change their lives, follow directions, influence decisions, and get involved in their community and the world so that all harmoniously work together to accomplish common goals (Rom 12:8; cf. Exod 18:13-16; Judg 3:10; Heb 13:7). Those with the gift of leadership inspire others to follow without feeling the need to command, threaten, or cajole. Those with the gift of leadership often become actual leaders in their communities, businesses, or countries.

Martyrdom: To give over one's life to death for the cause of Christ (1 Cor 13:3). Those who give their life in this way are called "martyrs," from the Greek word, *marturos,* meaning "witness." Giving one's life for Jesus is a great way to be a witness for Him. Nevertheless, while one can feel that they would be willing to die for Jesus Christ, it is not something which you can plan, prepare, or practice. Therefore, a person cannot know if they have the gift of martyrdom until they actually become a martyr. As a result, the Spiritual Gift inventory test at the end of this book does not contain any questions about martyrdom.

Mercy: To be sensitive toward those who are suffering, whether physically, mentally, or emotionally, so that you feel genuine empathy and compassion for others in their misery (Rom 12:8; cf. Luke 10:30-37). Those with the gift of mercy are able to empathize with those in pain, so that they speak words of compassion and offer acts of love to help alleviate others in their distress. Those with the gift of mercy often devote large amounts of time to help others in need, and can typically be found in the positions as counselors, mentors, and service positions where they work with the sick, elderly, mentally ill, and handicapped.

Miracles: To be enabled by God to perform mighty deeds which witnesses acknowledge to be of supernatural origin and means (1 Cor 12:10, 28). Those with the gift of miracles cannot promise that God will work miracles in their life, or the life of someone else, but often see God work the impossible in response to their prayers and acts of faith. This gift often works in coordination with the gifts of faith and healing.

Pastor-Teacher: To be responsible for the spiritual care, protection, guidance, and provision of a group of believers entrusted to one's care (Eph 4:11; cf. 1 Pet 5:1-11). Since the word *pastor* is related to the word for *shepherd,* the pastor-teacher often uses preaching and teaching as a way to lead, guide, and protect others (See Chapter 7 in my book, *God's Blueprints for Church Growth*). Those with the gift of pastor-teacher tend to be more relational than the teacher, and are therefore better at providing overall care for the spiritual well-being of the church.

Prophecy: To speak forth the message of God to His people (Rom 12:6; 1 Cor 12:10; Eph 4:11; cf. Isaiah–Malachi; 1 Cor 14:1-5, 30-40). The Greek word, *prophētēs,* refers to the forth-telling of the will and word of God. It does not primarily refer to foretelling the future, but to forth-telling God's will (See Chapter 7 in my book, *God's Blueprints for Church Growth*). One with the gift of prophecy will speak God's Word with boldness and clarity to call God's people to repent from sin and return to God's ways.

Service: To identify undone tasks in God's work, however menial, and use available resources to get the job done (Rom 12:7; cf. Gal 6:1-2). The Greek word, *diakonia,* means "servant, attendant," and refers to someone who runs errands for others. They take care of the day-to-day physical details for leaders and spiritual directors to free them up to take care of spiritual matters. Though this spiritual gift sounds lowly, it is one of the backbone gifts of any community or group. Without people to take care of these routine tasks, no business or organization would be able to properly function.

Teaching: To instruct others in a passionate, logical, succinct, and systematic way so as to communicate pertinent information for true understanding and personal growth in others (Rom 12:7; 1 Cor 12:28; cf. Heb 5:12-14). The gift of teaching differs from that of pastor-teacher in one main way: the pastor-teacher usually teaches with "pastoral" concerns in mind. The preaching and teaching of the pastor-teacher tends to be more practical, attempting to address the needs and concerns of the average Christian. The teacher, however, might be more academic and will often lack the interpersonal skills necessary to serve as a pastor-teacher. Most skilled teachers and professors have the gift of teaching.

Tongues: To speak in a language not previously learned so unbelievers can hear God's message in their own language (Acts 2:4; 1 Cor 12:10; 14:27-28). If those who are present do not understand what is said, tongues must always be interpreted. If there is no interpreter, the speaker must remain silent. There is no evidence anywhere in Scripture that the gift of tongues causes a person to speak in a secret prayer language. Speaking in tongues always involves speaking in another "tongue," or language. As such, it might be more precise to speak of people having the gift of *languages*, which helps them quickly learn foreign languages. (See the chapter on tongues later in this book.)

Voluntary Poverty: To purposely live in an impoverished lifestyle to serve and aid others with your material resources (1 Cor 13:3). Those with the gift of poverty love to give away their money and possessions so that they might live simply, generously, and sacrificially. They often view possessions and money as a hindrance to ministry, and use their money to meet the needs of those poorer than themselves. Voluntary poverty differs from the gift of giving in that those with the gift of giving might be rich, whereas those with the gift of voluntary poverty tend to live among the poor so that they might love, serve, and identify with them.

Wisdom: To apply knowledge to life in such a way as to make spiritual truths quite relevant and practical in proper decision-making and daily life situations (1 Cor 12:8; cf. Jas 3:13-17). Those with the gift of wisdom are often very good in counseling situations, and find that people often come to them for advice. They are very good at understanding God's will in various situations, and helping people understand the right decisions to make in life.

Related to the list of spiritual gifts, some try to categorize the gifts into various groupings. For example, many divide the gifts into two categories: ministry gifts and miraculous gifts. Yet are not miracles also a form of ministry? The gift of healing ministers to the physical body and the gift of tongues ministers to people who speak other languages. So this two-fold division is unsatisfactory, since all spiritual gifts are "ministry" gifts.

The same is true for the three-fold gift division of teaching gifts, service gifts, and sign gifts. While it is true that some gifts tend to use words (whether written or spoken) while other gifts focus on helping others with your hands, all uses of the gifts are still a form of service to others, and all the gifts serve as a sign to others that God is at work in our midst. A powerful sermon from Scripture that convicts hearts and calls people to follow Jesus is just as much a sign that the Holy Spirit is at work in our presence as is the gift of miracles or healing.

Furthermore, since most human learning is done through imitation of others and the vast majority of human communication is done through body language, one does not have to say a single word in order to teach and train others. By loving and serving others, you naturally teach them about the love of God and how they too can treat other people, even if you never say a single word to them about such subjects. Therefore, all gifts are sign gifts, and all gifts are service gifts, and all gifts are teaching gifts. Here too, the attempts to categorize and divide the gifts break down.

One reason that some people try to categorize the gifts is because they say that only some of the gifts are active today while others are no longer being used. This issue will be briefly addressed later, but for now, since we see that there is no good or logical way to categorize the gifts, this is one indication that all the gifts are likely still in use.

So rather than worrying about whether you have a ministry gift or a miraculous gift, the best approach is to simply figure out which gifts you have and then start using them for ministry. Thankfully, as we will learn in the next chapter, it is not too difficult to identify your spiritual gifts.

CHAPTER 4

HOW CAN I KNOW MY SPIRITUAL GIFT?

There are many ways to discover your spiritual gifts. I encourage you to use all of them as a way to identify and confirm your spiritual gifts. If you use just one method, there is a chance of improperly identifying your spiritual gifts, thereby leading to frustration in life and ministry. But if you start with one method of identification, and then use the other methods to confirm or change the results of the first method, you will often end up properly identifying your spiritual gifts.

SELF-ANALYSIS

The first (and preferred) method for identifying your spiritual gift is to look into your own heart and mind and consider which spiritual gifts you would like to have. Of course, when you do this, you are not just trusting your own heart and mind to "figure it out," but are actually looking for the still small voice of the Holy Spirit to point out to you which gifts you have been given. As these gifts are *spiritual* gifts, we must first look to the Holy Spirit for leading in this matter.

Even if you are uncomfortable or unaware of how to listen to the voice and leading of the Spirit, it is still important to try. The Spirit is always whispering to you, and you will only learn to sense His leading and direction as you attempt to listen to what He is saying. Furthermore, once you discover your spiritual gift, it will be important to continue to rely on the leading of the Holy Spirit for how He wants you to use your spiritual gift. So you might as well begin by seeking His input on the identification of your gifts.

To do this, just return to the previous chapter where the spiritual gifts are listed and read through them slowly, trying to discern which ones might be true of you. As you read the descriptions, look for ones that might be interesting or that sound intriguing. Look for gifts that pull on you heart or that seem to describe your interests and desires. The gifts that you feel drawn to are possibly the gifts that God has given to you.

Remember, of course, that there is a difference between the gifts you *want* and the gifts you *have*. You can be wrong in your feelings and desires. So as you read through the spiritual gifts, not only think about the gifts you would like to have, but also the sorts of things you have actually done in life which have given you joy and satisfaction. For example, almost everybody wants the gift of giving since it is often accompanied by wealth. But if you have never been rich, and do not see that you are likely to become rich, and do not have a history of giving away large sums of money, then these are good indications that even though you desire the gift of giving, you likely do not have it. Pairing the gifts you desire with the sorts of activities and actions you have actually done provides the best self-analysis of the spiritual gifts you might have.

Once you have done this self-analysis, you can move on to the next four ways of identifying your spiritual gifts, as they help confirm which spiritual gifts you might have.

SEEK THE INPUT OF OTHERS

Since the gifts are given for the edification of others, one way you can gain insight into which gifts you might have is by seeking the input of others. This is especially effective when you seek the input of people who know you well, and who have seen you serve and interact with other people.

This method of discovering your spiritual gifts is especially effective if you can ask someone who has the spiritual gift of discernment. God has specifically enabled those with the gift of discernment to see, understand, and recognize the various spiritual gifts in other people. Of course, they don't do this through some sort of magical "fortune-telling" experience where their eyes roll back in their head and they read tea leaves in a cup. No, they discern these things by getting to know you and observing your life. So even here, if you are going to ask for the input of others, you must not ask strangers.

This shows why it is important to be involved in the lives of other people. It is only with other people that you can practice your spiritual gifts, and it is only with other people that you can ask for their input about your gifts. If you are not part of a gathering of believers, it may be difficult for you to discover your spiritual gifts, or for others to provide input on what your gifts might be.

Remember, of course, that the smallest, most basic gathering of believers is your immediate family. So as you seek the input of others about your spiritual gifts, start with your parents, children, spouse, and siblings. They know you best, and will be able to provide some of the most helpful input and advice about your spiritual gifts. Other than family, you can also ask your close friends and coworkers. It will not be of any benefit to ask people who rarely see you or interact with you on a daily or weekly basis.

SPIRITUAL VOID ANALYSIS

One of the very best ways to discover your spiritual gifts is to take note of your criticisms and complaints about church. When you look at the local church body you are part of (or the worldwide church as a whole), and see areas of weakness, fault, or neglect, you have just discovered what God wants you to be doing in the church. In other words, if there is something you think that everybody in the church should be doing (but aren't), then you have just discovered what it is *you* should be doing.

For example, if you think the church is doing a poor job of teaching Scripture to others, then this likely means that you have the spiritual gift of teaching, and you are supposed to start using it. If you think the church should be serving the poor in your community, this probably means you have the gifts of service, mercy, or hospitality. If you complain that the church is not creative and artistic enough in its music, programs, or decorations, this likely means that you have the gift of creative communication.

As you can see, this method of discovering your spiritual gifts is extremely helpful, for it not only allows you to accurately identify your spiritual gifts, but it also spurs you on to actually use your gifts to meet the need that you see, rather than just sit on the sideline (or in the pew) complaining about all the things the church should do differently. If you see a void in the church, it is likely because God wants you to fill it and has specially gifted you to do so.

SPIRITUAL GIFT ANALYSIS

You can, of course, always take a spiritual gift inventory test as a way of discovering your spiritual gifts. There is one such test at the end of this book (see Appendix 1). Many of these tests are somewhat like personality tests, where the person answers a series of questions and then scores the test based on their answers. The scores provide insight into which spiritual gifts the person might have.

However, it is necessary to state a warning about these sorts of tests. Of the five available ways for discovering your spiritual gifts, this method is the least reliable. This is simply due to the fact that test results are easily undermined by various outside factors. Not only is it possible for the questions to be misunderstood, but when a person takes the test, a whole host of outside factors can drastically alter the outcome of these sorts of tests, such as where they took it, how they are feeling at the time they took it, and what they just heard or read before they took it.

I once ran a little experiment where I decided to test a group of men by giving them the same exact test two weeks apart. During the first week, I taught a 30-minute lesson about the miracles of Jesus and the importance of faith for seeing miracles today. Then I gave the men the test, and had them turn it in to me for scoring. The next week, I told the men that I had somehow misplaced the tests, and I apologetically asked them to take it again. But this time, I preceded the test with a 30-minute lesson on the importance of Scripture memorization, Bible study, and reading good books about theology. Then they took the test a second time.

The (unsurprising) results of these two tests were that even though the same men took it only two weeks apart, the results from the first week showed that the majority of the men had spiritual gifts of miracles and faith, while the results from the second week showed that the majority of them had spiritual gifts of teaching and knowledge. The clear influencing factor which explains the difference was the lesson they had just heard me teach.

So it is fine to take spiritual gift inventories like the one at the end of this book, but you must recognize that these tests are easily skewed by how you are feeling, what you have been reading or hearing, and a wide variety of other factors. If you take a spiritual gift inventory test, it is best to take it multiple times over the span of a several months or years, and to use it in coordination with the other four ways of discovering your spiritual gifts. It is especially important to use the fifth and final way, discussed below.

SERVE AND EXPERIMENT

The last and most important way of discovering your spiritual gifts is simply to use the spiritual gifts you think you have. There is no better way to discover and strengthen your spiritual gifts than by serving and experimenting with them in the context of a local body of believers. Regardless of what other method you might use for discovering your spiritual gifts, this is the one method you must not neglect.

The reason this method is so critical is because it will either confirm or contradict the initial identification of your spiritual gifts. When you find your spiritual gift and start putting it into practice, you will experience greater excitement and energy in the ways you interact with others, and find that they grow closer to Jesus as a result of your work with them. Furthermore, as you practice your gifts, you will get better and better at using them, and will begin to influence and edify more and more people.

The exact opposite happens, however, when you try to use gifts that you think you might have, but in fact do not. For example, if you think you have the spiritual gift of teaching, but people fall asleep when you teach, and few return to hear you teach, then this might be a good sign that teaching is not your gift. If you think you have the gift of mercy, but you get upset and angry at people who don't seem to take your advice and don't change fast enough to suit your expectations, then this might be a good sign that you don't have the gift of mercy.

So if you think you have certain spiritual gifts, but when you attempt to put them into practice, you get frustrated and angry while other people are not encouraged or edified, then this is a good sign that the spiritual gift you are trying to practice is not actually your spiritual gift. If you initially misdiagnose your spiritual gift, do not be discouraged, but simply go back and try to discover your spiritual gift again. It usually will not take more than two or three attempts before you find the spiritual gift God has given to you, and you begin to see Him work through your life to touch the lives of others.

One of the reasons that some people experience this initial misdiagnosis is because they have been taught that some spiritual gifts are better than others, and they want one of these "better" gifts. But is this true? The answer is "No," as we see in the next chapter.

CHAPTER 5

ARE SOME GIFTS BETTER THAN OTHERS?

Various groups of Christians seem to think that some spiritual gifts are better than others. For example, many charismatic and Pentecostal groups place a heavy emphasis on the gifts of tongues, miracles, and healing. They do this partly because these three gifts provide a good "show" to the people in the pew, but also because there are a few texts which seem to indicate the importance of these gifts. For example, Acts 2 shows that tongues came upon those who were in the Upper Room when they first received the Holy Spirit. Therefore, some teach that tongues is a sign that someone has received the Holy Spirit. Also, 1 Corinthians 14:22 says that tongues are a sign to unbelievers.

Related to this, miracles and healing are viewed as a way of verifying the truth of what someone is teaching. For example, when Jesus was challenged about the truth of His teachings, He pointed people to the signs He had performed as evidence of His authority and identity (cf. Luke 7:18-22). The apostles also seemed to follow a similar practice in the Book of Acts as they carried the gospel message to other regions of the Roman Empire.

Then there is Paul's statement in 1 Corinthians 12:31 where he seems to instruct the Corinthian Christians to eagerly desire the greater gifts. Some believe that since Paul has just mentioned tongues and healings (1 Cor 12:30), it is these gifts that are "best" or "greater" and therefore, it is these that Christians should seek after and desire. Supporters of this view point out that Paul's words in 1 Corinthians 12:31 are better translated as "You are eagerly desiring the best gifts." Further support for this view is found in 1 Corinthians 14, where Paul goes into great detail about the use of tongues in the meeting of the church. Some have used this text to say that tongues is one of the better gifts. After all, the Corinthian Christians were emphasizing tongues and Paul seems to say that they are eagerly desiring the best gifts. Furthermore, Paul then goes on to provide careful instruction of the use of tongues. So does this mean that tongues truly is one of the better spiritual gifts?

Mostly likely not. Many believe that while Paul does indeed spend a lot of time writing about tongues, the overall tone of Paul's discussion is corrective. Yes, the Corinthians are emphasizing tongues, but the overall purpose of Paul's letter, and the immediate context of these chapters, is to correct various Corinthian abuses. Tongues is one of those. And while some of these scholars agree that 1 Corinthians 12:31 could be translated as suggested above, they say that Paul's tone is one of sarcasm or irony. If so, Paul should be understood as saying, "But you are eagerly desiring *what you think to be* better gifts, *but they really are not.* Let me show you a more excellent way." Then Paul goes on to write about love (1 Cor 13), and how intelligible words are more loving and edifying than unintelligible words (1 Cor 14:12-19).

So in this second view, Paul is criticizing the Corinthian Christians for their overemphasis upon tongues and is instead instructing them to seek better gifts, such as those that edify and instruct the entire church (1 Cor 12:12-26; 14:12-19). Paul states later that it is better to speak five intelligible words than ten thousand words that cannot be understood. This seems to show that gifts such as prophecy and teaching are more important to Paul than gifts of tongues and miracles.

However, I believe that this debate about which gifts are better misses the entire point of Paul's overall argument. Paul's point is that no gift is better than another. Though the Corinthian Christians did indeed seem to place a higher degree of emphasis and importance on various "miraculous" gifts, Paul tries to rein them in by pointing out that all the gifts are equally important. This truth is especially seen in 1 Corinthians 12:12-26, where Paul uses body imagery to show that there are no lesser or greater parts of the body, for all parts depend and rely upon all the other parts. While it is true that some parts "seem to be weaker" (1 Cor 12:22) or "less honorable" (1 Cor 12:23), it is these parts that tend to be more important or bestowed with greater honor (1 Cor 12:23-25). All parts are equally necessary, important, and honorable, and if one part is despised, rejected, or neglected, the entire body suffers (1 Cor 12:26).

The overall message of Paul, therefore, is that no gift is better than another, for all gifts are given by God. All the gifts are required for the proper functioning of believers as the Body of Christ to love and serve others in this world. Those gifts that have the appearance of being less important or less honorable, are actually those who are given additional importance and honor so that they are raised up to equality and value with all the other gifts.

The bottom line is this: Whatever gifts you have been given by God are critically important for your life as a follower of Jesus as you use them in this world. But this does not make your spiritual gift more important than the gifts of others. The spiritual gifts of others are just as essential and important as yours. When we fail to remember this, we fall prey to the dangers of spiritual gifts, which we learn about in the next chapter.

CHAPTER 6

THE DANGERS OF THE SPIRITUAL GIFTS

As wonderful as spiritual gifts are, they come with inherent dangers. While there are specific dangers for each gift, there are also two general dangers that all the gifts have in common. Let us first look at these two general dangers, and then we will briefly consider the specific dangers of each individual gift.

TWO GENERAL DANGERS

The first danger that all the spiritual gifts have in common is the tendency of many to only use their spiritual gifts for other Christians, or "in the church" on Sunday morning. Frequently, when people start to think about how they can use their spiritual gifts, they limit their ideas to only those ministries or people which will help their local church body.

For example, evangelists might focus primarily on getting people to "come to church." Those with hospitality might only invite "church members" over for dinner. People who love to serve might only look for opportunities to help in the church functions and programs.

This is a danger because while it is true that the spiritual gifts help us function as the Body of Christ, the spiritual gifts *are not for the Body of Christ only*. Did Jesus come to this earth only for the religious and the righteous people? No. As He Himself frequently said, He came for the sick, the sinners, and the sheep of other pastures (Mark 2:17; Luke 5:32; John 10:16). Therefore, since believers are the physical Body of Christ here on earth now, we too must work and serve among the non-

Christian, non-religious world.

When you think about your spiritual gifts, don't think about how you can primarily use them to help other Christians. Instead, think about how you can use them to help those who are not Christians. Your spiritual gifts are primarily for the world—not for the church. Christians *are the church* only when we use our spiritual gifts to love and serve the world.

The great benefit to thinking about spiritual gifts this way is that the typical Sunday morning "church service" does not allow most people to use their spiritual gifts. Even when you factor in all of the various ministries and programs of a traditional church, there still are relatively few opportunities for most people to use their spiritual gifts. But this not the case when we avoid this pitfall and start to think about spiritual gifts as an opportunity to be Jesus to others in this world. When we think about spiritual gifts this way, then there is not a lack of opportunity to use our gifts, but a lack of available workers who are willing to go out and love and serve others like Jesus.

So avoid this first general danger of spiritual gifts. They are not primarily for the church. They are given to us so that we can be the church (or be Jesus) to the people of this world.

The second general danger that all spiritual gifts have in common is that each of us tends to think that our gift is the most important one. By their very nature, spiritual gifts cause a person to see the need and importance of their own ways of working with others and serving this world. As a result, however, we fail to see the need and importance of the gifts of other people, and therefore believe that anybody not practicing our spiritual gift is unspiritual. In other words, each person tends to think that their spiritual gift is the most important and that everybody else should be practicing the same thing.

For example, the person with the gift of teaching tends to think that strong biblical preaching and teaching is the most important thing a church can be doing. After all, they think to themselves, if the people don't know God's will and instructions from Scripture, how can they possibly follow and obey Him? And so they place a high emphasis on teaching the Scriptures through meaty sermons on Sunday and frequent Bible study during the week. When someone with the gift of teaching falls into this trap, they start thinking that anybody who doesn't like long, expository sermons is "less spiritual," and anybody who doesn't engage in frequent Bible reading and theological study is possibly not even a Christian.

All the other gifts can fall into the exact same trap. Those with the gifts of mercy or service might think that anybody who does not actively and frequently serve the poor, help the homeless, or provide food for the hungry is less spiritual than those who do. Those with the gift of hospitality might think that those who do not open their home to others are disobedient to God. Those with the gift of giving might think that those who do not generously give to others are being poor stewards of their money.

The solution to this universal problem is to remember what Paul wrote in 1 Corinthians 12, that God has given different spiritual gifts to different people. Each person is supposed to practice their own spiritual gift, and let others practice theirs. Let us not look down on others because they are not practicing our spiritual gifts. Instead, let each of us learn and practice our own spiritual gifts for the benefit of others, while giving them the freedom to do the same with theirs. Only in this way will we all grow in unity, power, and healthy spirituality.

Beyond these two general pitfalls that all the spiritual gifts have in common, there are also some unique dangers that go along with each individual gift. These specific dangers and weakness are considered below.

THE SPECIFIC DANGERS

Administration: Those with the gift of administration can sometimes treat others as if they were employees in a business. Rather than focusing on people and their needs, they might over-prioritize paperwork, "To-Do" lists, and goals. Furthermore, it is easy for someone with the gift of administration to get impatient with people when they do not move fast enough in accomplishing various assigned tasks and duties. Finally, those with the gift of administration sometimes equate their own personal goals and desires with those of God, thereby thinking that anybody who doesn't "get on board" is living contrary to the will of God.

Apostleship (Missionary): Those with the gift of apostleship can fall into the trap of lording their position over others. It is easy for those with the gift of apostleship to confuse their gift with the office of Apostle in the New Testament. When this happens, they tend to portray themselves as authoritative leaders, and then use this position to manipulate and control others for their own ends and purposes. Finally, those who serve as missionaries sometimes give the impression that "real" ministry requires a person to cross an ocean, while forgetting that God just as often calls His people to cross a hallway or a street. It is a sad reality that many of those who cross an ocean to share the gospel with others have never crossed the street to share it with their neighbors.

Craftsmanship: Those with the gift of craftsmanship sometimes think that their gifts are not really spiritual, and therefore, of little help to the Body of Christ. Therefore, they sometimes view their contributions as insignificant or unimportant. It is easy to think that making things with wood or metal does not actually help anyone in their spiritual life. But constructing items that help people live their lives in a community of others and with more ease are important ways of helping others see that God provides for them. These skills also allow the beauty and splendor of

God to be magnified on the earth.

Creative Communication: Those with the gift of creative communication must remember that while many often place great emphasis on the written and spoken word, God is a Creator, and has made people to be creative, and so the creative outlets of people help expand and strengthen the Body of Christ in new directions. Of course, since the church often places such an emphasis on the spoken and written word, those with creative communication often get critical of long sermons, deep Bible studies, and advanced theological education. These too are important ways that some people learn. At the same time, they must be patient with those who have trouble finding meaning in art, beauty in music, or symbolic significance in dance.

Celibacy: Those with the gift of celibacy can fall into the trap of judging those who struggle with lust or who need to live with a spouse for companionship and sexual intimacy. Additionally, it is easy for those with the gift of celibacy to look at the problems that married couples face and think that they have the solution. It is quite common for single people to provide unwanted marital advice to couples and parental advice to parents. Those who are not married or do not have children should avoid this urge. Finally, those with the gift of celibacy should not look down upon those who want to spend lots of time with their spouse or children instead of "at church doing ministry." Instead, they must remember that having a good marriage and family is the most central form of Christian ministry and evangelism.

Discernment: Those with the gift of discernment can sometimes be too critical of others. Since they often see faults and weaknesses in others, they might fail to recognize their own failures, or to show mercy to those who struggle. It is also easy for those with the gift of discernment to be overly dogmatic and assertive with their own beliefs and ideas. Therefore, those with the gift of discernment must make an extra effort to listen to the ideas and input of others, while also being patient with those who seem to take a long time to learn or discover truths that seem obvious to them.

Evangelism: Those with the gift of evangelism often feel that everybody should be actively sharing their faith with other people every chance they get. Additionally, they sometimes fail to remember that the best forms of evangelism do not always need to use words. How one lives their life can be a better form of evangelism than taking someone through a gospel tract. Finally, the evangelist must never forget that the task of evangelism does not stop when a person believes in Jesus for eternal life, but has only just begun. True evangelism carries on through discipleship.

Exhortation (Encouragement): Those with the gift of exhortation can sometimes be so focused on encouraging others and creating peace, that they avoid confrontation, even when it is necessary. They can also be too quick to offer advice, sometimes before they actually understand the problem. Furthermore, some with the gift of exhortation fail to understand the perspective and experiences of others before offering advice. As such, their advice can occasionally be simplistic and minimalistic, ignoring the complexity of issues that people often face. To avoid this problem, they must make sure to listen and understand before providing instruction or encouragement. Finally, those with the gift of exhortation or encouragement can be too cheerful and upbeat, even when the circumstances call for sadness. They must remember to mourn with those who mourn and let sorrow complete its cycle.

Faith: Those with the gift of faith often lack patience with those who see the difficulties in various situations, preferring to ignore their objections and instead just move forward, trusting God to work it all out. They need to remember that words of caution and careful planning are also important ways for the people of God to make progress in God's plan and purposes for their lives. Related to this, those with the gift of faith sometimes fall prey to thinking that faith is nothing more than sitting and waiting for God to act. Faith is not "letting go and letting God," but is the persuasion or conviction that God can work in desperate situations, even against impossible odds, but usually in coordination with human activity. So the one who has the gift of faith should listen to the objections offered, and then encourage people to move forward with tangible steps of faith that allow God's power to work and His name to be glorified.

Giving: Those with the gift of giving can sometimes be guilty of condemning or criticizing others who do not seem to give enough. Since those with the gift of giving often give more than 50% of their income away, it is easy for them to be critical of those who give much smaller amounts. Furthermore, since some with the gift of giving are often able to make lots of money, they must watch out for greed. They must remember that even if they give away 50% of their income, the remaining amount is still more than the average person makes. Those with the gift of giving also must ward off the temptation to influence or control how their money is spent when they give it away. The money must be given freely, with no strings or conditions attached. Finally, since their large donations often receive public praise and recognition, it is important that the giver not give in to pride.

Healing: Those with the gift of healing can sometimes go overboard in caring for others. Since the gift of healing can often manifest in providing physical care for others, those who have this gift will sometimes wear themselves out in taking care of others. Beyond this, some people need to learn from their own health mistakes, and so while they can be cared for in their pain and health problems, it is also important to let them experience the pain and hardship from their poor decisions so that they can learn to live healthier in the future. When healing is used in coordination with miracles, those with this gift combination often make the mistake of guaranteeing that someone will be miraculously healed. This can create false hope in others and also bring shame to the name of Jesus Christ if someone dies after they were promised healing. Therefore, those with the gift of healing must never promise that someone will be healed, but should leave all such decisions up to God.

Helping: Those with the gift of helping sometimes think that because they and their work rarely gets recognized, it is not very important. They must remember, however, that their gift of helping others is essential for the proper functioning of other gifts. Another caution for those with this gift is that they have trouble saying "No" to other people who ask for help, and have even greater trouble accepting help from other people. The one with the gift of helps must develop the freedom to say "No" and even to ask others for help when needed. Finally, those with the gift of helping must make sure they help their own family first and foremost. It is easy to see all the needs "out there," while neglecting the needs right within their own household.

Hospitality: Those with the gift of hospitality must ward against the danger of doing little more than entertaining. Hospitality is not simply the ability to make good food and provide a place to sleep for others, but is also the task of making them feel at home and safe. At the same time, the primary responsibility of the person with the gift of hospitality is their own family. It does no good to provide food and lodging for other people if the person's family feels neglected and unsafe in their own home. This is why it is often unwise to welcome complete strangers into one's home while there are still children in the home, as such a use of hospitality can endanger one's own family.

Interpretation of Tongues: Those with the gift of interpretation must be careful to protect themselves against pride when others are amazed at their ability to understand and translate the words of other people. This is especially true when the gift is used in a miraculous way to translate a language that has never been studied. Beyond this, the one with the gift of interpretation should also protect themselves from allowing their own desires or ideas to influence their interpretation. They must always provide an accurate interpretation that is in accordance with the revealed Word of God in Scripture.

Knowledge: Those with the gift of knowledge must watch out for pride (cf. 1 Cor 8:1). It is very easy for the one with knowledge to think that he or she knows more than everyone else, and is therefore correct in everything they teach. They must remain humble and teachable, recognizing that there are unknown flaws in their thinking and holes in their theology. It is important as well for the person with the gift of knowledge to never look down upon those who have little interest in studying Scripture or reading theology. Those with the gift of knowledge often forget that widespread literacy is a recent historical phenomenon, and so they often use Scripture to inflict guilt upon others for not spending plenty of time every day in the study of Scripture. Such Bible study guilt trips must stop.

Leadership: Those with the gift of leadership are often "Type A" personalities who can be abrasive, impatient, abusive, and demanding in their treatment of others. While it is true that those with the gift of leadership often know where people need to go and the steps they need to take to get there, those in leadership positions must be patient with people, leading by example and in love, rather than with fear, manipulation, and control. They must remember that leadership is not loudership, so that the one who is loudest gets to lead. Instead, leadership is loving influence, so that people naturally and willingly follow those who provide and care for them in love.

Martyrdom: Since the person with the gift of martyrdom doesn't really know they have the gift until they are put to death for the cause of Christ, it is difficult for such a person to watch out for their weaknesses. Nevertheless, some people *feel* that they might be asked to give their life for Jesus Christ, and end up being a martyr. In such cases, those who think they have the gift of martyrdom must be wary of thinking that they are being persecuted for Christ just because someone is rude to them. It is quite common for Christians to behave toward others in the meanest and rudest ways imaginable, and then when they receive rude and mean treatment in return, they praise God for being "persecuted for Christ." But this is not what is happening. To the contrary, such Christians are persecuting others in the name of Christ, which is completely contrary to Christ and the gospel. So the primary danger with the gift of martyrdom is in thinking that you have it, and then assuming that others are persecuting you as a result of being a Christian. If you think you have the gift of martyrdom, don't announce it to others or claim that you are being persecuted by others. Instead, suffer silently for the cause of Christ, speaking only when asked to give a reason for the hope that you have (1 Pet 3:14-15).

Mercy: Those with the gift of mercy need to be careful that they do not burn themselves out emotionally. Since they are often dealing with the pain and tragedy in the lives of other people, it is important that they also receive emotional support from others. Of course, it is important for them to recognize as well that God is the ultimate source of comfort, and so while they can help others in their time of need, they must make sure to direct people to God as well, who will never leave them nor forsake them. Finally, those with the gift of mercy must ward themselves against being taken advantage of by others. They are often people-pleasers who want to help everybody who asks, but they need to remember that the best way to help some people is to help them learn from their mistakes and take responsibility for their own actions.

Miracles: Those with the gift of miracles can sometimes fall into the trap of spiritual pride. Since their gift is so awe-inspiring, it is easy for them to turn it into a circus sideshow for wide-eyed onlookers. In other words, the gift of miracles is not for the stage and the crowd, but for the individual person with the need or sickness. Furthermore, the one with the gift of miracles must never promise or guarantee that a miracle will occur. God is the one who sends the miracles, and it is not a sign of "great faith" to promise a sick or dying person that God will make them well. This is instead a sign of little faith, for such a promise reveals a misunderstanding of the nature, character, and power of God. Far too much damage has been done to the cause of Christ by people who promise miracles of healing or financial blessing to others that never come true. So those with the gift of miracles should never make such promises, but should instead allow God to decide when and where miracles occur.

Pastor-Teacher: Those with the gift of pastor-teacher can sometimes develop pride and arrogance, because their ministry often takes place in public venues, in front of adoring crowds. As a result, it is easy for pastor-teachers to take themselves too seriously, forgetting that they are only under-shepherds to the Good Shepherd, Jesus Christ. So the pastor-teacher must remain humble, and must lead, tend, guide, and care for the flock under their care. It is also important to recognize that since the entire church is the flock of God, there must not be competition between individual local churches. There is nothing wrong with a person sitting under the care of one pastor-teacher for a while, and then after a time moving to sit under the care of someone else. As each person matures in their walk with God, they need different types of teaching and encouragement at different times, and so the pastor-teacher must be willing to release people to follow Jesus wherever it is He leads, even if it is to another church or away from Sunday morning gatherings altogether.

Prophecy: Those with the gift of prophecy can sometimes neglect the greater aspect of their gift (the forthtelling of God's will) for the lesser aspect (foretelling the future) because the latter is more spectacular. So the person with the gift of prophecy must maintain the correct balance, as did the Prophets of Scripture, by spending most of their time calling people away from sin and back to obedience. At the same time, however, the prophet must make their call to repentance with love and mercy. They should seek to protect themselves from being too harsh or critical toward others when their sin is pointed out, or too impatient when people do not repent or change as quickly as the prophet expects. The prophetic call must reflect the heart of God, which is full of tender, loving care, and limitless patience for His straying children.

Service: Those with the gift of service might be tempted to think that their gift is not very important, since they rarely receive any praise or recognition from others. It is also easy for those with the gift of service to let themselves be taken advantage of by others, taking on too much work. Therefore, the servant should set boundaries, protecting their time and energy, so they can provide quality service over a longer period of time for those who truly need it. Finally, since the needs of others are vast and varied and can become all-consuming, the servant must always remember to serve at home first. The servant must not neglect their family while in the service of others.

Teaching: Those with the gift of teaching can sometimes get bogged down with insignificant details of the biblical text or the theological topic they are studying, so that what they teach to others has very little practical application for people's daily lives. Therefore, the one who teaches should always try to make their teaching relevant and applicable to life. Also, the one who teaches must always be learning as well, for the best teachers are also teachable. A teachable person is humble and inquisitive, so that they always have fresh ideas and new insights to teach to others (cf. 2 Tim 2:2).

Tongues: Those with the gift of tongues must first of all make sure they actually have it. Since tongues is sought after by so many people in the church, many people think they have the gift of tongues when they really do not. Related to this, many who have the gift of tongues are tempted to use it as a way to make themselves look more spiritual in the eyes of others. Therefore, the one with the gift of tongues should never speak in a public setting in a showy or dramatic way, and especially when there is no interpreter present.

Voluntary Poverty: Those with the gift of voluntary poverty often struggle with the consumerism and materialism that pervades the surrounding culture, church, and other Christians. It is easy, therefore, to condemn and criticize others who spend money on cars, houses, clothes, or vacations when there is so much poverty, hunger, and sickness in the world. The one who has chosen the life of voluntary poverty should remember that not all are called to this same lifestyle, and so it is not wrong or sinful for other Christians to enjoy some of the blessings of God's creation.

Wisdom: Those with the gift of wisdom tend to become very frustrated at the foolish choices, decisions, and lifestyles of other people. They can also struggle with selfishness, as they tend to make decisions that benefit themselves personally in their jobs, finances, and relationships. Therefore, the one with the gift of wisdom should treat others with patience and love, providing counsel and insight into the types of decisions they can make which will help their life turn out for the best. They must remember that what appears to them as "common sense" is not commonly known to other people.

As you read the warnings above for your spiritual gifts, you might have recognized some things you struggle with and some things you don't. This is okay. As stated previously, not everyone struggles with the same things in each gift, and the best thing you can do with your spiritual gift is practice and experiment with it as you serve others and edify the Body of Christ. As you do this, you will strengthen the effectiveness of your spiritual gift while avoiding some of its weaknesses. So keep practicing and ministering, so that the entire church will be knit together in unity and love until we all come to the fullness of Jesus Christ.

Most of all, use your gifts so that the world can reap the benefits of these gifts. Jesus came to love and serve the world, and as followers of Jesus, we must do the same. We must seek to show God's love to a lost and hurting world.

But this raises a question. You might have heard that some of the spiritual gifts are no longer in use. Is this true? This is the question we consider next.

CHAPTER 7

HAVE SOME OF THE GIFTS CEASED?

There are many within Christianity who believe and teach that various spiritual gifts have ceased to be given by God or practiced by the church. Those who hold this view believe that some of the "sign" gifts such as tongues, prophecy, miracles, and healing were important for the birth and initial expansion of the church, but once the church was founded, these sorts of gifts faded away from use.

Various arguments are given in support of this idea. For example, some look at the frequent accounts of tongues, miracles, and healing in the Book of Acts, and then look at the relative infrequent use of such things today, and conclude that something must have changed between then and now. But of course, the frequency of such miraculous events depends entirely on who you ask. Certain groups claim that prophecy, tongues, and miracles are even *more common* today than they were in the Book of Acts. So this argument for the cessation of certain gifts is somewhat arbitrary.

Some people also point to Jesus' statement in Matthew 12 that only a wicked and adulterous generation asks for a sign (Matt 12:39). Since these so-called "sign gifts" are often sought out by large audiences of relatively new Christians, some apply Jesus' statements from Matthew 12 to the similar crowds today who only seem to seek after signs. While the warning is probably appropriate, the fact that people seek signs doesn't necessarily mean that the "signs gifts" have ceased. It just means that people can abuse them, both then and now.

The main reason some think various gifts have ceased is because of what Paul wrote in 1 Corinthians 13:8-13. He said that prophecy will fail and tongues will cease when "that which is perfect has come" (1 Cor 13:8-13). Some people see this as a reference to the birthing of the church and its expansion around the world. Once the church was fully formed in the first century, there was no longer any need for some of the foundational and miraculous gifts. Therefore, these gifts ceased to function.

But this view has several problems. For example, along with prophecy and tongues, Paul also lists knowledge (1 Cor 13:8). Few who believe that tongues and prophecy have ceased also believe that knowledge has ceased. To the contrary, nearly all Christians believe that the spiritual gift of knowledge is very much in use today. So why would tongues and prophesy cease while knowledge did not, when Paul mentions all three together?

Another problem, of course, is that Paul does not explain what he means when he writes about "that which is perfect." But whatever he meant, it doesn't seem logical that he would have meant the coming of the church. After all, the church had already been born by the time Paul wrote this. And if Paul meant that these gifts would end when the church spread over the entire earth, this still hasn't happened in our own day, which means the gifts should still be in effect.

The most likely explanation of Paul's statement, therefore, is that he was thinking of the perfect future state that will exist in the new heavens and new earth after the old have passed away and God makes everything new (Rev 21:1-5). The new heavens and new earth will be different and better than this current sin-filled planet we live in. As a result, how we live and work together as humans will also be different, and so there will be no need for any of the spiritual gifts. I assume that we will each still have different interests, hobbies, and talents, but God has not provided many details about our future eternal existence, and so we must be careful about making assumptions. The bottom line is that as long as we are on this earth and in these non-perfect bodies, all the spiritual gifts will be in use.

This doesn't necessarily mean that when someone claims to be speaking in tongues, giving a prophecy, or healing the sick, they are actually doing so. Due to the nature of spiritual gifts, they can be easily abused or faked. This is, in fact, one of the reasons that some people think some of the gifts have ceased. When they see how some gifts are misunderstood, misapplied, and abused, they want to correct these problems, and the easiest way to do so is to simply claim that the gifts have ceased functioning.

It is indeed true that some groups twist and distort various spiritual gifts (such as tongues, prophecies, and miracles) so that they are used to put on a "magic" show in front of large audiences. This is not the way spiritual gifts were ever used in the Bible, and is not the way such gifts are to be used today. But the solution is not to ban the gifts or say they have ceased from use, for this would only bring harm to the rest of the Body (1 Cor 12:21, 25-26). The solution to the abuse of spiritual gifts is to properly understand what they are (and are not), and how to use them for the edification of others, while also avoiding the problems which the gifts can cause.

It is also critical to understand that while all the gifts are still in use, some of the gifts (such as apostleship and tongues) have changed in how they are implemented within the Body of Christ. Ultimately, when properly understood and practiced, we conclude that all the spiritual gifts are still in use today, including those of apostleship, healing, miracles, and tongues.

Nevertheless, since so many people have questions about the gift of tongues, let me briefly try to address some of the main issues related to this confusing spiritual gift.

CHAPTER 8

WHAT ABOUT TONGUES?

The gift of tongues is a tricky topic. Most Christians have strong opinions about it one way or the other. Some think it was in use in the early church era but has now completely ceased, while others think it is a gift that all Christians should practice as a means to spiritual growth. Some think it is a gift that can be taught and learned, while others say it is only miraculously received. The following short chapter on tongues will not solve all these differences, but will hopefully provide a middle-ground perspective that will create some peace between the opposing sides while also giving a brief explanation for how the gift of tongues is presented in Scripture.

TONGUES IN THE OLD TESTAMENT

The main point to recognize regarding tongues is that the New Testament is not the first place they are mentioned. Speaking in tongues is first referenced in various places in the Old Testament. Genesis 11 reveals that God judged the people building the tower to the heavens by causing people to speak in different tongues so that they could not understand each other. As a result of this divine discipline, the people spread out over the face of the earth. This first use of tongues in the Bible reveals a theme that is found elsewhere as well. People speaking in other tongues is a symbolic sign of divine discipline which leads to the scattering and dispersion of the people. This same cycle is found elsewhere in the Old Testament where speaking in foreign tongues is mentioned (cf.

Deut 28:15, 49, 64-65; Isa 28:9-13; 33:19; Jer 5:15, 19).

So the consistent theme in all these texts is that speaking in tongues is a sign to the Jewish people that God's divine discipline is coming, and that if they do not change their ways, they will be scattered and dispersed upon the earth. And this is exactly what happened following the ministry of Jesus. He announced that God's kingdom was coming, but most Jewish people rejected Jesus as the Messiah. So following the death, resurrection, and ascension of Jesus, the Jews in Jerusalem at Pentecost heard others speaking in tongues (Acts 2:4, 8). The Jewish people were then scattered and dispersed in AD 70 after Jerusalem and the temple were destroyed by the Roman Empire.[12]

The first point to recognize about tongues, therefore, is that they are not a sign of God's blessing, but a sign of God's discipline. They serve as a warning about impending destruction and dispersion. Why does God send the warning this way? It is so that the people who hear the warning in other languages know that the message is not of human origin, but comes directly from God. In Isaiah 28, for example, the Jewish people criticize Isaiah for saying the same thing to them over and over and over. They mock Isaiah as if he were a child. The statement in Isaiah 28:13 could be translated as "But the word of the Lord to them was, 'Blah blah blah yada yada yada.'" It is with this sort of scornful mockery that they criticized Isaiah's words.[13]

This is why God said that He will send foreigners to speak to the Jews in another tongue (Isa 28:11). The implication is that when they hear the translation of these other words, they will discover that these others are saying the same thing Isaiah said. This would prove that the message was from God, for foreigners would not have collaborated with the prophet

---

[12] For a good summary of this view, see George W. Zeller, *God's Gift of Tongues* (Eugene OR: Wipf & Stock, 1978), 77-90. He goes on to argue that as a result of the dispersion, tongues has ceased. But this does not necessarily follow, for there were several cycles of tongues and dispersion prior to the events of Acts. Therefore, it seems logical that the cycle could repeat after AD 70 as well.

[13] See my book, *Cruciform Pastoral Leadership* (Dallas, OR: Redeeming Press, 2019), for further explanation of Isaiah 28:13.

to speak the same message he had spoken. If, therefore, the Jewish people did not respond either to the message of Isaiah or the message spoken in a foreign tongue, this would then lead to scattering and dispersion. And this is exactly what has happened over and over throughout Israelite history.

TONGUES ARE HUMAN LANGUAGES

Following this truth about the biblical nature and purpose of tongues, we also learn that biblical tongues are always a human language. Most of the biblical texts that describe tongues also point out that the tongues are other human languages (cf. Gen 11:7-9; Deut 28:49; Isa 28:9-13; 33:19; Jer 5:15; Acts 2:6, 8). Also, the fact that Paul writes in 1 Corinthians 14 that tongues should never be spoken unless an interpreter is present indicates that tongues are an actual human language which can be interpreted. There is no evidence in Scripture anywhere that tongues is a "heavenly" or "angelic" language that sounds like gibberish.

As a side note, the texts of Romans 8:26 and Jude 20 are likely not referring to speaking in tongues. Both of these texts refer to "praying in the Spirit" and Paul even mentions praying with "groaning which cannot be uttered" (Rom 8:26). But neither of these texts mention anything about tongues, and so they should be taken literally, as having nothing to do with speaking in another language. Sometimes, when people pray, they struggle with knowing what words to use, or even how to pray for a certain situation. In such cases, trust the Holy Spirit to give you the actual words you should say (this is praying in the Spirit ... with an actual language you understand), and in some cases, to maybe even pray without words at all, but instead with emotional utterances of groans and sighs. These groans and sighs are not words, but are the same sort of sounds anyone might make in times of deep physical pain, mental need, or emotional distress. So these texts are not referring to speaking in tongues. In

Scripture, tongues always refers to speaking another human language.

TONGUES AS A SIGN OF THE KINGDOM

One final line of evidence to understand about the gift of tongues is how it is related to the spread of the gospel in the Book of Acts. It is critical to recognize that the Book of Acts does not describe the perfect church in the way God wanted it to be forevermore, but instead describes the birth of the church and its initial growth upon the earth. If the church were a human being, the Book of Acts would describe its infancy years. But just as a human must grow up and mature, so also must the church. The Book of Acts, therefore, does not offer a prescription for how the church should behave, but simply offers a description of how the early church was born and began to function.

At the beginning, Jesus instructed the disciples to carry the gospel to the ends of the earth, beginning in Jerusalem, Judea, and Samaria (Acts 1:8). They were to spread the rule and reign of God (i.e., the Kingdom of God), as inaugurated and exemplified by Jesus, to the ends of the earth. And Peter himself was given the keys of the kingdom for this very purpose (Matt 16:19). So it was Peter's responsibility to unlock the door of the Kingdom to the various people groups on earth. This was to begin with the Jews in Jerusalem and Judea, and then spread outward to the Samaritans and the Gentiles. And this is indeed exactly what happens in the Book of Acts.

After Jesus ascended, the disciples were in the Upper Room when the Holy Spirit came upon them, and many of them started speaking in tongues (Acts 2:5-8). Peter was present, and he explained to the multitude what was happening and what it meant (Acts 2:14-39). In Acts 8, the gospel spreads to the Samaritans (Acts 8:4-8). But note that nobody in Samaria received the Holy Spirit (and presumably started speaking in tongues, though the text doesn't say this) until Peter arrived and "unlocked the door of the Kingdom" to the Samaritans by laying hands on them (Acts 8:14-17).

Later, Peter is similarly instructed by God to preach the gospel to a Gentile convert to Judaism, Cornelius (Acts 10:1-16). So Peter goes and after he preaches the gospel to them, Cornelius and his household receive the Holy Spirit and start speaking in tongues (Acts 10:33-48). This indicates that the door to the Kingdom had now been flung open to the Gentiles as well. Peter's task was finished, and we do not hear much more about Peter in the Book of Acts.

However, the church debated whether or not the gospel could truly be preached to the Gentiles. Though Paul was traveling around the Roman Empire preaching Jesus and proclaiming peace to all (Acts 13ff), not all Jewish Christians were convinced that all Gentiles were welcome. For although Cornelius had been a Gentile, he had converted to Judaism, and so many Jews believed that before a Gentile could accept the gospel and believe in Jesus, they must first convert to Judaism. This is what the church leaders discussed in Acts 15. So when Paul encountered a group of Gentiles in Ephesus who had heard bits and pieces of the gospel, he laid hands on them so that they might receive the Holy Spirit. When they did, they also began to speak in tongues (Acts 19:1-6). Paul was able to do this because Peter had already unlocked the door to the Gentiles. Paul's actions only confirmed that the door was indeed unlocked to any and all who would believe.

Other than these incidents, we do not hear about the gift of tongues in the Book of Acts. It is only mentioned in these critical transitionary accounts which show the fulfillment of Jesus' instructions in Acts 1:8. In each case, the gift of tongues was a sign to the Jewish leaders that God's discipline was coming, which would be followed by a dispersion, and therefore, the gospel of Jesus Christ should be spread far and wide so that the church as the people of God on earth might survive and thrive. In this case, the dispersion had been redeemed by God, so that it was no longer a form of discipline and judgment. It became a form of blessing, as it showed that God was working in the world to reverse Babel and spread the Gospel far and wide within the seeds of the scattered church.

TONGUES AND 1 CORINTHIANS 14

All of these ideas about tongues are reinforced by what Paul writes in 1 Corinthians 12–14. He points out that tongues are a sign (1 Cor 14:21-22). The unbelievers he mentioned are not general unbelievers of the world, but unbelieving *Jews* as indicated by Paul's quote from Isaiah 28:11-12. He also indicates that tongues are a spoken human language when he indicates that there must be a translation if someone speaks in another tongue during a church gathering (1 Cor 14:6-19). And of course, the ultimate goal is love (1 Cor 13) and edification of the Body (1 Cor 14:1-5). Paul even states that he would rather speak 10,000 words that can be understood by himself and others than 5 words which cannot be understood (1 Cor 14:19).

The spread of the gospel and the advancement of the Kingdom requires that what we say be understood by those who hear it. The bottom line truth about tongues, therefore, is that if a person speaks in tongues, it must be translated so that those who hear are instructed and edified. Otherwise, where there is no understanding, there is no benefit to the one who speaks or the one who hears (1 Cor 14:15-17). Note that according to Paul, even the one who speaks in tongues is not edified by tongues if he or she does not know what they are saying. Even the personal use of tongues requires a translation if it is going to be helpful and beneficial to the speaker (1 Cor 14:13).

ARE TONGUES FOR TODAY?

Due to the transitionary and redemptive use of tongues in the Book of Acts, it appears that the gift of tongues might very well be in use today. However, whenever and wherever God allows this gift to be used, the basic principles of tongues still stand. Tongues are always a human language that is spoken to a group of people as a way of introducing them to the gospel and indicating the truthfulness and divine origin of what is said. Therefore, when an interpreter is not present, tongues serve no purpose, and the speaker should remain silent (1 Cor 14:28).

So I think that the gift of tongues could still be in use today, albeit in a slightly different way than commonly practiced in many modern church gatherings, and also somewhat different than the way it is used and described in Scripture. The Old Testament use of tongues was a sign to the Jewish people that God was disciplining them for their failure to hear and respond to His message. In these situations, God sent an identical message to what the prophets had preached, but He sent it through people who spoke another language. If the Jewish people still did not hear and respond, then further discipline would come in the form of scattering and dispersion.

But in the Book of Acts, while the gift of tongues still served as a sign to Jewish people that discipline and judgment were coming, it also helped spread the gospel to other people groups, showing the Jewish people and the world that the Kingdom of God was open to all. This transitionary and redemptive use of tongues helps us understand how tongues might be in use today.

Since we no longer need evidence or proof (the way the early Jewish Christians did) that the gospel is available to all people around the world we should not expect to see the widespread use of tongues as a sign to verify that the door to the Kingdom of God has been opened to these other groups. We know it is open, and we don't need a sign to prove it. Therefore, the only remaining purpose for the use of tongues is to help spread the gospel message of Jesus to those who have not yet heard it in their own language.

If the gift of tongues is in use today, it would be used in evangelistic settings where the speaker is specially gifted by God to speak in another language (or quickly learn another language) for the sake of sharing the gospel message with others. This is how it was used in Acts 2, and it appears that this might be what Paul was referring to in 1 Corinthians 14 when he wrote about speaking in tongues more than anyone else (1 Cor 14:18). Paul's evangelistic and missionary travels likely put him in situations where he needed to convey the gospel message to people who spoke other languages. The gift of tongues enabled him to do so.

So do you think you have the gift of tongues? If so, don't use it for personal reasons, and also don't think that this gift somehow makes you more spiritual than others. All the gifts are equally important for the health and growth of the Body. Instead, pray that God will help you use your ability to speak in other languages so that those who have not heard the gospel will come to understand it and believe in Jesus for eternal life. Though tongues is one of the "stranger" gifts, go ahead and embrace your strangeness for Jesus, as all of us should do with the gifts we have been given.

CHAPTER 9

EMBRACE YOUR GIFTS

The beautiful thing about spiritual gifts is that they make you unique. Due to your spiritual gift mix (along with your abilities, desires, talents, experience, and skills), there is nobody else in the world who is just like you, nor will there ever be. This is incredibly liberating when you think about it.

Most people in this world spend large amounts of time trying to act like everyone else. They try to behave like the popular kids at school, talk like the actors on TV, dress like the sports stars on the playing field, and look like the pretty people in the magazines. But we can never be someone else ... and they can never be us. Each person is completely and majestically unique. And until you recognize and embrace this, you will always struggle in this life. You will always fail at trying to measure up. You will always feel insignificant and overlooked.

But once you embrace who God made you to be, you will then be set free to be as strange and unique as you possibly can. You will begin to realize that since nobody can ever be you, you might as well be the best you that you can be. This comes by embracing your quirks, reveling in your differences, and strengthening the things that make you stand out in a crowd. Learning and using your spiritual gifts allows you to become and "own" who you are.

THE FRUSTRATION OF CONFORMITY

A few years ago my wife and I had a conversation in which we both discovered that we were each trying to be the other person. My wife, Wendy, is a lover and a server. She is very passionate and emotional. She nearly always speaks and acts before she thinks. Whatever she does, she dives in head first and with both feet. I don't know how she does this, since it's logically impossible, but she does. Logic has never stopped Wendy from doing the impossible. I, on the other hand, am a thinker and a writer. I am even-keeled to the point of being emotionless. I never speak unless I have thought through what I am going to say and all the possible ways the other person might respond. I tend to approach everything logically, as if it were a puzzle to be solved. I tend to prefer books over people.

For many years in our marriage, I felt terribly guilty that I did not spend enough time getting to know our neighbors, taking baked-goods over to friends, or playing with children down at the park the way my wife did. I thought that a "true" follower of Jesus would be out volunteering at the soup-kitchen, chatting with the neighbors about tomato-growing tips, and learning the names of the children down at the local park. I used to think that a "true" follower of Jesus would go about with a spirit and attitude of prayer and grace as they spend their days washing, serving, scrubbing, praying, befriending, and talking.

But that was never me. Not ever.

Within a week of moving into a new neighborhood, my wife has taken fresh-baked loaves of bread and cookies to our neighbors and has had hour-long conversations with all of them, learning about their dogs, their jobs, and their children. When I talk to the neighbors, however, I am barely able to talk about anything more than the weather. I fear going to get the mail, because I am afraid I will meet a neighbor. I dread running into a coworker at Wal-Mart because I will probably forget their name or not know what to say.

If Wendy goes to the local park, she will have a crowd of children around her in ten minutes, all of them laughing, cheering, and giggling. In a few minutes more, she will know their names. She will know their dog's names. They even ask her when she is coming back to the park. I call her a modern-day Pied Piper (but in a good way). When I have tried this in the past, I am pretty sure I scared the kids. I know I scared the parents, because when they saw a long-haired strange man trying to talk nicely to their children, they immediately call the kids over because "It's time to go home!" I am not making this up.

When Wendy stands in line at the grocery store, people just talk to her about things. Sometimes, she strikes up conversations with them, but more often than not, they start conversations with her. This has never happened to me. Not once in my entire life. Nobody ever starts a conversation with me at the grocery store. I have tried to start a conversation with others, and they usually look at me like I'm some sort of freak.

So it was a shock for me to discover a few years back that my wife felt just as guilty as I did, but about the opposite things. While she was great with people, she felt guilty that she wasn't spending as much time studying Scripture and reading theology as I did. She saw me reading a couple theology books per week and studying several hours each day, and felt that she wasn't spending enough time "in the Word." She feared that she wasn't being "spiritual" enough to be a strong Christian. After all, she attended the same Bible College I did, where we learned that "disciple" means "student, pupil, learner." As a result, she thought that if she was a fully-committed disciple of Jesus Christ, she needed to be studying and learning every day.

In fact, during our first ten years of marriage, while I was a pastor, my wife tried to wear the "Bible and theology student hat." She attended every Bible study, every theology conference, and made sure she read and studied the Bible every day. It slowly killed her, for all of this study and reading kept her from having time to love and serve other people. She stopped all of her people-focused activities to make sure she had adequate time to become the "disciple-student" that good Christians were supposed to become. It wasn't until years later when we followed Jesus out of institutional Christianity that she felt the freedom to focus more on people than on Bible study. But she still felt guilty for not spending more time studying the way I was.

So when we discovered that each of us was trying to be the other person, it is then that we realized that both of us were perfect just as we were. We realized that God made Wendy to be Wendy, and He made me to be me. We also realized that rather than fight who God made us to be, we must instead revel in it. Best of all, since we are married, we can work together as a team to both do the things that each of us is uniquely suited to do.

Wendy shines when we have people over to our house. She almost literally glows, especially when the company includes children. I swear that I sometimes see beams of light coming out of her eyes and smile. She is specially gifted by God to love and serve others with her whole being. She bakes, cooks, talks, serves, and loves people in a way I have never seen anybody else match.

I, on the other hand, will sit for hours with my nose in a pile of books, chasing down insights into various Greek words, information about the historical background of a biblical event, and ideas about how to understand a particular text. This reasoning ability also allows me to fix problems around the house. I have often dismantled and then fixed lawn mowers and dishwashers. I built a state-of-the-art chicken coop, complete with heated water and a slide-out cleaning tray, simply by looking at a picture online. I taught myself to design and code websites, create and sell books, and publish a Bible study podcast and online theology courses.

Wendy looks at me and says, "How can you sit and study so long? How can you know what needs to be fixed on the dishwasher?" I look at her and say, "How can you love to bake and entertain children so often?" And for many years, when each of us tried to be the other person, both of us were miserable. But now that we have recognized that each of us has specific gifts, talents, strengths, and abilities, and that we are each supposed to strengthen, develop, and use our *own* gifts (rather than those of someone else), life has become much more enjoyable. And so has our marriage.

Since we are married, I get to join Wendy as she cooks and converses with friends and neighbors. By myself, I could never do this. But I am happy to join her when she does it. And Wendy gets to hear my ideas and insight into Scripture as we discuss what is going on inside my head. As different as we are, we need each other, and we help each other do things that we could not do on our own. I need her to lead me in practical ways to put my ideas into practice, and she needs me to help theologically affirm and encourage her actions in loving others. We learned to accept who God made us to be. We learned that it was better to revel in our strengths than to resist them.

The Olympic runner, Eric Liddell, once said, "I believe God made me for a purpose, but he also made me fast. And when I run I feel His pleasure." My wife feels God's pleasure when she bakes for other people, plays with children, ministers to the neighbors, and laughs with friends. I feel God's pleasure when I discover something new about a certain Greek word, when I read an intriguing idea in someone else's book, or when I am able to help someone in their Christian life by answering a tricky theological question. My wife is not me, and she shouldn't try to be me. Similarly, I am not my wife, and shouldn't try to be her. Yet we both need each other. I do the studying for her and she learns from me. She does the love and service and helps me make friends and love others in ways I could never do on my own.

BE WHO YOU ARE

The same thing is true for you. God made you to be who you are. So embrace it! Discover your gifts, throw caution to the wind, and fling yourself into your strange, unique life with wild abandon. Rather than seeking to become a clone of somebody else, become who God uniquely gifted you to be. Only then will you find satisfaction in life and fulfillment in this world. Only then will the Body of Christ develop in healthy and beautiful ways as you contribute as only you can.

Of course, you must let others do the same. Just as each of us must be who God made us to be, we must allow others to be whom God made them to be. I must not expect others to tirelessly read and study, and they must not expect me to be invigorated by baking a cake or listening to our neighbor talk about his dog. Imagine the beauty and glory that would enter into this world if we all embraced our gifts and allowed others to do the same? It is only because of this beautiful diversity that the church exists in this world. The beauty of Christianity is not that we are all the same or that we are all "balanced," but instead, that we are all so dissimilar and opposite, and that in Christ, we are unified and can celebrate the differences and insanities of others rather than calling them to "become like us."

So don't try to be balanced. Don't try to fit in. Don't try to be someone else. Be the best "you" that you can be, for you cannot be anyone else, and nobody else can be "you" either. God created you to do something, so go do it! Don't turn to the left or the right by pious-sounding talk about wearing the "right" clothes, using the "right" language, hanging out with the "right" people, or acting in the "right" way. Instead, find your divine spark of "madness" and fully embrace it until it turns into a raging inferno. Then people will come from miles away just to watch you burn.

EMBRACE YOUR INSANITY

When you live the way God made you to live, some people might think you're insane. At times, you might agree with them. But learn to accept your insanity. Embrace it. Enjoy it. Live it. Be different and be proud.

I dive fully into reading, writing, and studying. This is why people are often amazed at how I publish 2-3 books per year. But that's my insanity and I love it. My wife is always full-steam ahead with cooking and helping others. It is so insane sometimes, that I tell my daughters, "Remember … when you grow up and become a mother, you don't have to do everything your mother does in order to be a good mother. She's insane."

What is your insanity? What are the passions, interests, and gifts that make you "you"? Fling yourself into these whole-heartedly for your own satisfaction and for the glory of God. As you exercise you spiritual gifts, you might find yourself neck-deep in one of the following areas:

- Loving your family and friends
- Caring for children
- Cooking, baking, and hospitality
- Ministry to prostitutes
- Providing for the homeless
- Serving the elderly
- Conserving nature
- Tending to animals
- Involving yourself in politics
- Studying and teaching Scripture
- Learning and writing about theology
- Helping others live a healthy life
- Giving generously to others
- Cleaning your town and neighborhood
- Researching medical and scientific advances
- Healing the sick and injured
- And millions of other possibilities

By learning about your spiritual gifts and choosing to put them into practice, you will be allowing God to form and shape you into the amazing and astonishing person He made you to be. Embrace your gifts and let the world see the light and the glory of God shining through you.

APPENDIX

SPIRITUAL GIFTS INVENTORY

Instructions for Use:

1. There are a total of 125 statements below. For each statement, circle whether you *Strongly Agree, Somewhat Agree,* are *Undecided, Somewhat Disagree,* or *Completely Disagree.* Try to use *Undecided* no more than five times.

2. When you have completed all 125 statements, transfer your answers to the profile sheet at the end of this document.

3. Total your scores for each of the gifts. Each gift will have a score between ZERO and TWENTY.

4. Order the gifts in descending order of score. Higher scores indicate your more dominant gifts.

5. For more information on your gift and how to use it, look at the chapter titled "What Are the Spiritual Gifts?"

1) *I enjoy the responsibility of making important decisions that affect others.*

     4-Strongly Agree
     3-Somewhat Agree
     2-Undecided

1-Somewhat Disagree
0-Completely Disagree

2) *I often think God is calling me to take the gospel to people who haven't heard about Jesus.*

4-Strongly Agree
3-Somewhat Agree
2-Undecided
1-Somewhat Disagree
0-Completely Disagree

3) *I enjoy working creatively with wood, cloth, paints, metal, glass, or other materials.*

4-Strongly Agree
3-Somewhat Agree
2-Undecided
1-Somewhat Disagree
0-Completely Disagree

4) *I enjoy developing and using my artistic skills (art, drama, music, photography, etc.).*

4-Strongly Agree
3-Somewhat Agree
2-Undecided
1-Somewhat Disagree
0-Completely Disagree

5) *It is easy for me to recognize talents and gifts in other people.*

4-Strongly Agree
3-Somewhat Agree
2-Undecided
1-Somewhat Disagree
0-Completely Disagree

6) *I live out the truths of gospel with words and actions so that others see and understand God's love and grace in their lives.*

4-Strongly Agree
3-Somewhat Agree
2-Undecided
1-Somewhat Disagree
0-Completely Disagree

7) *It is enjoyable to motivate people to help them take the next step in following Jesus.*

4-Strongly Agree
3-Somewhat Agree
2-Undecided
1-Somewhat Disagree
0-Completely Disagree

8) *I often step out to attempt the impossible.*

4-Strongly Agree
3-Somewhat Agree
2-Undecided
1-Somewhat Disagree
0-Completely Disagree

9) *I give liberally and joyfully to people in financial need or to projects requiring support.*

    4-Strongly Agree
    3-Somewhat Agree
    2-Undecided
    1-Somewhat Disagree
    0-Completely Disagree

10) *I often know what is wrong with people physically, and know what steps are needed to help them recover to full health.*

    4-Strongly Agree
    3-Somewhat Agree
    2-Undecided
    1-Somewhat Disagree
    0-Completely Disagree

11) *I enjoy working behind the scenes in order to support the work of others.*

    4-Strongly Agree
    3-Somewhat Agree
    2-Undecided
    1-Somewhat Disagree
    0-Completely Disagree

12) *I view my home as a place to love and serve other people.*

    4-Strongly Agree
    3-Somewhat Agree
    2-Undecided

1-Somewhat Disagree
0-Completely Disagree

13) *I often wonder why people struggle with sexual urges, since these are not a temptation for me.*

4-Strongly Agree
3-Somewhat Agree
2-Undecided
1-Somewhat Disagree
0-Completely Disagree

14) *It is easy for me to learn foreign languages.*

4-Strongly Agree
3-Somewhat Agree
2-Undecided
1-Somewhat Disagree
0-Completely Disagree

15) *I am often approached by people who want to know my perspective on a certain Bible passage or theological concept.*

4-Strongly Agree
3-Somewhat Agree
2-Undecided
1-Somewhat Disagree
0-Completely Disagree

16) *I am able to motivate others to accomplish a goal.*

4-Strongly Agree
3-Somewhat Agree
2-Undecided
1-Somewhat Disagree
0-Completely Disagree

17) *I empathize with hurting people and desire to help in their healing process.*

4-Strongly Agree
3-Somewhat Agree
2-Undecided
1-Somewhat Disagree
0-Completely Disagree

18) *I very frequently see God miraculously alter circumstances when I pray.*

4-Strongly Agree
3-Somewhat Agree
2-Undecided
1-Somewhat Disagree
0-Completely Disagree

19) *My wallet and bank account are nearly always empty because I give so much money away.*

4-Strongly Agree
3-Somewhat Agree
2-Undecided
1-Somewhat Disagree
0-Completely Disagree

20) *It is enjoyable to have the responsibility of leading other people in their spiritual life.*

    4-Strongly Agree
    3-Somewhat Agree
    2-Undecided
    1-Somewhat Disagree
    0-Completely Disagree

21) *I often speak in a way that results in conviction and a change of life in others.*

    4-Strongly Agree
    3-Somewhat Agree
    2-Undecided
    1-Somewhat Disagree
    0-Completely Disagree

22) *There is great joy in doing little jobs for other people and helping with day-to-day tasks.*

    4-Strongly Agree
    3-Somewhat Agree
    2-Undecided
    1-Somewhat Disagree
    0-Completely Disagree

23) *I love to read and study God's Word and then share with others what I have learned.*

    4-Strongly Agree

3-Somewhat Agree
2-Undecided
1-Somewhat Disagree
0-Completely Disagree

24) *Sometimes I am able to speak to a person in their own language even though I have never studied it.*

4-Strongly Agree
3-Somewhat Agree
2-Undecided
1-Somewhat Disagree
0-Completely Disagree

25) *I am often sought out for advice on personal or spiritual matters.*

4-Strongly Agree
3-Somewhat Agree
2-Undecided
1-Somewhat Disagree
0-Completely Disagree

26) *I enjoy organizing people and harnessing their gifts and talents to solve a particular problem.*

4-Strongly Agree
3-Somewhat Agree
2-Undecided
1-Somewhat Disagree
0-Completely Disagree

27) *I have a strong burden to share the gospel with the unreached people*

groups of the world.

> 4-Strongly Agree
> 3-Somewhat Agree
> 2-Undecided
> 1-Somewhat Disagree
> 0-Completely Disagree

28) *I am skilled in working with different kinds of tools.*

> 4-Strongly Agree
> 3-Somewhat Agree
> 2-Undecided
> 1-Somewhat Disagree
> 0-Completely Disagree

29) *I use art, plays, pictures, or music to help people understand God, themselves, this world, and their relationships.*

> 4-Strongly Agree
> 3-Somewhat Agree
> 2-Undecided
> 1-Somewhat Disagree
> 0-Completely Disagree

30) *I usually detect spiritual truth from spiritual error before fellow believers.*

> 4-Strongly Agree
> 3-Somewhat Agree
> 2-Undecided

1-Somewhat Disagree
0-Completely Disagree

31) *I find it easier to build relationships with non-believers than with believers.*

4-Strongly Agree
3-Somewhat Agree
2-Undecided
1-Somewhat Disagree
0-Completely Disagree

32) *I like to encourage people to revitalize their spiritual life through Bible study, prayer, or getting involved in community service.*

4-Strongly Agree
3-Somewhat Agree
2-Undecided
1-Somewhat Disagree
0-Completely Disagree

33) *I find it natural and easy to know that God is hearing and answering my prayers.*

4-Strongly Agree
3-Somewhat Agree
2-Undecided
1-Somewhat Disagree
0-Completely Disagree

34) *I manage my money well in order to free more of it for giving.*

4-Strongly Agree
3-Somewhat Agree
2-Undecided
1-Somewhat Disagree
0-Completely Disagree

35) *When someone is sick or injured, I pray for them and check up on them until they recover.*

4-Strongly Agree
3-Somewhat Agree
2-Undecided
1-Somewhat Disagree
0-Completely Disagree

36) *In life, I gravitate toward undone work, even if unpopular.*

4-Strongly Agree
3-Somewhat Agree
2-Undecided
1-Somewhat Disagree
0-Completely Disagree

37) *I enjoy meeting new people and helping them feel welcomed.*

4-Strongly Agree
3-Somewhat Agree
2-Undecided
1-Somewhat Disagree
0-Completely Disagree

38) *I want to serve God with all my time and energy, and am sometimes afraid that marriage or children might get in the way.*

    4-Strongly Agree
    3-Somewhat Agree
    2-Undecided
    1-Somewhat Disagree
    0-Completely Disagree

39) *I often feel like I can understand what a person from another country is saying even though I have never studied their language.*

    4-Strongly Agree
    3-Somewhat Agree
    2-Undecided
    1-Somewhat Disagree
    0-Completely Disagree

40) *I am committed to spending large blocks of time on reading and studying Scripture so that I might know biblical truth more fully and accurately.*

    4-Strongly Agree
    3-Somewhat Agree
    2-Undecided
    1-Somewhat Disagree
    0-Completely Disagree

41) *I know where groups of people should be headed and the steps they need to take to accomplish the goals of the group.*

    4-Strongly Agree
    3-Somewhat Agree

2-Undecided
1-Somewhat Disagree
0-Completely Disagree

42) *I can patiently support those going through painful experiences as they try to stabilize their lives.*

4-Strongly Agree
3-Somewhat Agree
2-Undecided
1-Somewhat Disagree
0-Completely Disagree

43) *I have often seen God work in desperate life situations by miraculous intervention when I pray.*

4-Strongly Agree
3-Somewhat Agree
2-Undecided
1-Somewhat Disagree
0-Completely Disagree

44) *I have no desire to own a car, wear nice clothes, buy a house, or go on vacations.*

4-Strongly Agree
3-Somewhat Agree
2-Undecided
1-Somewhat Disagree
0-Completely Disagree

45) *I have a strong desire to seek out wayward believers and restore them to fellowship with Jesus and the church.*

    4-Strongly Agree
    3-Somewhat Agree
    2-Undecided
    1-Somewhat Disagree
    0-Completely Disagree

46) *I often am able to predict the consequences of a particular sinful behavior if a person continues engaging in it.*

    4-Strongly Agree
    3-Somewhat Agree
    2-Undecided
    1-Somewhat Disagree
    0-Completely Disagree

47) *I enjoy doing routine tasks to help others.*

    4-Strongly Agree
    3-Somewhat Agree
    2-Undecided
    1-Somewhat Disagree
    0-Completely Disagree

48) *People often tell me I am able to share difficult truths in ways that are easy to understand.*

    4-Strongly Agree
    3-Somewhat Agree
    2-Undecided

1-Somewhat Disagree

0-Completely Disagree

49) *Sometimes when I do not know what to pray, words come out of my mouth which I do not understand.*

4-Strongly Agree

3-Somewhat Agree

2-Undecided

1-Somewhat Disagree

0-Completely Disagree

50) *I often find simple, practical solutions in the midst of conflict or confusion.*

4-Strongly Agree

3-Somewhat Agree

2-Undecided

1-Somewhat Disagree

0-Completely Disagree

51) *People often look to me for guidance in coordination, organization, and ministry opportunities.*

4-Strongly Agree

3-Somewhat Agree

2-Undecided

1-Somewhat Disagree

0-Completely Disagree

52) *I desire to learn another language, culture, or religion so that I can bet-*

ter connect the truths of the gospel with the people in that culture.

> 4-Strongly Agree
> 3-Somewhat Agree
> 2-Undecided
> 1-Somewhat Disagree
> 0-Completely Disagree

53) *I enjoy making things with my hands.*

> 4-Strongly Agree
> 3-Somewhat Agree
> 2-Undecided
> 1-Somewhat Disagree
> 0-Completely Disagree

54) *I have enjoyed being involved in local musical productions or plays.*

> 4-Strongly Agree
> 3-Somewhat Agree
> 2-Undecided
> 1-Somewhat Disagree
> 0-Completely Disagree

55) *It is easy for me to tell if a person is honest or dishonest.*

> 4-Strongly Agree
> 3-Somewhat Agree
> 2-Undecided
> 1-Somewhat Disagree
> 0-Completely Disagree

56) *I am effective at adapting the gospel message to fit a person's needs or current situation.*

> 4-Strongly Agree
> 3-Somewhat Agree
> 2-Undecided
> 1-Somewhat Disagree
> 0-Completely Disagree

57) *I can challenge others without making them feel condemned.*

> 4-Strongly Agree
> 3-Somewhat Agree
> 2-Undecided
> 1-Somewhat Disagree
> 0-Completely Disagree

58) *I have unwavering confidence in God's continuing provision to help, even in difficult times.*

> 4-Strongly Agree
> 3-Somewhat Agree
> 2-Undecided
> 1-Somewhat Disagree
> 0-Completely Disagree

59) *I like knowing my financial support is making a real difference in the lives of others.*

> 4-Strongly Agree
> 3-Somewhat Agree

2-Undecided
1-Somewhat Disagree
0-Completely Disagree

60) *I have prayed for an emotionally ill person and seen the person get better.*

4-Strongly Agree
3-Somewhat Agree
2-Undecided
1-Somewhat Disagree
0-Completely Disagree

61) *I cannot stand idly by while things go undone.*

4-Strongly Agree
3-Somewhat Agree
2-Undecided
1-Somewhat Disagree
0-Completely Disagree

62) *I like to create a place where people do not feel they are alone.*

4-Strongly Agree
3-Somewhat Agree
2-Undecided
1-Somewhat Disagree
0-Completely Disagree

63) *I have never had problems with lust or strong sexual desires.*

4-Strongly Agree

3-Somewhat Agree

2-Undecided

1-Somewhat Disagree

0-Completely Disagree

64) *It is a strong desire of mine to have all Christians of all languages communicate together.*

4-Strongly Agree

3-Somewhat Agree

2-Undecided

1-Somewhat Disagree

0-Completely Disagree

65) *I am able to grasp and understand passages in Scripture which others find difficult.*

4-Strongly Agree

3-Somewhat Agree

2-Undecided

1-Somewhat Disagree

0-Completely Disagree

66) *I am able to influence others to achieve a goal.*

4-Strongly Agree

3-Somewhat Agree

2-Undecided

1-Somewhat Disagree

0-Completely Disagree

67) *I enjoy helping people sometimes regarded as undeserving or beyond help.*

    4-Strongly Agree
    3-Somewhat Agree
    2-Undecided
    1-Somewhat Disagree
    0-Completely Disagree

68) *I believe that if we trusted God more, we would see dramatic, public miracles like in the New Testament.*

    4-Strongly Agree
    3-Somewhat Agree
    2-Undecided
    1-Somewhat Disagree
    0-Completely Disagree

69) *I live in communal housing and get my clothes from thrift shops so that I can give more of my income away.*

    4-Strongly Agree
    3-Somewhat Agree
    2-Undecided
    1-Somewhat Disagree
    0-Completely Disagree

70) *In the past, when helping someone, I try to provide direction for the whole person—relationally, emotionally, spiritually, etc.*

    4-Strongly Agree
    3-Somewhat Agree
    2-Undecided

1-Somewhat Disagree
0-Completely Disagree

71) *I frequently, boldly, and verbally expose cultural trends, teachings, or events to other Christians which contradict biblical principles.*

4-Strongly Agree
3-Somewhat Agree
2-Undecided
1-Somewhat Disagree
0-Completely Disagree

72) *I receive great satisfaction in doing small or trivial tasks for others that need to be done.*

4-Strongly Agree
3-Somewhat Agree
2-Undecided
1-Somewhat Disagree
0-Completely Disagree

73) *I pay close attention to the words, phrases and meanings of those who teach God's Word.*

4-Strongly Agree
3-Somewhat Agree
2-Undecided
1-Somewhat Disagree
0-Completely Disagree

74) *I frequently speak or pray in a language that I have not learned.*

4-Strongly Agree
3-Somewhat Agree
2-Undecided
1-Somewhat Disagree
0-Completely Disagree

75) *I can anticipate the likely consequence of an individual's or group's action.*

4-Strongly Agree
3-Somewhat Agree
2-Undecided
1-Somewhat Disagree
0-Completely Disagree

76) *The development of effective plans for church ministry or community service gives me great satisfaction.*

4-Strongly Agree
3-Somewhat Agree
2-Undecided
1-Somewhat Disagree
0-Completely Disagree

77) *It is easy for me to move into a new community and make friends.*

4-Strongly Agree
3-Somewhat Agree
2-Undecided
1-Somewhat Disagree
0-Completely Disagree

78) *I am good at and enjoy working with my hands.*

    4-Strongly Agree
    3-Somewhat Agree
    2-Undecided
    1-Somewhat Disagree
    0-Completely Disagree

79) *If a truth cannot be presented creatively, it would be better to not present it at all.*

    4-Strongly Agree
    3-Somewhat Agree
    2-Undecided
    1-Somewhat Disagree
    0-Completely Disagree

80) *God has used me to warn others of the danger of a certain teaching.*

    4-Strongly Agree
    3-Somewhat Agree
    2-Undecided
    1-Somewhat Disagree
    0-Completely Disagree

81) *I openly and confidently tell others what Jesus has done for me, and want others to ask me about my faith.*

    4-Strongly Agree
    3-Somewhat Agree

2-Undecided

1-Somewhat Disagree

0-Completely Disagree

82) *People express to me how much I've helped or encouraged them in a time of need.*

4-Strongly Agree

3-Somewhat Agree

2-Undecided

1-Somewhat Disagree

0-Completely Disagree

83) *I believe God will help me accomplish great things.*

4-Strongly Agree

3-Somewhat Agree

2-Undecided

1-Somewhat Disagree

0-Completely Disagree

84) *I believe I have been given an abundance of resources so that I may give more to help with the financial needs of others.*

4-Strongly Agree

3-Somewhat Agree

2-Undecided

1-Somewhat Disagree

0-Completely Disagree

85) *When I visit and help those who are sick and pray that God would make them physically whole, they nearly always recover.*

4-Strongly Agree
3-Somewhat Agree
2-Undecided
1-Somewhat Disagree
0-Completely Disagree

86) *The church needs to stop talking so much and start helping people in practical ways.*

4-Strongly Agree
3-Somewhat Agree
2-Undecided
1-Somewhat Disagree
0-Completely Disagree

87) *I make people feel at ease even in unfamiliar surroundings.*

4-Strongly Agree
3-Somewhat Agree
2-Undecided
1-Somewhat Disagree
0-Completely Disagree

88) *When I imagine my future, I rarely envision a spouse or family,*

4-Strongly Agree
3-Somewhat Agree
2-Undecided
1-Somewhat Disagree
0-Completely Disagree

89) *If I hear a Christian speaking in a different language, I find I can understand what they are saying.*

    4-Strongly Agree
    3-Somewhat Agree
    2-Undecided
    1-Somewhat Disagree
    0-Completely Disagree

90) *I discover important biblical truths when reading or studying Scripture which benefit others in the church.*

    4-Strongly Agree
    3-Somewhat Agree
    2-Undecided
    1-Somewhat Disagree
    0-Completely Disagree

91) *I can manage people and resources effectively to accomplish set goals.*

    4-Strongly Agree
    3-Somewhat Agree
    2-Undecided
    1-Somewhat Disagree
    0-Completely Disagree

92) *I enjoy doing practical things for people who are in need.*

    4-Strongly Agree
    3-Somewhat Agree
    2-Undecided

1-Somewhat Disagree
0-Completely Disagree

93) *I often pray for impossible things which actually come true.*

4-Strongly Agree
3-Somewhat Agree
2-Undecided
1-Somewhat Disagree
0-Completely Disagree

94) *I think that materialism, consumerism, capitalism, and greed are some of the greatest problems in the world today.*

4-Strongly Agree
3-Somewhat Agree
2-Undecided
1-Somewhat Disagree
0-Completely Disagree

95) *I often see other believers respond spiritually to my direction and leadership.*

4-Strongly Agree
3-Somewhat Agree
2-Undecided
1-Somewhat Disagree
0-Completely Disagree

96) *I am able to understand how key current events around the world tie into Bible prophecy and how these events will affect the future.*

4-Strongly Agree
3-Somewhat Agree
2-Undecided
1-Somewhat Disagree
0-Completely Disagree

97) *I often recognize ways that I can care for others indirectly without speaking or teaching.*

4-Strongly Agree
3-Somewhat Agree
2-Undecided
1-Somewhat Disagree
0-Completely Disagree

98) *I take a systematic approach to my daily study of the Bible.*

4-Strongly Agree
3-Somewhat Agree
2-Undecided
1-Somewhat Disagree
0-Completely Disagree

99) *God has used me to witness to other people whose language I did not know.*

4-Strongly Agree
3-Somewhat Agree
2-Undecided
1-Somewhat Disagree
0-Completely Disagree

100) *I have a strong sense of confidence in my solution to problems.*

    4-Strongly Agree
    3-Somewhat Agree
    2-Undecided
    1-Somewhat Disagree
    0-Completely Disagree

101) *I would rather make a decision for a group than persuade them to reach the same decision.*

    4-Strongly Agree
    3-Somewhat Agree
    2-Undecided
    1-Somewhat Disagree
    0-Completely Disagree

102) *The thought of moving to a new community and making new friends is exciting to me.*

    4-Strongly Agree
    3-Somewhat Agree
    2-Undecided
    1-Somewhat Disagree
    0-Completely Disagree

103) *I am able to design and construct things that help others.*

    4-Strongly Agree
    3-Somewhat Agree

2-Undecided
1-Somewhat Disagree
0-Completely Disagree

104) *I regularly need to get away from people so that I can reflect and develop my imagination.*

4-Strongly Agree
3-Somewhat Agree
2-Undecided
1-Somewhat Disagree
0-Completely Disagree

105) *I often have insights into a person's character or motives, and receive confirmation of my perceptions at a later date.*

4-Strongly Agree
3-Somewhat Agree
2-Undecided
1-Somewhat Disagree
0-Completely Disagree

106) *I seem to be able to determine when a person is prepared to receive Jesus Christ.*

4-Strongly Agree
3-Somewhat Agree
2-Undecided
1-Somewhat Disagree
0-Completely Disagree

107) *I would rather develop a friendship with a Christian person than a*

non-Christian.

    4-Strongly Agree
    3-Somewhat Agree
    2-Undecided
    1-Somewhat Disagree
    0-Completely Disagree

108) *I am regularly challenging others to trust God and step out in faith to do difficult things.*

    4-Strongly Agree
    3-Somewhat Agree
    2-Undecided
    1-Somewhat Disagree
    0-Completely Disagree

109) *I have great satisfaction in giving large amounts of money to others in need.*

    4-Strongly Agree
    3-Somewhat Agree
    2-Undecided
    1-Somewhat Disagree
    0-Completely Disagree

110) *I feel strongly that my prayers for a sick person bring wholeness to that person.*

    4-Strongly Agree
    3-Somewhat Agree

2-Undecided
1-Somewhat Disagree
0-Completely Disagree

111) *I would rather support someone in their ministry than lead a ministry of my own.*

4-Strongly Agree
3-Somewhat Agree
2-Undecided
1-Somewhat Disagree
0-Completely Disagree

112) *I enjoy cooking meals and preparing my house so that I can share my house with other people.*

4-Strongly Agree
3-Somewhat Agree
2-Undecided
1-Somewhat Disagree
0-Completely Disagree

113) *I am currently single, and am fine with never being married or having children.*

4-Strongly Agree
3-Somewhat Agree
2-Undecided
1-Somewhat Disagree
0-Completely Disagree

114) *When visiting other countries, I find it easy to communicate even*

though I don't know the language.

    4-Strongly Agree
    3-Somewhat Agree
    2-Undecided
    1-Somewhat Disagree
    0-Completely Disagree

115) *It is easy for me to learn difficult truths.*

    4-Strongly Agree
    3-Somewhat Agree
    2-Undecided
    1-Somewhat Disagree
    0-Completely Disagree

116) *People seem to enjoy following me to do an important task.*

    4-Strongly Agree
    3-Somewhat Agree
    2-Undecided
    1-Somewhat Disagree
    0-Completely Disagree

117) *I enjoy ministering to a person who is sick in the hospital.*

    4-Strongly Agree
    3-Somewhat Agree
    2-Undecided
    1-Somewhat Disagree
    0-Completely Disagree

118) *God often provides answers to my prayers with unordinary means.*

    4-Strongly Agree
    3-Somewhat Agree
    2-Undecided
    1-Somewhat Disagree
    0-Completely Disagree

119) *If I die with more than $1000 to my name, I will consider my ministry a failure.*

    4-Strongly Agree
    3-Somewhat Agree
    2-Undecided
    1-Somewhat Disagree
    0-Completely Disagree

120) *Other Christians frequently come to me with their cares and spiritual worries.*

    4-Strongly Agree
    3-Somewhat Agree
    2-Undecided
    1-Somewhat Disagree
    0-Completely Disagree

121) *I often speak the truth, even in places where it is unpopular or difficult for people to accept.*

    4-Strongly Agree
    3-Somewhat Agree

2-Undecided
1-Somewhat Disagree
0-Completely Disagree

122) *I don't mind helping others even if they are undeserving or take advantage of me.*

4-Strongly Agree
3-Somewhat Agree
2-Undecided
1-Somewhat Disagree
0-Completely Disagree

123) *I am always looking for better ways to explain things to people so they can grow spiritually and personally.*

4-Strongly Agree
3-Somewhat Agree
2-Undecided
1-Somewhat Disagree
0-Completely Disagree

124) *I find it easy to quickly learn foreign languages.*

4-Strongly Agree
3-Somewhat Agree
2-Undecided
1-Somewhat Disagree
0-Completely Disagree

125) *When people follow my advice in difficult situations, things often turn*

out well.

        4-Strongly Agree
        3-Somewhat Agree
        2-Undecided
        1-Somewhat Disagree
        0-Completely Disagree

GIFT PROFILE ANSWER SHEET

1	Administration	1	26	51	76	101	=
2	Apostleship (Missionary)	2	27	52	77	102	=
3	Craftsmanship	3	28	53	78	103	=
4	Creative Communication	4	29	54	79	104	=
5	Discernment	5	30	55	80	105	=
6	Evangelism	6	31	56	81	106	=
7	Exhortation or Encouragement	7	32	57	82	107	=
8	Faith	8	33	58	83	108	=
9	Giving	9	34	59	84	109	=
10	Healing	10	35	60	85	110	=
11	Helping	11	36	61	86	111	=
12	Hospitality	12	37	62	87	112	=
13	Celibacy	13	38	63	88	113	=
14	Interpretation	14	39	64	89	114	=
15	Knowledge	15	40	65	90	115	=

16	Leadership	16	41	66	91	116	=
17	Mercy or Compassion	17	42	67	92	117	=
18	Miracles	18	43	68	93	118	=
19	Voluntary Poverty	19	44	69	94	119	=
20	Pastor-Teacher	20	45	70	95	120	=
21	Prophecy	21	46	71	96	121	=
22	Service	22	47	72	97	122	=
23	Teaching	23	48	73	98	123	=
24	Tongues	24	49	74	99	124	=
25	Wisdom	25	50	75	100	125	=

PLEASE NOTE:

This test is not infallible.

Confirmation comes only through repeated cycles of practice and reassessment.

DOMINANT GIFTS

_____

_____

_____

_____

CHRISTIAN QUESTIONS
VOLUME 3

WHAT IS FAITH?

HOW TO KNOW THAT YOU BELIEVE

J. D. MYERS

WHAT IS FAITH?
How to Know that You Believe
© 2019 by J. D. Myers

Published by Redeeming Press
Dallas, OR 97338
RedeemingPress.com

978-1-939992-60-4 (Paperback)
978-1-939992-61-1 (Mobi)
978-1-939992-62-8 (ePub)

Learn more about J. D. Myers by visiting RedeemingGod.com
Discover similar authors by visiting TheGracelings.com

All rights reserved. No part of this publication may be reproduced, stored in or introduced into a retrieval system, or transmitted, in any form, or by any means—electronic, mechanical, photocopying, recording, or otherwise—except for brief quotations, without the prior written permission of both the copyright owner and the publisher of this book.

Unless otherwise noted, Scripture quotations are taken from the New King James Version®. Copyright © 1982 by Thomas Nelson, Inc. Used by permission. All rights reserved.

Scripture quotations marked "NIV" are from The Holy Bible, New International Version®, NIV® Copyright © 1973, 1978, 1984, 2011 by Biblica, Inc.® Used by permission. All rights reserved worldwide.

Scripture quotations marked "NASB" are taken from the New American Standard Bible®, Copyright © 1960, 1962, 1963, 1968, 1971, 1972, 1973, 1975, 1977, 1995 by The Lockman Foundation. Used by permission. All rights reserved.

Cover Design by Taylor Myers
TaylorGraceGraphics.com

JOIN JEREMY MYERS AND LEARN MORE
Take Bible and theology courses by joining Jeremy at
RedeemingGod.com/join/

WANT TO LEARN MORE?

Take the online Gospel Dictionary course
which defines 52 key words of the gospel.

One of the words in this course is "faith" but it also
defines words like salvation, sin, forgiveness, and grace.

Learn more at RedeemingGod.com/Courses/

The course is normally $297, but you can
take it for free by joining the Discipleship Group at
RedeemingGod.com/join/

For those who want to know that
they *really* do believe.

ACKNOWLEDGEMENTS

Thanks goes to my parents, Bill and Alana Myers, for buying me stacks of theology books when I was young. Books were all I ever wanted for Christmas and birthdays, and they accommodated my strange request with an overabundance of good reading. I am especially grateful for the books by C. S. Lewis and Josh McDowell, who show showed me that we have a reasonable faith.

Thanks goes as well to Bob Wilkin of the Grace Evangelical Society for being the first person in my life to explain that faith is certainty and does not come in degrees or percentages. I also want to thank Dave Anderson of the Free Grace Alliance for teaching about the Excel spreadsheet illustration for faith which I prominently use in this book.

I also must never forget the members of my Advance Reader Team who helped proofread and prepare this book for publication. Nizam Khan, Wesley Rostoll, Mike Edwards, David DeMille, Pete Nellmapius, Michael Rans, Taco Verhoef, Wickus Hendriks, John Flegg, Radu Dumitru, Bernard Shuford, Craig Duncan, Bernard Shuford, and Jim Maus, thank you for your help on my books. Please let me know how I can help you on any books or projects in the future.

Finally, and most of all, thanks goes to my wife, Wendy, who has never stopped believing.

FOREWORD

How many times have you heard an altar call and you walked down the aisle thinking, "This time I *really* believe"?

How many times have you been baptized, thinking, "I'm not sure I had genuine faith the last time, but now I feel like I mean it"?

How many times have you been confused about the nature of faith and wondered if you were just a hypocrite in disguise?

Isn't that tragic?

Would you like to be sure that you believe?

After all, the New Testament calls Christians "believers" (1 Tim 6:2). And no wonder. Your eternal destiny turns on your faith in Christ. Jesus promised everlasting life to whoever would simply believe in Him for it (John 3:15-18, 36). That's as simple as the offer of eternal life gets ... assuming you know what it means to believe in Jesus!

Sadly, not everyone does.

In fact, there is widespread confusion about the nature of faith. And that means there is also widespread confusion about the nature of the message of eternal life.

You see, the doctrine of eternal life by faith alone has always been under attack in obvious ways. Through the centuries, many denominations and teachers have openly added works, rituals, sacraments, ascetic practices, and spiritual encounters to the one condition of receiving everlasting life.

But a more subtle kind of attack has also been underway.

Rather than openly teach that eternal life is by faith plus works, this strategy has tried to redefine faith itself to include good works. Hence, I have often heard preachers publicly claim to believe in justification by faith apart from works, and deny a works-based gospel, but when they were asked what it means to believe, they answered: "If you *really* believe, then you'll *do* this ..."

Belief became behavior.

In that way, works get smuggled in through the back door.

Do you see that teaching eternal life "by faith *plus* circumcision" and teaching eternal life "by a faith *that* circumcises" is a distinction without a difference? The result is the same either way: works become part of the condition of receiving eternal life.

Both are false gospels.

Hence, to defend the gospel, you have to defend faith itself.

In the recent past, Gordon H. Clark's book *Faith and Saving Faith* helped to clear away the fog that has surrounded the nature of believing. Clark explained that to believe is to understand and to be persuaded that a proposition is true. But Clark's book had some faults. He was mostly concerned with the statements of other theologians in the Reformed tradition, making it less accessible to the general public. And Clark himself was unsure of what you needed to believe to receive eternal life. Clark advanced the cause, but there was further to go.

I tried to present a modern defense of Clark's position in my book *Beyond Doubt: How to Be Sure of Your Salvation.* However, since that book was not directly about the nature of faith, I had planned to write another on the topic. It is with a mixture of relief, sadness, joy, and not a little envy that I can say Jeremy beat me to it!

And he's done an excellent job.

In *What Is Faith?*, all the most common doubts, questions, concerns, and objections about faith are treated concisely, clearly, and biblically, using simple language anyone can understand.

If the message of eternal life by faith apart from works is to prevail in the churches today, we need to be clear about the nature of faith itself.

We need the message of this book to be more widely known.

Whether you're confused about your faith or currently take a different position on how faith should be defined, you should read this book. I think Jeremy can persuade you to change your mind.

–Shawn Lazar
Editor of "Grace in Focus" Magazine and Radio
Author of *Beyond Doubt* and *Chosen to Serve*

AUTHOR'S PREFACE

When I was a teenager, I read the books *Know What You Believe* and *Know Why You Believe* by Paul E. Little. I found them to be helpful as a basic introduction to Christian doctrine and apologetics. I believed what I read (most of it, anyway). But then I read some other books which began to challenge my beliefs. Specifically, the ideas in these other books made me begin to wonder if I had *really* believed. They talked about "head faith" vs. "heart faith" and how our faith must be a "living and active faith" rather than a "dead faith." After all, we should all make sure we don't have the faith that demons have (Jas 2:14-26). These books challenged me to move beyond a mere "intellectual faith" based on "mental assent" and instead develop a "real faith."

As a result of reading these later books, I began to worry. How could I know if I had really believed? The question was critical, for my eternal destiny hung in the balance. If I only had a "temporary faith," a "spurious faith," or a "head faith" then I could think my whole life that I was headed for heaven, and would only discover after death that I ended up in hell … when it was too late. So how could I know? More importantly, how could I know *now*?

I eventually discovered answers to all such questions.

This book shows what I learned along the way.

If you have similar questions as the ones I had, this book will help you find the answers. If you seek to not only know what you believe and why you believe, but also *that* you believe, this book is for you. Don't believe me? Read it and see!

INTRODUCTION

How often have you heard someone say that "Salvation is by faith alone, but not by a faith that is alone"? Or how about this one: "You can't say that salvation is by faith alone! After all, even the demons believe!" And of course, we must not forget the famous evangelistic appeal about missing heaven by eighteen inches because you have "head faith" instead of "heart faith." As a result of statements like these, many people struggle with whether or not they have believed.[1]

With all this confusion about faith, it is no wonder that when people hear that Jesus gives eternal life to anyone and everyone who simply and only believes in Him for it, some object by saying, "Yes, but how do I know if I've *really* believed?" Some people are afraid of having dead faith, little faith, empty faith, head faith, false faith, or temporary faith. Others wonder if they have believed the right things, or believed enough. Others think that their actions prove that they never really had faith in the first place.

And on and on it goes.

The problem with this general befuddlement about faith is that it leads to uncertainty about where people stand in their relationship with God. Since eternal life is given to those who believe in Jesus for it, a person cannot really know whether or not they have eternal life if they cannot first know that they have believed in Jesus for it. So where there is uncertainty about faith itself, there is also uncertainty in the object of

---

[1] Robert N. Wilkin, *Confident in Christ: Living by Faith Really Works* (Irving, TX: Grace Evangelical Society, 1999), 12f.

faith (Jesus) and the promise of faith (eternal life). In other words, Jesus's promise to give eternal life to those who believe in Him for it (John 3:16; 5:24; 6:47; etc.) is worthless if we cannot know whether or not we have believed. It is pointless to say that eternal life is by faith alone in Christ alone if we don't know what faith is.

For these reasons, the word "faith" may be one of the most important words in the Bible. The word is not only used in numerous passages and a wide variety of contexts, "faith" is also said to be instrumental in how we receive eternal life. Beyond simply receiving eternal life, faith is also taught to be a key element of living the Christian life as a follower of Jesus. In other words, we not only receive eternal life by faith in Jesus, but we live out our Christian life by faith as well. Numerous other truths of Scripture are also experienced and applied by faith. This is why faith is so important. It allows us to gain eternal life, live the Christian life, and better understand Scripture.

If you have ever struggled with the question of whether or not you *really* believe, or whether or not you are *truly* a Christian, this book is for you. By reading this book, you will learn how faith is defined in Scripture. Once you learn this, you will discover that you can *know* that you have believed, and therefore, *know* that you have eternal life through Jesus Christ. You don't need to wonder any longer. You don't need to fear that maybe you didn't believe *enough*. Yes, you can know for sure that you have believed in Jesus for everlasting life. Best of all, you can know today.

Toward this end, the following book will clarify what the Bible teaches about faith. Chapter 1 will define faith according to how the word is used in Scripture and how it is defined in the lexicons. Chapter 2 will then discuss how we come to believe things. Understanding what faith is and how faith operates will then enable us to clarify some of the prevalent misconceptions about faith (Chapter 3). Once all this is cleared up, Chapter 4 reveals how to know that we actually do believe. The book then closes out in Chapter 5 by applying all of these insights about faith to various passages from Scripture.

So are you ready to discover what faith is and whether or not you believe? We begin by defining faith.

CHAPTER 1

DEFINING FAITH

Almost everybody has heard the story of the man who walked across Niagara Falls on a tightrope. After the tightrope had been fixed in place, he started gathering a crowd to watch his daring and dangerous feat. "Come one! Come all!" he shouted into his bullhorn. "Watch me walk above Niagara Falls, balancing on nothing more than this little rope!"

As people started gathering, he passed around a sample of the rope so people could see how small it was. "One little slip, and I will tumble to my death in the waters below!" he shouted. "You never know when I might fall. The rope is getting wet from the misting water. A wind is coming up the gorge. I don't want to die, but today could be the day!"

As the crowd swelled even more, he shouted to those who had gathered, "Who believes I can walk across the falls and back without falling to my death below?"

Most of the crowd shouted that they believed he could do it. Many of them cheered him on to try it. So he climbed up onto the rope, and balanced his way across Niagara Falls. When he reached the far side, he turned around and came back. He didn't slip. He didn't fall. In fact, he barely wobbled or wavered. So when he returned to the safety of the shore, he motioned with his hands for the cheering crowd to quiet down.

"That was too easy!" he yelled. "That wasn't a challenge for me at all! Let's make it more difficult! Who believes I can do again, but this time, while pushing a wheelbarrow? If my hands are on the wheelbarrow, I will not be able to use them to balance on the rope. Shall I give it a try? Do you believe I can do it?" He motioned to a nearby wheelbarrow, which he had brought for this very purpose.

The crowd cheered their approval, which caused the number of gathering people to swell even further. So with the help of two nearby men, he lifted a wheelbarrow up onto the rope, and then started pushing it across the Falls. He went more slowly this time, and even had a few wobbles, which caused the crowd to gasp and cry out with fear, but he made it to the other side and back without any great problem.

The crowd went wild.

"That was too easy!" he yelled. "Who believes I can do it again, but this time, with another person inside the wheelbarrow?" The crowd roared their approval. "I would not only be risking my own life, but also the life of the person in the wheelbarrow," the man shouted to the crowd. "With a show of hands, let me see how many of you believe I can do this!" Almost every person in the large crowd raised their hand. It was nearly unanimous.

"Wonderful! I am so glad to see that you have such faith in me! I think I will give it a shot!" the man yelled. "Now ... among all of you who raised your hand, do I have a volunteer to get into the wheelbarrow?" Every hand in the large crowd went down. "What?" said the man. "You've seen me walk across Niagara Falls twice without any problems, once while pushing this wheelbarrow! And most of you believe I can do it with someone else in the wheelbarrow with me! But when I ask which of you wants to get into the wheelbarrow, none of you volunteer? Do you believe I can do it or not?"

But there were no takers, so the crowd did not see him push someone across Niagara Falls in a wheelbarrow that day.

This story is likely fictional, but it is often used by pastors and preachers as an example of faith. They say, "You see? It's not true faith unless you get into the wheelbarrow. Those people didn't *really* believe. They just *said* they believed. They raised their hand claiming they had faith the man could do it. But it is not enough to *say* you believe. It is not enough to *claim* you have faith. If you *really* believe, you have to get into the wheelbarrow. Otherwise, you have false faith. Spurious faith."

Then the pastor goes on to tell the audience how they can have true and effective faith. Usually the pastor says that they need to "prove" the reality of their faith by their good works. If they don't have the good works which proves the existence of their faith, then they are just like the people who claimed to have faith, but didn't prove it by getting into the wheelbarrow. Most people go away from such a sermon wondering if they've *really* believed, and therefore, whether they are *really* a Christian.

But you can know that you are really a Christian and that you have really believed. You can know that you have eternal life. You can know that you are already in the wheelbarrow, and that it is the safest place you can be. This knowledge of your safety and security in Jesus Christ begins by properly defining the word "faith."

THE DEFINITION OF "FAITH"

When we begin to define the word "faith," it is important to recognize that modern, English usage of the word "faith" does not match the ancient Hebrew or Greek usage. The way this word is used today bears little resemblance to the way the word was used in biblical times.

The word "faith" is sort of like the word "love," though somewhat in reverse. In modern English, we have one word for love, and we use it in reference to a wide variety of objects, including sports, spouses, occupations, and vacations. But in Greek, as nearly everyone knows, there are four words for love. Each word has a different shade of meaning, and is used in reference to different types of objects. Yet when people do not know about the different types of love in the Greek language, and they read about "love" in the Bible, they might confuse the way the word is used in the Bible with how we sometimes use it today. Therefore, when the Bible talks about God's love for us, some people might think that God just temporarily "likes" us, as when a person "loves" a song they hear on the radio.

Something similar happens with faith, though in reverse. Greek only has one root word for faith, whereas English has several. The Greek noun is *pistis* and the verb is *pisteuō* (with the root for both being *pist-*),[1] but English Bibles tend to translate the first as "faith" and the second as "believe." Sometimes the noun even gets translated as "faithfulness," which most would agree is quite different in meaning than "faith" itself. Furthermore, there are even cases where the Greek word will get translated as "trust." So here we have one Greek root word, with at least four different English words used to translate it. For consistency, it might be best to use only one English root word as a translation for the one Greek root. I suggest "belief" and "believing." This in itself would clear up a lot of the confusion about "faith."

But this would not clear up all the problems. Even if we take the main two English translations, "faith" and "belief," our modern English usage of these words does not come close to matching the ancient Greek usage. Today, when we talk about "faith" or "belief" we generally use the words as a synonym for hope. We might say, "I believe the Cubs will win the World Series this year," but we don't really know for sure that they will. In fact, such a "belief" is closer to wishful thinking.

Or we might say, "I have faith that the government will keep me safe." But this is closer to hope. There is a good chance that the government will do its job to protect us, but it cannot protect us from everything all the time, especially not from natural disasters and rogue terrorist attacks. In sentences such as these, the words "believe" and "faith" are equivalent to "wish" and "hope."

In light of these sorts of problems about faith, people get confused—and rightfully so—when they read about faith and belief in the Bible. They are not sure whether they should understand faith to be more like

---

[1] It is no wonder that Christians argue so much about the nature of faith ... the Greek root is *pist*. So why are some Christians so angry when they defend their faith? Because they're *pist*. But that's okay. Since faith, hope, and love are the three greatest Christian virtues (1 Cor 13:13), this means that it is good to be *pist*. Ok, I'll stop now.

hope, wishful thinking, trust, faithful actions, or maybe something else.

A lot of the confusion arises from something Plato taught more than 2000 years ago. N. T. Wright summarizes it well:

> Plato declared that belief was a kind of second-rate knowing, more or less halfway between knowing and not knowing, so that the objects of belief possessed a kind of intermediate ontology, halfway between existence and nonexistence. This way of thinking has colored popular usage, so that when we say, "I believe it's raining," we are cushioning ourselves against the possibility that we might be wrong, whereas when we say, "I know it's raining," we are open to straightforward contradiction. But this usage has slid, over the last centuries, to the point where, with a kind of implicit positivism, we use *know* and *knowledge* for things we think we can in some sense prove, and *believe* and its cognates for things that we perceive as degenerating into more private opinion without much purchase on the wider world.[2]

Whether or not Plato was right (and I don't think he was), his way of thinking about faith and belief is the way people use the words today. "Faith" is more of a hope, or a possibility, that something might or might not be true. In the minds of many, their beliefs do not need facts to back them up, and sometimes, their beliefs can even contradict the facts.

But this is not the way faith is described in Scripture or in the writings of early Christians. In the Greek New Testament, the word "faith" is most commonly used in reference to something that a person knows to be true. This is where N. T. Wright is headed in the quote above. For New Testament era Christians, to believe something, or to have faith, meant that they were persuaded or convinced of the truth of it. They *knew* it to be true. Good synonyms for "faith," therefore, are not "hope or wish" but rather "persuasion, conviction, or knowing."

New Testament Greek Lexicons such as BDAG typically provides three basic definitions for *pistis*. When used with an article, as in "*the*

---

[2] N. T. Wright, *Surprised by Scripture: Engaging Contemporary Issues* (New York: HarperOne, 2014), 42-43.

faith," it typically refers to the body of Christian beliefs that separates Christianity from other religious faiths. It is used this way thirteen times in the New Testament (cf. Acts 6:7; Rom 4:11; Gal 1:23). Second, the word can be translated as "faithfulness" or "fidelity." BDAG lists six possible verses with this meaning, but not all English translations of these passages translate it in such a way. In fact, "major contemporary English versions translate *pistis* as 'faithfulness' or 'fidelity' in only three or four New Testament verses."[3] And even these could arguably be translated as "faith" (Matt 23:23; Rom 3:3; Gal 5:22; Titus 2:10). This point will be discussed further in Chapter 4.

The third possible definition for *pistis* is also the most common. Over 180 times in the New Testament, *pistis* refers to "believing." In context, this belief occurs when a person knows something to be true based on the reliability of the one who teaches it. The last part of this understanding is critically important, as we will shortly see. This understanding is by far the most common way of defining and translating *pistis* in the New Testament, and is also closely related to the lexical definition of the Greek verb, *pisteō*.

Therefore, the primary lexical definition for the verb is "to consider something to be true, to believe."[4] Faith (and the verb "believe") is a confidence, persuasion, or conviction that something is true.[5] We have faith when we are fully persuaded by the evidence presented to us. "To believe is to be persuaded that some declaration is true. ... If you think something is true, you believe it."[6] Joseph Dillow says,

> Faith is located in the mind and is persuasion or belief. It is something which "happens" to us as a result of reflection upon sufficient evidence ...

[3] Wayne A. Brindle, "Faith in Christ Does Not Mean Faithfulness or Fidelity," *Grace in Focus* (Jan/Feb 2018), 24. This article does an excellent job summarizing the lexical data for *pistis*.

[4] Walter Bauer et al., *A Greek-English Lexicon of the New Testament and Other Early Christian Literature*, 3rd ed. (Chicago: University of Chicago Press, 2000), 816.

[5] Wilkin, *Confident in Christ*, 5, 7.

[6] Shawn Lazar, *Beyond Doubt: How to Be Sure of Your Salvation* (Denton, TX: GES, 2017), 106.

Saving faith is reliance upon God for salvation. It does not include within its compass the determination of the will to obey, nor does it include a commitment to a life of works. To believe is to be persuaded and be reliant and includes nothing else.[7]

Dr. Robert Wilkin, founder of the Grace Evangelical Society and author of numerous books, writes this about the definition of faith:

> Faith is the persuasion or conviction that something is true. In Acts 17:4 Luke tells us concerning Jews at the synagogue in Thessalonica. "And some of them *were persuaded.*" Then in the next verse he reports, "But the Jews who were *not persuaded* ... attacked the house of Jason ..." A few verses later Luke reports on the response of the Jews at the synagogue in Berea: "Therefore many of them *believed* ..." (v 12). Clearly *the persuasion* of vv 4-5 is synonymous with *the unbelief* of v 12. Faith is persuasion of the truth of a fact or proposition, in this case, that Jesus is the Messiah who guarantees everlasting life to all who believe in Him.[8]

So what then is biblical faith (or belief)? We can do no better at defining faith than does the author of Hebrews, who writes: "Faith is the substance of things hoped for, the evidence of things not seen" (Heb 11:1). The author of Hebrews is saying that faith substantiates, or sees as reality, that which we have previously only hoped to be true. Faith is the evidence, conviction, or confidence in things we cannot see. Certainly, we also believe the things we have seen, but the faith described in the rest of Hebrews 11 is the faith that is confident in God's promises based on what is known about God's character and God's Word.

---

[7] Joseph C. Dillow, *The Reign of the Servant Kings: A Study of Eternal Security and the Final Significance of Man* (Miami Springs, FL: Schoettle Publishing, 1992), 276.
[8] Bob Wilkin, "Should we Rethink the Idea of Degrees of Faith?" *JOTGES* (Autumn 2006), 3.

FAITH IN THE PROMISES OF GOD

Many people struggle with thinking about faith as a persuasion or conviction that something is true because they have often discovered that their faith in humans is misplaced. They believe that someone is going to do something, only to discover later that this other person did not follow through on what they promised. So it is sadly true that we cannot always believe in humans for the promises they make.

But God is not a human that He should lie (Num 23:19). We can always believe in God for the promises He makes. This is why faith toward God is a certain and sure faith. Such faith is not about us, but is all about Him. Since faith is the confidence or conviction that something is true based on the evidence presented,[9] and since God can fully be trusted, faith in the promises of God is a sure and certain faith. So believing in the statements of God is the same as knowing with certainty that what God says is true.

But is believing in what God says the same thing as believing what Scripture says? In other words, although we can know for sure that what God says is true, does this mean that we can know for sure that what the Bible says is true? The answer is yes … and no. While we can always have *absolute* certainty in the promises, instructions, and ideas of God, an honest bit of self-reflection reveals that sometimes we humans do not always properly understand what God has said. There is often a difference between what God has said and what we humans *think* God has said.[10] Ideally, what the Bible actually says and what we think the Bible says should be the same, but this is not always the case. One goal of sanctification and Christian maturity is to find and discover where our understanding of God and His Word is wrong, and then change our views to match what is actually true.

---

[9] Cf. a similar definition in Grant Hawley, *The Guts of Grace: Preparing Ordinary Saints for Extraordinary Ministry* (Allen, TX: BoldGrace, 2013), 125. He writes, "… to have faith is to be persuaded that something is true. It is to be fully convinced that what God says is true."

[10] See J. D. Myers, *How Can I Study the Bible* (Dallas, OR: Redeeming Press, 2019).

So are the truth claims of Scripture absolutely true? Yes, they are, because they are of divine origin.[11] But since we humans often misunderstand what other people are saying, this means that it is also quite possible that we will misunderstand some of what God is saying through Scripture. While God is infallible and His Word can be trusted, we humans are not infallible, so that our understanding of God's Word cannot always be trusted. Therefore, to some degree, even when we are talking about our beliefs in what God has said in Scripture, it is wise to always retain a bit of humility, recognizing that maybe, somewhere along the way in our thinking and study, we might slightly (or greatly) misunderstand something about God and what He teaches in Scripture. God and His Word are infallible; our understanding of God and His Word are not.

Nevertheless, this is not to say that we cannot be certain about what we believe. We can. This is also not to say that our beliefs always contain an element of doubt. They don't. By definition, faith is the opposite of doubt (cf. Jas 1:6). If you doubt something, you don't believe it. When you doubt something is true, it is because you have not been presented with enough evidence to persuade or convince you that the statement or proposition is true. When you doubt, you don't believe. Indeed, when you doubt, you *can't* believe.

Are you confused yet? On the one hand, I say that our beliefs do not include any elements of doubt, but on the other hand, I argue that we cannot always be absolutely certain about our beliefs. So which is it? It is illogical to say that faith is certainty when it comes to the promises of God, but faith is uncertainty when it comes to the claims of humans. If we are going to properly define and understand faith, the definition of faith must stay the same whether we are talking about faith in God or faith in humans.

---

[11] Obviously, this depends on the inspiration and inerrancy of Scripture. If someone does not believe in inspiration and inerrancy, then their views of the reliability of Scripture will be much different.

The solution is to recognize that while faith is indeed certainty, it might be best to think of faith as *reasonable* certainty.

FAITH IS REASONABLE CERTAINTY

Even though faith can be defined or understood as "knowing with certainty that something is true," this doesn't exactly mean that faith is *absolute* certainty. For example, when it comes to believing the truth claims made by other people, we may not always be absolutely certain that what they say is true or that they can follow through on what they promise. Unlike God, people are not infallible. People make mistakes. People have errors in judgment and logic. Unlike God, people are not omniscient, omnipresent, or omnipotent. And so there is a degree of uncertainty that sometimes enters into faith when we are dealing with beliefs that are not the promises of God. While I believe, and am persuaded or convinced, of the truth claim made by Einstein that $E=MC^2$, I also recognize the remote possibility that Einstein made a mistake and was therefore wrong.

This hesitancy to claim absolutely certainty about any particular fact is what causes some people to state that we cannot be *absolutely* certain about anything. But such reasoning reveals a misunderstanding about how faith works, and how the various truths we believe interact with one another. This interaction of beliefs will be discussed further in the next chapter. For now, I am willing to admit that when it comes to a discussion about the certainty of our beliefs, it might be better to speak of *reasonable* certainty rather than *absolute* certainty. Or maybe we could say that faith is educated and informed certainty.

With this basic understanding of faith, note what we have just discovered about faith. While faith (by definition) does not include any element of doubt, it is nevertheless true that doubt is often a pre-condition to faith. In other words, it is quite often true that you cannot believe something unless you first doubt it. Very often, the only way you will investigate a particular truth is if you first question it. Questions and doubt, then, are not the enemy of faith, but the catalyst that leads to true faith. In life and theology, your beliefs are not likely to change unless you first question and doubt what you believe. But this does not mean that faith includes an element of doubt. There is a vast difference between saying that faith follows doubt and faith includes doubt.

This means, of course, that doubt can actually be healthy and helpful. Sometimes, it is only through doubt that we come to properly believe. By doubting and questioning the various truth claims presented to us, we examine the reasonableness of these claims to see whether or not they are true. And when we are persuaded or convinced of their truthfulness, it is then that we come to believe them.

You have likely seen this in your own experience. All people are able to look back to the past and remember something they once wholeheartedly believed, but no longer do. There is no person in the world who has believed the same thing their entire life and never had any of their beliefs change. And if you think about how some of your beliefs changed, you will notice that they changed in one of two ways. Either you questioned what you believed and came to see that what you believed was wrong, or you questioned what someone else believed, and in the attempt to prove them wrong, discovered that they were correct after all. Either way, the act of questioning and doubting changed your beliefs.

But the process of questioning and doubting can also solidify your beliefs. When we question and doubt the things we believe, and then seek to find answers to these questions, we often end up realizing that what we believe truly does have a solid factual and logical foundation. During this process of questioning and doubting, we do not actually believe what we are investigating (for we cannot doubt and believe something at the same time), but the end result will either be a further solidification of this belief through additional facts and arguments to support it, or a rejection of this belief in favor of something else.

As you approach faith in this way, you will develop a humble confidence that what you believe, you believe because you have investigated the truth and understand the facts to the best of your ability. This doesn't mean that you have read every book, talked to every expert, and turned over every stone in your quest for certainty. It does mean, however, that you have a reasonable explanation for what you believe. And if part of these reasons is that you trust another person to have done the necessary research and work for you so that you believe what they tell you, then this also is a reasonable faith.

This is even true when it comes to faith in the promises of God. As suggested previously, while we can know with absolute certainty that everything God says is true, we cannot know with absolute certainty that we have properly understood everything God has said. But rather than say that faith is doubt (for the two are opposites), it is best to say that faith is *reasonable* certainty. And we gain this reasonable certainty through an ongoing questioning and thorough investigation into the vast network of beliefs that connect with and surround each and every other belief we hold. Again, we will discuss this idea more in the following chapter.

But let us first take what we have learned about faith and apply it to one of the most pressing questions that Christians have about faith. Many people wonder whether or not they have eternal life. Many wonder if they have *truly* believed. Now that we have a basic understanding of what faith is and how faith works, we are in a position to address this all-important question. Based on what we know about faith, we are able to know with certainty that we have believed, and therefore, also know with certainty that we have eternal life. Let us take these two points one at a time.

HOW TO KNOW YOU BELIEVE

Some people struggle with knowing whether or not they believe certain theological truths. Specifically, many people wonder whether or not they have believed in Jesus for eternal life. But before a person can know whether or not they have believed in Jesus for eternal life, they first need to know how to recognize faith (or belief) when they have it. That is, they need to know they have believed before they can know they have believed in Jesus for eternal life.

Strangely, it is usually only in this area that people struggle with knowing whether or not they have believed. People never wonder about whether or not they have *truly* believed other truth statements. For example, do you believe that 2+2=4? Of course you do. You know that this is a mathematical fact. Do you believe that the sun is hot and rain is wet? I hope so. These are scientific truths. Do you believe that Donald Trump was elected as the 45th President of the United States? Whether or not you like him, it is a historical fact that he was elected, so of course you believe it.

And how do you *know* that you believe these statements? You know that you believe them simply because you know that they are true. When you were a toddler, you didn't believe that 2+2=4, but you were taught this truth and came to believe it. You know that the sun is hot and rain is wet through personal experience. When you first heard that Donald Trump had been elected President, you might not have immediately believed it, but as the evidence was presented to you, you were persuaded or convinced by the evidence, and so came to believe it. So with all three statements, you believe them because you know they are true.

When it comes to theological truths, faith works exactly the same way. You know you believe something when you can substitute the word "know" for "believe." Thus, the statement "I believe that God exists" becomes "I know that God exists." The opposite is also true. If you do not know or if you doubt that God exists, then you do not believe that God exists.

So "belief" is just another way of speaking about knowledge. If you know something, you believe it. When someone says, "I believe that such and such is true" they were saying, "I know for a fact that such and such is true." Since faith is defined as a confidence, persuasion, or conviction that something is true, you can know that you have believed something if you know it to be true. So how do you know whether or not you believe something? You know you have believed something if you know it is true.

This understanding of faith is quite helpful when it comes to the central truth claims of Scripture, and especially the most important truth claim of all, which is that Jesus gives eternal life to those who believe in Him for it. If you know that this is true, then you know that you have eternal life. Let us consider this idea a little more carefully.

HOW TO KNOW YOU HAVE ETERNAL LIFE

There are numerous truth claims in Scripture related to the gospel. The central truth claim of the gospel is that Jesus gives eternal life to anyone who believes in Him for it (cf. John 3:16; 5:24; 6:47).

Although this central gospel claim is simple to understand, it is not easy to believe. That is, it is not easy to know that Jesus gives eternal life to everyone and anyone who simply and only believes in Him for it. In fact, this truth is so difficult to believe, most people don't believe it! Most people, even many within Christianity, believe that good works are somehow required in order to receive eternal life and entrance into heaven when they die. The human mind does not naturally know (or believe) that God freely gives eternal life to humans simply out of His love for them and grace toward them. We tend to believe the opposite instead.

So how is it that people come to believe in Jesus for eternal life? How is it that you can believe in Jesus for eternal life? More importantly, how is it that you can *know* that you have eternal life in Jesus? These are critically important questions.

To show you how these questions are answered, and therefore, how you can know that you have eternal life, let me present an alternate scenario. Imagine that your neighbor came up to you one afternoon, and told you that if you believed in him, he would give you eternal life. Would you believe him? I think not. Furthermore, it is unlikely that he could provide any amount of persuasive arguments that would convince you to believe in him for eternal life. It is a ludicrous claim. If he made such a claim, you would be more likely to believe that he was insane than to believe in him for eternal life.

Yet when someone knows nothing about Scripture or any of the historical and theological facts surrounding the person and work of Jesus, this is exactly what they think of the initial offer of eternal life for those who believe in Jesus for it. It literally sounds insane. If a person knows nothing about Jesus, and they are told that Jesus will give them eternal life if they believe in Him for it, their initial response might be "Who is this Jesus to make such a claim?" If they believe that there is no life after death, then they might have questions about eternal life, what it is, and why it is being offered. Their ability to believe this truth claim from Jesus might also require investigation into the existence of God, the issue of sin, why Jesus died on the cross, how we can know He rose from the dead, and what all this means in relation to His promise of eternal life.

Do you see how the simple truth claim that "Jesus gives eternal life to anyone who believes in Him for it" leads to a wide-ranging discussion about numerous other truth claims that must also be believed before someone will be persuaded or convinced to believe in Jesus for eternal life? So although the truth claim that Jesus gives eternal life to those who believe in Him for it is simple, it is not easy to believe. Before a person can be persuaded or convinced that what Jesus said is true, they must first come to understand and believe a whole host of additional and supporting truth claims that lead up to this central gospel concept.

In my book, *The Gospel According to Scripture,* I separate these gospel truths into various categories, such as Preparation truths, Proof truths,

Presentation truth, and Purification truths.[12] The Preparation truths and Proof truths help lay the foundation and provide evidence for the truthfulness of the Presentation truth, which is that Jesus gives eternal life to those who believe in Him for it. The Purification truths are for those who have already believed in Jesus, and provide ways that we can purify our lives and live in light of the eternal life we have been given in Jesus Christ.

Some people need to believe more of these Presentation truths; others need to believe fewer. Some people will believe various Preparation truths of the gospel based on the authority and trustworthiness of the person who taught it to them (such as a child believing what a parent says). In other cases, a person might need to investigate, research, analyze, and consider all the various arguments and ideas surrounding a truth claim before they come to believe it. Neither approach is better or worse than the other. But eventually, when a person comes to believe in Jesus for eternal life, it is because they have recognized the truth that Jesus has given them eternal life, not because they have earned it or deserved it, but because God loves them, forgives them, and accepts them into His family.[13] When a person comes to believe in Jesus for eternal life, it is because they have come to *know* that they have eternal life in Jesus.

This means that if you know that you have eternal life in Jesus, and not because of anything you have done, then you have it. It is that simple.

BELIEVE IN JESUS FOR ETERNAL LIFE

Let me offer a few points of clarification. First, note that people do not receive eternal life simply by faith alone. Yes, people receive eternal life by faith alone in Jesus Christ alone, but this is not the same thing as saying that eternal life is by faith alone. Do you see the difference? When it

---

[12] J. D. Myers, *The Gospel According to Scripture* (Dallas, OR: Redeeming Press, 2019).

[13] God accepts and invites us into His life; we do not accept or invite Him into ours.

comes to receiving eternal life, the object of our faith is of paramount importance. One does not receive eternal life simply because they have faith. No, we receive eternal life by believing *in Jesus* for it. To believe in Jesus means to believe certain propositions about Jesus, namely, that Jesus is the sole provider and protector of eternal life.[14]

If eternal life were by faith alone, then everybody would have eternal life, for everyone believes something. Atheists believe that there is no God. They are persuaded and convinced that God does not exist. So even atheists believe. If eternal life is gained simply by believing, then atheists have eternal life. Similarly, it is not enough to have beliefs about the color of your car, the existence of the Milky Way galaxy, or the historical reality of Abraham Lincoln. People believe all sorts of things, but belief itself does not grant eternal life to anyone.

Taking this a step further, it is not even enough to believe that God exists. For other than atheists, almost everyone believes in the existence of God (or gods). Muslims believe that Allah exists. Pagans believe in Odin, Thor, Loki, and others. Hindus believe in millions of deities. Though many Buddhists don't exactly believe in a god, they do believe that humans are working toward an infinitely divine, enlightened state of being. It is not even enough to believe in the God of the Bible, for many cults and religious groups believe in the existence of the biblical God.

Note that it is also not enough to believe that you have eternal life. Lots of people believe they have eternal life, but they believe in something other than Jesus for it. Maybe they believe that they have eternal life because they are "a pretty good person." In this case, they believe in their own good works for eternal life. Or maybe a person believes in the god of some other religion for eternal life. Here again, such people are not believing *in Jesus*, and therefore, do not have eternal life.

---

[14] Shawn Lazar provides some good clarification that the phrase "believe in Jesus" means to believe certain propositions about Jesus. See his article "Is Faith Trust in a Person?" https://faithalone.org/blog/is-faith-trust-in-a-person/ Last Accessed March 17, 2018.

We can clarify even further. Lots of people believe all sorts of things about Jesus, and even say that they "believe in Jesus," and might also believe that they have eternal life. But many of these people do not believe in Jesus *for* eternal life. They believe all sorts of historical and theological facts about Jesus, but do not believe in Him for eternal life. They might correctly believe that Jesus existed, that He was God incarnate, that He lived a sinless life, died on the cross, and rose again from the dead three days later.

Such beliefs are good, important, and correct, but Scripture does not teach anywhere that those who believe such things will receive eternal life. After all, there are many people who believe many good things about Jesus, yet still believe that in order to receive eternal life they have to live a life of good works and faithful obedience to God. While such people do believe in Jesus and believe many things about Jesus, and may even believe that they have eternal life, they do not *believe in Jesus for eternal life*, but instead believe in themselves and their own good works for eternal life.

The bottom line truth of Scripture and the central message of the gospel is this: God gives eternal life to those who believe in Jesus for it (cf. John 3:16; 5:24; 6:47). Each word in the central gospel truth claim is important. We must believe in a person for a promise. Scripture invites us to believe that a person, Jesus Christ, can fulfill a promise, which is everlasting life. So do you believe that Jesus has given you eternal life? Do you know that you can have eternal life simply because Jesus promises to give it to you, and not because of anything you have done or will do? If you know this, then you have eternal life! Jesus guarantees it.

CONCLUSION

This brings us back to the illustration of the tightrope walker pushing a wheelbarrow across Niagara Falls. The people truly believed that the man could walk across the tightrope above Niagara Falls. They had seen him do it. They also believed that he could do it with a wheelbarrow. They had seen him do this as well. In both cases, their faith was real and genuine. Based on what they had seen him do, they also stated their belief that he would be able to push someone across Niagara Falls in a wheelbarrow. However, none of them were willing to get into the wheelbarrow themselves. Does this mean that they didn't actually believe? No, it does not.

First, walking across Niagara Falls on a tightrope has inherent risks. This is why it is so thrilling to watch. And given all the various things that can go wrong in such a situation—many of which are completely out of the control of the man on the tightrope—there is no guarantee that he will make it across. Even if he performed this feat a thousand times in a row and became so good at it that he could run across while blindfolded, there is still no guarantee that he would be able to do the one-thousand-and-first time. Maybe a stronger than normal gust of wind would knock him off balance. Maybe it would start to rain and he would slip. Maybe a reckless bird would hit him in the head. There are just too many variables.

No matter how many times the man completes this feat, it is a statistical certainty that eventually he will slip and fall to his death. So while the crowd could state their genuine belief every time that the man will make it across the falls, they also believe that a time will come when the man will fall. None of the people on the shore wanted to be in the wheelbarrow when that happened.

So the people on the shore had two genuine, but conflicting, beliefs. They believed that the man could walk across Niagara Falls, and would be able to do it many times, even with a person in a wheelbarrow. However, they also believed in statistics and science, both of which say that eventually, the tightrope walker will fall.

Related to this, while the people on the shore might have had full faith in the tightrope walker's ability to maintain his balance, none of them had faith in their own ability. It is logical and reasonable to think that the man could take someone across the Falls in a wheelbarrow if the person stayed completely still and did not move. After all, if the person in the wheelbarrow starts flailing about, screaming in terror, or even sneezes, such movement could throw off the balance, causing both people to plunge to their death below. And as all people know, we cannot always keep fear at bay, nor can we easily hold back a sneeze. Therefore, here again, while a person might properly believe that a well-trained tightrope walker can push a person in a wheelbarrow across Niagara Falls, there are too many unknown and uncontrollable variables for any person to believe that they themselves could hold still enough to complete such a dangerous journey.

The bottom line truth is that that this fictional illustration about how nobody from a watching crowd would get into a wheelbarrow so that they might be pushed across Niagara Falls on a tightrope does not illustrate the lack of faith in the watching crowd. To the contrary, it shows their true and genuine faith in a variety of truth claims. They believed the man could do it. But they did not believe in their own ability to sit still enough inside the wheelbarrow. They also knew (i.e., believed) that there were millions of random variables in nature that could create problems as well.

So did they believe the man could push a person across Niagara Falls in a wheelbarrow? Yes, they firmly believed that the man could do it. But did each individual person believe the man *would* do this for themselves if they got into the wheelbarrow? No, they did not believe this, for the various reasons mentioned above. They probably had somewhere over fifty percent certainty that he would, maybe even approaching ninety percent certainty in some cases. But this was not enough *reasonable certainty* for them to gamble their lives on it.

But notice how different it is when it comes to the promises of God made to us through Jesus Christ. God is not a tightrope walker who will eventually make a mistake if we just give Him enough time. If He promises to take us across a spiritual tightrope, He will fulfill that promise every single time forever and ever without fail. There are no spiritual or natural variables which can wreak havoc with the promises of God. The same goes for Jesus. When Jesus makes a promise, it is a promise with a 100% guarantee. Like God, Jesus is fully reliable.

Furthermore, many of the promises of God are not at all dependent upon our own effort or involvement. If we were to equate eternal life to getting into a wheelbarrow for a trip across Niagara Falls, then we would also have to say that on this trip, we could jump around and do flips inside the wheelbarrow and Jesus will still not lose His balance or let us fall into the waters below. We could even try to jump out, but He will not let us fall. Eternal life is His gift to us, and this gift has an everlasting guarantee. We are safe and secure in His hands, and He will never let us go (John 10:27-29). This is His promise. When we refuse to believe His promises, it is simply because we are refusing to believe that Jesus knows what He is talking about and can be trusted to do what He says.

Jesus is fully trustworthy and reliable. So you can believe in Him for what He says. And when He offers eternal life to anyone who believes in Him for it, you can know that if you have believed in Jesus, then you have eternal life. When you believe in Jesus, you are already in the wheelbarrow and He is taking you across the falls, and there is nothing that you, or anyone (or anything) else can do to stop Him (Rom 8:38-39).

Nevertheless, I imagine that you still have some questions about the nature of faith and how faith works. You also might still have some lingering doubts about whether or not you *really* believe. Maybe you have also heard people talk about head faith, heart faith, true faith, false faith, small faith, and great faith, and you want to know how these sorts of descriptions fit with what we have learned in this chapter. So the next chapter will continue to address the issue of how faith works, and specifically, how we come to believe something and why our beliefs can change.

CHAPTER 2

HOW FAITH WORKS

When my wife and I were newly married, we both served tables in a Mexican restaurant. One of the other servers was named Jesus Lopez (His first name followed the Spanish pronunciation "*Haysoos*"). But this Jesus we worked with was not very much like Jesus of the Bible. Jesus (the server) loved to work on Sundays when all the Christians came in to eat after their church services. He would go up to tables after they had finished praying over their meal and say, "I'm Jesus. Is everything okay?" (He would pronounce his name with the English pronunciation, "*Geesus*"). Most church-going Christians weren't quite sure how to respond.

But it was worse on Halloween. Those of us who served that night were supposed to dress up as some character. I don't remember what my wife and I dressed up as, but Jesus came dressed up as Satan. That night, while dressed as Satan and using the English pronunciation for Jesus, he greeted every table by saying, "I'm Jesus. I'll be your server tonight." Some tables laughed, while others looked shocked. I remember thinking that his statement bordered on blasphemy. Clearly, Jesus Lopez was nothing like Jesus Christ.

A few years later I was working as the pastor of a small church in Northwest Montana. One summer the church participated in a community children's outreach. I remember being shocked at the response of two neighborhood children (ages 8 and 10) when I asked them if they had believed in Jesus for eternal life. "Who's Jesus?" the older boy asked. Through further conversation, I discovered that they had never heard any story from the Bible about Jesus. They had also never heard about some of the other most famous Bible characters, such as Noah, Moses, or Jonah.

As I came to the realization that there were genuinely "unreached" people groups right in my own United States neighborhood, I thought about our fellow server from the Mexican restaurant. Imagine the response of these children if the only Jesus they knew had been Jesus Lopez. What would they have said, if they had never heard of Jesus Christ, but Jesus Lopez had been a teacher, friend, or neighbor? What would they have said if I invited them to "Believe in Jesus for eternal life"? Aside from his twisted sense of religious humor, Jesus Lopez was a nice enough guy, but I still think the children would have found it incredulous for some stranger to suggest that they "Believe in Jesus for eternal life." If Jesus Lopez was the only Jesus they knew, they would have looked at me like I was crazy. They were not ready (or able) to believe in Jesus because they didn't know or believe anything accurate about Jesus.

I share these two stories, and how they came together in my mind, as a way of illustrating how faith works. While it is absolutely true that Jesus gives eternal life to anyone who believes in Him for it, nobody in their right mind is going to believe in Jesus for eternal life unless they first know and believe many additional truths about Jesus.

What are these truths? Well, the set of necessary truths will be different for each and every person.[1] Consider the following statement: "Jesus is God." Do you believe this? (I do.) If you do believe this, have you ever stopped to consider *why* you believe that Jesus is God, or *how* you first came to believe it? (I have.) The belief that "Jesus is God" is an incredibly important belief for Christian life and doctrine. Our eternal destinies quite literally depend upon this truth.

So why and how do you believe that Jesus is God? You cannot say

---

[1] I am *not* saying that each person has their own truth. I am not teaching relativism. I am saying that of all the *available* myriad of truths which support the claim that Jesus gives eternal life to those who believe in Him for it, different people will find different sets of truths persuasive. There is no single set of truths that will be persuasive for all people.

that you "Just believe it," for this is not true. Nobody is born into this world "just believing" anything. Quite likely, you initially came to believe that Jesus is God because some authority figure taught this truth to you. Maybe it was your parents or a Sunday school teacher. It might have been a Christian pastor or author. Yet before you believed that Jesus is God, you first came to believe that there is a God, and also came to believe in the authority of Scripture. You likely also learned some of the basic Bible stories, including several stories about Jesus. There was a whole series of truths you came to believe before you believed that Jesus is God.

Furthermore, after you believed that Jesus is God, this belief was likely challenged in various ways and at various times throughout your life. During those times, you probably read some books or heard some sermons that provided a defense of this central Christian belief. Maybe you had an experience which helped solidify your belief that Jesus is God. Maybe this belief wavered, and you stopped believing it for a while, but eventually, came back to the realization that Jesus truly is God.

It is also possible that you have gone through several cycles of this sort of questioning, study, and solidification of your belief that Jesus is God. As you went through these cycles of solidification, it is not that you *didn't believe* before. You did. But these cycles of questioning and investigating help you shore up your belief that Jesus is God by addressing the questions and issues that could potentially undermine it. If you are unable to address or find answers for the issues and questions about this central belief, then you would likely stop believing it. Sadly, some people do indeed stop believing that Jesus is God.

Are you beginning to see how faith works? Are you starting to understand how we come to believe certain truths? Each individual truth we believe is built upon the foundation of other truths and is intricately connected to a wide network of related truths. One cannot believe something unless they first believe several of the foundational and preliminary truths, and if a person eventually stops believing some of these other foundational beliefs, then this change has a ripple effect through a large number of other related beliefs.

In my experience, before a person can believe in Jesus for eternal life, they will not only need to believe several truths about the identity and character of Jesus, they will likely also need to believe in the authority of the person who is telling them about Jesus, and also the authority of Scripture which contains these truths. Furthermore, they will likely need to believe that there is a God, that humans are sinners, and that we humans will in some way answer to God for how we live this life. There might need to be some sort of belief about life after death and also a basic understanding of why and how Jesus took care of our sin.[2] There is a whole set of truths that must be understood and believed before a person can believe in Jesus for eternal life.

Do you see how each individual belief is dependent upon and connected with a wide variety of other beliefs? There is not one colossal, all-inclusive, comprehensive "belief" that makes a person a Christian. While a person does receive eternal life at the moment they believe in Jesus for it, there are always a whole series of beliefs that lead up to (and follow) that moment when a person believes in Jesus. These various beliefs are all connected and intertwined to create a vast network of beliefs that shift and change as new ideas are understood and then either accepted or rejected.

This understanding of faith is getting somewhat complex, so let me provide an illustration which might better explain how this network of beliefs actually works.

THE GIANT EXCEL SPREADSHEET

In the previous chapter I defined faith as a certainty or conviction that

---

[2] As mentioned previously, my book *The Gospel According to Scripture* (Dallas, OR: Redeeming Press, 2018), refers to these truths as Preparation truths. These foundational gospel beliefs help *prepare* a person to believe in Jesus for eternal life.

something is true. Some do not like the idea of faith as certainty. For example, author and pastor Greg Boyd once criticized the idea that faith is certainty by comparing faith to a house of cards.³ He argued that if we believe that our faith must be certain, then any time a challenge or question comes along which threatens this certainty, our entire belief system comes tumbling down like a house of cards. Boyd talks about his own experience with this, saying that every time he stopped believing something he had been taught as a youth, he felt like his entire belief structure collapsed like a house of cards, and he had to painstakingly rebuild it from the ground up.⁴ Boyd rightly points out that this is a dangerous and damaging way to live life, and it leads many people to abandon or reject Christianity altogether.

While I share Boyd's concern for the spiritual health and vitality of others, he goes on in the sermon to teach that rather than define faith as certainty, it is better to allow faith to include an element of doubt. According to him, the inclusion of doubt into faith allows people to embrace their doubts without feeling that they need to reject all of Christianity. In this way, a person can still be a Christian even if they have doubts that Methuselah lived to be 969 years old. (This is the reason my grandmother gave for rejecting the Bible and Christianity.)

I completely agree with Greg Boyd that Christianity is not an "all or nothing" belief system. I completely agree that people should be able to have doubts. I always encourage people to question everything. However, none of this means that faith includes doubt, as Boyd suggests. Faith is actually the opposite of doubt. You either doubt or you believe, but it is nonsense to say that you have a belief that you doubt. You either doubt something or you believe it; but you cannot do both simultaneously.

---

[3] Greg Boyd, "Toppling the House of Cards," A Sermon by Greg Boyd, delivered on January 30, 2011 at Woodland Hills Church. See https://whchurch.org/sermon/toppling-the-house-of-cards/. Last Accessed February 24, 2018.

[4] Gregory A. Boyd, *Benefit of the Doubt: Breaking the Idol of Certainty* (Grand Rapids: Baker, 2013).

Logically and linguistically, faith must be defined as certainty and conviction. And if you have certainty about something, you do not doubt it. When you do doubt, you do not have certainty, and therefore, do not believe.

So how then do we avoid the "house of cards" disaster that Greg Boyd talks about? Like Greg Boyd, I also know people who think that if they cannot believe that the world was created in seven 24-hour days, this means they must reject all of Christianity. I even know some Christians who teach this very thing! So I agree with Greg Boyd that we cannot have a "house of cards" faith in which all of our beliefs stand or fall together. But how can we avoid this if faith truly is defined as certainty?

The solution is to use a better analogy.

Rather than thinking about faith as a house of cards, a better analogy is to think about our network of beliefs as a giant Excel spreadsheet.[5] If you are not familiar with a Microsoft Excel spreadsheet, it is an accounting tool which contains a series of rows and columns. At the intersection of each row and column, there is a "cell." This cell can contain a bit of data. For example, a cell could contain a number or some sort of mathematical calculation. Spreadsheets are usually set up so that as you enter data into the cells, it automatically makes calculations in other cells. Advanced Excel spreadsheets might contain thousands of cells set in a way so that a change in one single cell might affect the numbers or calculations in thousands of other cells. Each little change can have a ripple or cascading effect throughout the rest of the spreadsheet.

It is helpful to think about our network of beliefs in a similar way. We can think of our belief system as a giant Excel spreadsheet. But rather than numbers and math calculations, each cell contains an individual fact. Since there are a nearly infinite number of facts, this giant spreadsheet has a nearly infinite number of cells. "The sky is blue" is in one cell, "I exist" is in another, and "There is a God" is in third. Furthermore, just

---

[5] I first heard this analogy from Dave Anderson, a pastor in The Woodlands, TX, in one of his podcast sermons. I cannot recall which sermon it was in. I think he termed this idea "Spreadsheet theology."

like on any complex Excel spreadsheet, nearly all the cells are interconnected by functions, so that when one cell changes, it causes a cascading, rippling effect throughout the rest of the spreadsheet.

If we think about our beliefs in this way, we can see that when it comes to each individual statement, we can either believe it or disbelieve it. We can either know it to be true, or we can doubt that it is true. We can either assent and agree with the statement in the cell, or dissent and disagree. While we will be reasonably certain about several statements on this spreadsheet, we will be either ignorant or uncertain about the vast majority of statements. And as we change what we think about any particular fact, this change will have a cascading, ripple effect through the related and connected cells on the spreadsheet of beliefs.

What this means is that as we come to believe new ideas, some of the beliefs which have not changed for decades might need to be reconsidered in light of new evidence. Therefore, while we can have reasonable conviction or confidence about the accuracy of any single cell (or belief), we nevertheless know that the content of that cell is based upon the ideas of other related cells, about which we are less confident. To put it another way, the complete confidence of one belief in one "cell" can be based upon less confident beliefs of other "cells."

This way of thinking about faith provides adequate responses to many of the objections that some pastors and theologians have to the concept of faith as certainty. Many who criticize the idea of "faith as certainty" seem to think that the entire system stands or falls together.[6] But this is not the true nature of faith. It is impossible for the entire system of faith to collapse. Instead, our beliefs constantly shift and change as additional information is presented to us, so that new beliefs are turned "On" in the spreadsheet while other beliefs are corrected and turned "Off."

If you are not fond of this "accounting" spreadsheet metaphor, you could also think of our network of beliefs as a giant network of walking

---

[6] For example, see Peter Enns, *The Sin of Certainty* (New York: Harper Collins, 2016).

trails that spans the entire globe. At each fork in the road there is a sign with a "fact" written on it. You can either believe or disbelieve this fact, based on everything else you know to be true. What you believe about that fact determines the path you will take next on the trail. Sometimes, your later beliefs cause you to circle back around to earlier beliefs so that they can be reconsidered. This doesn't mean you didn't believe this idea before. You did. But now that you are presented with new evidence, new ideas, and new beliefs, the turn in the trail leads you back to revisit some earlier beliefs so that you make different turns and head down different, unexplored paths. When you think about your beliefs in this way, you see that they do not make a house of cards that tumbles down around you when one belief changes, but rather a world of possibilities with each and every fork in the trail that opens up new vistas and horizons to explore.

Regardless of which analogy you prefer, the end result is the same. While many people fear the experience of changing their beliefs, it can actually be embraced as a journey into the great unknown. The investigation of truth is a quest to be enjoyed and anticipated. You can look forward to the changes and adjustments in your faith with great excitement. Each change is a little miniature adventure. Yes, the first few times are scary. Yes, it sometimes seems like the floor dropped out beneath you, or that you jumped out of an airplane without a parachute. But if you trust the process you will soon discover that examining your faith is nothing more than the greatest roller coaster ride of a lifetime. Yes, your stomach may jump into your throat from time to time, but after a while, you begin to really enjoy the ride. Eventually, as you allow the doubts and fears to resolve, you soon discover that Christianity is a reasonable faith, that there are answers to all questions that might come, and that no matter what, God will never let you fall.

Best of all, with each cell that changes (or fork in the trail that you travel) you gain a spreadsheet (or trail map) that is more accurate than it was before. One of these truths you discover quite soon (if you allow

God to teach it to you), is that God does not require a spreadsheet of beliefs that is free of error. Quite to the contrary, He desires a spreadsheet of beliefs that is constantly shifting and changing as we bring our life and thoughts into conformity with Jesus Christ and the revelation of Scripture. But this is a process, a journey, or an adventure that will last a lifetime (I suspect this adventure will last into eternity as well, as we forever unravel the infinite mysteries of glorious vistas of God), and so God is patient with us as we fill out our spreadsheet of beliefs with Him by our side.

Viewing faith in this way helps you see that although one changed belief often does cause a change in many other related beliefs, your entire belief system never collapses like a house of cards. It may initially feel like this has happened, but by taking a deep breath and examining the new evidence you have been given, you will discover that most of your beliefs remain intact. You will also discover that you now have a better and more accurate belief system through which to view God, Scripture, yourself, others, and life in general.

THE SPREADSHEET AT WORK

Let us briefly see how this works with the truth claim that "Jesus gives eternal life to those who believe in Him for it." I believe this truth with absolute certainty. I have many reasons for this belief, all of which reside in their own individual cells. For example, I believe that there is a God, and that only He gets to decide who has eternal life with Him and how they get it. I furthermore believe that Jesus is God, and so He knew what He was talking about when He offered eternal life. I also believe that the Bible can be trusted as an authoritative revelation from God. I believe that I have properly understood the simple promises of Jesus to give eternal life to those who believe in Him (cf. John 3:16; 5:24; 6:47). I believe that Jesus does not lie. I believe that I am not able to earn or work for my eternal life on my own, because I can never be good enough to qualify for God's perfect standard of complete righteousness. If all these things are true, as I believe they are, then it is completely logical to be convinced and persuaded that Jesus gives eternal life to those who believe in Him for it. And since I believe in Jesus, I know that I have eternal life.

But if any of these beliefs were to change, then this would likely cause me to stop believing that Jesus gives eternal life to those who believe in Him for it. If I stopped believing that God existed, or that the Bible accurately records the teachings of Jesus, I might stop believing in Jesus for eternal life. However, the more I study and learn, the more evidence I find that supports all these beliefs. I now know too much to turn back on any of these truths and cannot imagine a situation that would cause me to reject them. The more I study and learn, the more beliefs I gain, each of which further supports the belief that Jesus gives me eternal life.

Is it possible that the authors of the Gospels failed to accurately record what Jesus said? It's possible, but not likely, so I don't believe this. Is it possible that those who copied the Bible and passed it down through the generations made a mistake? It's possible, but manuscript evidence proves that this is unlikely, and so I don't believe it. Is it possible that I have incorrectly understood what Jesus said and meant? Well, this is the most likely factor that could cause me to stop believing in Jesus. But since the teachings from Jesus about how to receive eternal life are some of the simplest teachings He gave (even a child can understand and believe these promises), I do not think this is likely, and therefore, I believe I have properly understood His promises.

Since my belief in Jesus for eternal life is based on a large number of other reasonable beliefs, if any one of these other beliefs were to change, there would indeed be a cascading effect of changing beliefs. As numerous beliefs changed, it might indeed feel like Greg Boyd's house of cards, as if everything I thought I knew was tumbling down around me.

However, note that there are many beliefs that can safely change without affecting my belief in Jesus whatsoever. My belief in Jesus is not affected at all by belief (or lack thereof) that Methuselah lived to be 969, that the universe was created in seven 24-hour days, or that Jesus is going to return in the future to slaughter all His enemies with a reign of terror and blood (I actually don't believe this). These beliefs can change back and forth numerous times (as they have over the years), but such changes will not cause my entire belief system to come tumbling down like a house of cards. Note that if someone feels that changes in these beliefs *will* cause their entire belief system to come tumbling down, this is likely because they believe the false idea that "All Christian beliefs stand or fall together." As soon as a Christian stops believing this, they will be able to investigate their beliefs with freedom and joy.

Now the same sort of belief changes can be observed even with beliefs that are not "theological." The "network of belief" concept applies to any individual belief. For example, I believe the sky is blue because I believe I know what "blue" is, and because I believe my eyes are not deceiving me. I furthermore believe that I truly exist in this world rather than in a dream world or computer simulation as in "The Matrix." Since all of these are reasonable beliefs, I can confidently believe (know) that the sky is blue.

However, if someone could persuade me that I did not exist, or that this world was a computer simulation, or that I have color-blindness and so do not accurately understand "blue," then I might realize that I am wrong about the blueness of the sky. But until these other beliefs change (which is extremely unlikely), I am fully confident that the sky is blue. (Keep reading, because later in this chapter, I do, in fact, stop believing that the sky is blue. I will even show you how it happened, which might convince you too.)

So based on this understanding of our beliefs as a vast network of truths about which we have reasonable certainty, we are able to discover five foundational truths about any one particular belief. In other words, since each belief depends and relies upon various other beliefs, but also affects and influences numerous other beliefs, this reveals five facts about how faith actually works. Some of these five truths about faith were briefly mentioned above, but let us consider each in more detail.

1. THERE ARE NO DEGREES OF FAITH

When we begin to think of our network of beliefs as a vast Excel spreadsheet, we realize that there is no such thing as "degrees" of faith. In other words, you cannot "partly believe" something. If you only "partly believe" something, then you do not yet believe it. Since each individual cell contains a single factual statement, you can only agree or disagree with that statement. You either know that it is true, or you don't. If you know it is true, then you believe it. If you don't know, or are unsure that the statement is true, then you don't believe it.

At the risk of mixing metaphors, you could think of each individual belief as a light switch. The switch (or belief) is either "On" or "Off." And there are no dimmer switches to faith. You either believe something or you don't. Individual beliefs do not come in "quantities." You cannot have 50% faith, or even 99% faith about a particular statement. Yes, various passages from Scripture talk about having "great faith" or "small faith" (cf. Matt 8:10, 26), but such texts should not be understood as referring to degrees or percentages of faith.[7] Instead, "great" faith occurs when people believe something that is hard to believe, while "small" faith occurs when they don't even believe things that are easy to believe.[8] This concept will be discussed later in more detail.

To apply this to the spreadsheet analogy, since each individual belief

---

[7] For an excellent explanation of the difference between great faith and little faith and many of the passages that are often used to defend the ideas of "degrees of faith," see Bob Wilkin, "Should We Rethink the Idea of Degrees of Faith?" *JOTGES* (Fall, 2006), https://faithalone.org/journal/2006ii/01%20Wilkin%20-%20great%20faith.pdf Last Accessed April 2, 2008.

[8] For more on this, see the article I published on this topic here: Jeremy Myers, "Now That's Faith!" Grace in Focus Newsletter (January-February 2008). http://www.faithalone.org/magazine/y2008/ faith.html Last Accessed July 20, 2014.

resides in its own cell, you can either believe or disbelieve the statement of that cell. In computer terminology, the cell is either a "0" or a "1." There are no decimals or percentages in the Excel spreadsheet of beliefs. If you lack confidence about the truth of a certain cell, then you don't believe it, and it is "Off." Quite often, the reason you do not believe the statement within that cell is not because of the content of the cell itself, but because it relies upon and is related to the beliefs and statements of other supporting cells. Similarly, this "Off" switch blocks you from believing other ideas down the line, which depend on your belief in the original cell. This idea about the interplay of the various cells on the spreadsheet helps us see the second truth about our beliefs.

2. THERE ARE COUNTLESS TRUTHS WE CAN BELIEVE

The second truth about the network of beliefs, or our spreadsheet of faith, is that there are countless cells on this spreadsheet. Since there are a nearly infinite number of possible beliefs, there are countless statements we can either believe or disbelieve. And since each cell is either "On" or "Off," what we believe about the statement in that cell leads us to go one way or the other for all connected beliefs.

Consider again my earlier example of the statement "The sky is blue." This statement depends on me believing that I exist and that I can actually see. It depends upon me knowing that the sky actually exists. It depends on me knowing what the color "blue" is. It depends on me believing I have a decent grasp of the English language so that I know what the four words "They sky is blue" all mean.

Furthermore, if, for some reason, I come to believe that the sky is not blue, then this could have ramifications on other connected beliefs. For me to stop believing that the sky is blue, maybe I would have to believe that the sky was a giant TV screen set up by aliens. Or maybe (as some of the ancients believed) that we were actually living inside a giant bubble, and the sky wasn't sky at all, but was water, which helped them explain why rain fell from the sky. Do you see how changing one belief causes you to change others?

In fact, immediately after writing that previous paragraph, I decided to do some quick research to see if the sky really was blue. It turns out it isn't! The sky is not blue after all! It's violet.[9] But our eyes are unable to see the particular type of violet that is the color of the sky, and so it appears "blue" to us. Therefore, I now believe that the sky is violet. The science behind this fact persuaded me of this truth.

But as this belief changed in my mind, I did not observe all my other beliefs tumbling around me like a house of cards. Instead, my network of beliefs quickly adapted and adjusted to the new information I received, and (as far as I can tell), I only had to change a few minor other beliefs to accommodate this new belief. As a result, I now believe some ideas I did not believe before. I now believe that our atmosphere scatters the violet wavelength of light more than the other colors, and so the sky is violet. But since human eyes only have red, blue, and green receptors, we have trouble seeing the violet wavelength of light. So although the sky is violet, we see the violet sky as blue.

As a result of this little experiment, I have now switched the cell "Off" which says "The sky is blue" and switched "On" the cell which says "The sky is violet." However, the cell which says "I see the sky is blue" is still turned "On" for that belief has not changed. Though the sky is scientifically violet, our eyes observe it as blue.

Don't be confused by all of this. The point is to show you that there is a nearly infinite number of beliefs on your spreadsheet of faith, with each possible statement residing in its own cell. As you consider each individual statement, such as "The sky is blue," your assent (or lack of assent) to that statement both depends upon and influences numerous other beliefs on the spreadsheet. As your beliefs change and evolve, your

[9] Brian Koberlein, "Earth's Skies are Violet, We Just See Them as Blue," https://www.forbes.com/sites/briankoberlein/2017/ 01/11/earths-skies-are-violet-we-just-see-them-as-blue/ Last Accessed March 9, 2018.

spreadsheet is modified to accommodate these changes. This introduces a third truth about our beliefs.

3. SOME THINGS ARE EASY TO BELIEVE; OTHERS ARE HARD

Earlier in this chapter, it was stated that there are no such thing as degrees of faith. We either believe something or we don't. A cell is either "On" or it is "Off." If you are uncertain or unsure about a particular statement, then you don't believe it.

Some people think that the Bible does teach about degrees of faith because it occasionally mentions "little faith" and "great faith" (cf. Matt 6:30; 8:26; 14:31; 16:8; Luke 4:14-30; 12:28). There are also numerous passages in the Bible which seem to indicate that we must have "enough faith" before God answers our prayers (cf. Matt 13:58; 21:22; Mark 11:24; Luke 7:9, 50; 18:42; Jas 5:15-16). If there are no degrees of faith, then what do these descriptions of faith mean?

These descriptions refer to the fact that some truths are easy to believe while others are difficult. Since faith is the conviction or persuasion that something is true, people who have little faith have not been persuaded or convinced of even the basic truths, whereas, people who have great faith have been persuaded or convinced of some of the hard and difficult truths which few people come to believe. You and I do not have faith containers in our souls which overflow when our faith is great, but are nearly empty when our faith is little. Faith does not work like that. Great faith and little faith have nothing to do with the *size, amount,* or *degree* of faith. Rather, the terms "great faith" and "little faith" describe the difficulty of the truths that are believed. "Great faith is not some higher level of conviction. It is believing something that is harder to believe, something that is contrary to what most people believe."[10]

When a person fails to believe even some of the simple or easy truths,

---

[10] Wilkin, "Should We Rethink the Idea of Degrees of Faith?", 10.

this means that some of the basic, fundamental cells in their network of beliefs are turned "Off." Since they do not believe these simple truths, vast segments of their spreadsheet are also turned "Off." Their spreadsheet is darkened with unbelief because they don't even believe some of the simple, foundational, basic truths of life or Christianity. They have little faith, that is, an undeveloped and unexamined spreadsheet of beliefs. On such a spreadsheet of faith, most of the basic truths are still turned "Off."

On the other hand, there are some people who have great faith. These are those people who are persuaded or convinced of some difficult things to believe. People who have great faith believe truths and ideas that relatively few people understand and believe. There are truths in Scripture, life, and theology that are hard to believe, but people with great faith believe them. Such ideas often take great thought, insight, understanding, research, investigation, or deep spiritual experiences in order to believe them. When people come to believe these things, they believe something that few others believe, and can therefore be described as having great faith. Vast segments of their spreadsheet of beliefs are lit up with the light of the truth of God.

Some examples from Scripture might be helpful. There are numerous truths from Scripture that are easy to believe. These might include the statements that "A man named Jesus existed" or that "I am a sinner." Almost everybody believes these, including most non-Christians. Yet people with little faith do not even understand or believe these truths. People with little faith have trouble believing some of the simple, elementary, and introductory truths of Scripture, such as "God is love" or "Jesus gives eternal life to anyone who believes in Him for it." It is a telling fact of the condition of faith in our churches when most Christians don't truly believe these things. As simple as these truths are, many do not believe them.

However, there are other truths in Scripture which are hard to believe. People who believe these difficult truths have great faith. For example, it is difficult to believe that "God will supply all of your needs according to His riches in glory" (Php 4:19). Frankly, since I often worry about tomorrow, this means that I don't believe this promise. I don't believe that God will supply all my needs, and often find myself trying to supply for my own needs. So this means I don't yet believe this statement. But those who have great faith believe it.[11]

So great faith and little faith have nothing to do with the amount of faith one has, or the percentage to which one believes a particular fact. Faith does not come in degrees or amounts. Therefore, we must not feel bad when we discover we have little faith. Instead, if we discover that we have little faith, we must seek to learn, study, and grow in our relationship with God so that we can turn "On" more cells in our spreadsheet of faith, thereby gaining great faith.

In the Gospels, the people of Israel and Jesus' own disciples are often chided for having little faith. Ironically, though they prided themselves in being men and women of faith as descendants of the father of faith, Abraham, they were chastised over and over for their lack of faith.

In these instances, note that that while Jesus did speak of their little faith, He often turned around and praised the Roman guards and Gentiles for their great faith. Yet He never once invited people to have "more faith." Why not? Because, as we have already seen, faith does not come in percentages or degrees. We do not have "faith containers" in our souls which fill up bit by bit until they overflow when our faith is great. Faith does not work like that. Scripture invites us to believe more truths, and provides us with the evidence to do so, but we are not called or challenged to grow more faith. The reason for this is because of the fourth truth about faith.

---

[11] Some of these ideas are drawn from my article, "Now That's Faith!" http://faithalone.org/magazine/y2008/faith.html Last accessed December 19, 2018.

4. WE CANNOT CHOOSE TO BELIEVE ANYTHING

Since faith occurs when we are persuaded or convinced by the evidence presented to us, this means that we cannot choose to believe. Belief, or faith, is not a decision we make.[12] Faith is something that happens to us when presented with convincing and persuasive arguments or experiences in favor of the belief. Faith occurs when we are persuaded about the truth of something. Each truth we come to believe is formed by building upon other truths we already believe. But the level of verification required can change from person to person.

For example, some people might not be able to believe certain truths until they verify it with their own eyes. Others, however, might be able to believe that same fact simply on the word or testimony of someone they trust. All historical facts are of this second type. Any historical fact can only be believed on the testimony of others. But with other types of facts, we might come to faith through reason, logic, and the weight of argumentation.

Occasionally, we might even come to believe something despite our desire to not believe it. If a father was told that his son was a mass-murderer, the father would not want to believe it, and would likely not believe it. But if this father sat through the trial of his son, and saw the weight of evidence, and maybe even heard the confession of his son to these crimes, the father would be forced to believe what he did not want to believe. In such an instance, the father did not choose to believe, but was persuaded or convinced by the evidence presented, and came to believe something he did not wish to be true.

Or consider once again the "Sky is blue" illustration. If you had simply told me that the sky was violet, I would not have believed it. But once I was presented with the evidence, I was persuaded to believe that the sky is violet. This belief even goes against what I see with my own eyes. Although I *see* that the sky is blue, I know that something is going on with the light receptors in my eyes that causes it to appear blue, when in fact it

---

[12] Wilkin, *Confident in Christ*, 6.

is violet. So despite all the *visible* evidence, the scientific facts persuaded me to believe that the sky is violet. I did not choose to believe that the sky is violet; I was persuaded by the evidence.

This is how faith works. Every fact we believe, we believe because we are persuaded by the evidence. We did not choose to believe or make a decision to believe. Belief happens to us as the evidence is presented before us.

> Belief is not something we conjure up by strength of will. The key to believing something is the proof in favor of it. Faith is not really a choice. You don't choose to believe anything. Either you believe that two plus two equals four, or you don't. You can't *choose* to believe it. When the evidence that something is true persuades people, they believe it. When the evidence is insufficient, people don't believe it. ... Therefore, faith is not a decision. It is the conviction that something is true.[13]

Since we cannot choose to believe anything, but are only persuaded by the evidence presented to us, we can never judge or condemn someone for their lack of faith on a particular topic or idea. All we can do is present evidence to them and engage with them in conversations about what they believe. The same is true for our own beliefs. We cannot feel proud of our beliefs, nor can we feel guilty about things we don't believe. All we can do is think, reason, discuss, learn, and investigate the truth. As we do this, faith will blossom in us as we come to know, understand, and agree with the various propositions that we learn. Here is what Dallas Willard writes about this process:

> Our beliefs ... cannot be changed by choice. We cannot just choose to have different beliefs ... But we do have some liberty to take in different ideas and information and to think about things in different ways. We can choose to take in the Word of God, and when we do that, [our] beliefs ... will be

---

[13] Cf. Bob Wilkin, *The Ten Most Misunderstood Words in the Bible* (Denton, TX: GES, 2012), 20.

steadily pulled in a godly direction.

> We never *choose* to believe, and we must not try to get ourselves or others to choose to believe. ... We can try to understand and try to help others to understand. And beyond that—God must work. Once we understand this and stop trying to get people to choose to believe or to do things they really don't believe, He will certainly work as we do our part.[14]

C. S. Lewis agrees. In many of his letters to various people, Lewis wrote about how he became a Christian. He writes that was persuaded against his will about the existence of God and the truth of Christianity. He did not choose to believe or even want to believe, but was persuaded to believe by the evidence.

As people faced similar experiences of faith in their own life, Lewis wrote to them with counsel that just as they cannot fight faith, so also, they cannot force it. Faith happens to us as the light of God shines in our life. This does not mean we have no responsibility in faith, but that we must respond positively to the revelation God has given to us so that we can receive more revelation from Him. Here are a few examples of what Lewis wrote to various people:

> If you think [Christianity] is false you needn't bother about all the things in it that seem terrible. If you decide it is true, you needn't worry about not having faith, for apparently you have.[15]

> If you don't think [Christianity] is true why do you want to believe it? If you do think it is true, then you believe it already.[16]

> No one can make himself believe anything and the effort does harm. Nor make himself feel anything, and that effort also does harm. What is under

---

[14] Dallas Willard, *Renovation of the Heart* (Colorado Springs: NavPress, 2012), 248.
[15] C. S. Lewis, *Yours, Jack: Spiritual Direction from C. S. Lewis* (New York: HarperCollins, 2008), 91.
[16] Ibid., 125.

our own control is action and intellectual inquiry. Stick to that.[17]

C. S. Lewis is right. We cannot force ourselves to believe something. But at the same time, nor can we fight it. Faith happens to us when we are persuaded by the evidence presented. Of course, faith is not always the result of evidence and logic, but can also come through experience and emotions. While facts, logic, and reason can lead to faith, so also can experience, relationships, and revelation. Even hope and trust, which are not themselves faith, can be transformed into faith. Even faith itself can lead to greater faith, for once we believe some things about God, it becomes easier to believe other things. Divine revelation itself can lead us to believe things about God, ourselves, and eternity which we may not have believed otherwise (cf. Rom 10:17).

Note that to some degree, our beliefs depend on the reliability of the person who made a particular truth claim to us. When we believe, we not only believe based on the evidence of the facts presented, but also on the reliability of the source of those facts. For example, I believe that $E=MC^2$ because I believe that Einstein was smart enough to figure it out. If a kindergarten student tells me that Einstein was wrong, I am not likely to believe him. We use reason and logic to judge what we hear, so that we are either persuaded or unpersuaded by the truth claims of other people. Because I have more trust in Einstein than a 6-year old when it comes to the Theory of Relativity, I believe what Einstein says. However, I am more likely to believe a six-year old than Einstein when it comes to the best tasting candy.

The spreadsheet analogy is of further aid in this regard. One cell the spreadsheet of beliefs contains the truth claim that $E=MC^2$. I believe this. But the truth of this cell is dependent upon another cell which says "Einstein was a genius." Based on what I have read and learned about him, I also believe this. There is another spreadsheet cell which says "Einstein was infallible." I do not believe this. However, even though I do not be-

[17] Ibid., 126.

lieve Einstein was infallible, I can be reasonably certain of many of the other truth claims from Einstein, as well as nearly all of the things he taught related to the Theory of Relativity, and so when it comes to the truth claim that $E=MC^2$, I am persuaded to believe it.

Do you see how this works? Faith is a persuasion or conviction that something is true. Some people require more persuasion; some less. Some truth claims require more reasoning; some less. But in all cases, we cannot choose to believe something that we do not think is true. Furthermore, in no case does God invite us to turn off our brains and "just believe it." Quite to the contrary, God invites us to think and use reason to figure things out. God does not call us to turn off our minds. He gave us our minds for a reason ... which is reason.

We cannot, of course, always depend upon reason to properly guide us. It is as John Donne once wrote in "Holy Sonnet XIV":

> *I, like an usurp'd town, to another due,*
> *Labor to admit you, but O, to no end.*
> *Reason, your viceroy in me, me should defend,*
> *But is captive, and proves weak or untrue.*

Reason and logic are helpful in the development of faith, but reason can often lead us astray, partly because we are not omniscient, as God is. If we had all facts and knowledge, then our reason and logic would be infallible as well. But since there are great chasms of ignorance in our understanding of all things, our reason often leads us astray.

But even though reason is not entirely reasonable, God has not left us to our own devices. Due to the unreliability of reason, God has given us numerous allies to help reason in our quest for truth. God does not leave us alone in this process to figure things out on our own.

Along with Scripture and other humans to help guide our reasoning process, God has also given Himself in the person and work of the Holy Spirit. Prior to conversion, the Holy Spirit works upon the minds of unbelievers to convict them that they are sinners, that they need righteousness in order to get to receive eternal life, and that judgment is coming (John 16:8-11). This convicting work of the Holy Spirit involves persuading unbelievers to believe things that they did not previously believe. Even after we become Christians, the teaching and illuminating work of the Holy Spirit continues. Through Scripture, by the Spirit, and in the midst of life experiences and human relationships, God works to continually "renew our minds" (Rom 12:1-2; cf. 10:17) so that we come to know, understand, and believe the truth.[18]

In light of this fact that we cannot choose to believe or change our beliefs with a simple act of the will, but are instead persuaded to believe by the evidence presented to us, we see the fifth and final truth about faith.

5. WHEN A BELIEF CHANGES, OTHER BELIEFS ALSO CHANGE

This final insight about how faith works has already been mentioned numerous times in this chapter. Since our system of beliefs is like a giant spreadsheet of interconnected cells, it makes perfect sense that a change in one belief will cause a change in numerous other beliefs as well. When we come to believe something that we previously did not, this new belief has a cascading effect throughout our spreadsheet of beliefs so that we stop believing some things and start believing others. Note, however, that when a belief changes, we do not stop believing everything else on the spreadsheet. Our network of beliefs do not all stand or fall together. When one belief changes, it simply causes several other beliefs to change as well, which in turn causes more beliefs to change. So yes, these changes can sometimes occur on a large scale, but these changes are usually for best.

For example, on everybody's spreadsheet of beliefs there is a cell which says, "God exists." For some people, this cell is switched "Off"

---

[18] Gordon Clark, *Faith and Saving Faith* (Jefferson, MD: Trinity, 1983), 107. Cf. Also Zane Hodges, "The New Puritanism, Part 2" *JOTGES* 6:11 (Autumn 1993), http://www.faithalone.org /journal/1993ii/J11-93b.htm. Last Accessed January 29, 2004.

because they don't believe it is true. Others are uncertain about whether or not this statement is true. For them, the cell is also "Off." But for many people, myself included, this cell is switched "On" because we believe it to be true.

But this belief is not based on an illogical "blind leap of faith" (a terrible term!) into the dark void. This belief in the existence of God is based on a large number of beliefs that reside in other cells. Among these other cells are the beliefs that "Matter exists," "Matter cannot come from nothing," "Matter is not eternal," and "Matter had to have been 'created' by something outside of matter." These sorts of beliefs are turned "On" in my spreadsheet, and ultimately, are some of the beliefs that lead me to believe that "God exists." When taken as a belief *all by itself*, I could never believe that "God exists." But since this belief is based on other reasonable beliefs, I am able to state with full confidence that "God exists."

Many people think that believing in the existence of God is a blind leap of faith. But it isn't. People who believe that God exists maybe have not thought through all the rational arguments for the existence of God, but the only way that anyone comes to believe that God exists is by being persuaded of this truth in some way. Their new belief in the existence of God was due to some preliminary, foundational beliefs also changing. Maybe they heard some of the logical and rational arguments for the existence of God. Maybe they were persuaded by a personal experience, or the experience of someone else whom they trust. Maybe they simply excluded all other possibilities, and came to realize that a belief in the existence of God was the only remaining and reasonable possibility.

But regardless of how a person comes to believe in the existence of God, as soon as they believe this, numerous other beliefs will also start to change. They will eventually realize that since God exists, then God has authority (to some degree) over humans. And when they come to realize this, they will also come to believe that God would seek to exert that authority by telling us how to live our lives. This leads to a belief in some form of divine revelation from God.

Do you see how one belief starts to cascade and ripple through the rest of the spreadsheet of beliefs? This cascading ripple of changing beliefs is not instantaneous, but often takes some time to fully work its way through the spreadsheet. Sometimes this process can take an entire lifetime.

The process of changing beliefs can also be stopped, short-circuited, and even reversed. If a person comes to believe in the existence of God, but then someone else comes along and starts to challenge the various foundational beliefs that support the idea of the existence of God, this challenge might cause the person's faith in God to unravel and reverse. If a person recognizes that their feelings cannot always be trusted, that sometimes their pastor and parents are wrong, and that the Bible seems to contain some apparent contradictions about God (which I think can be rationally explained), then the person might end up turning their "God exists" cell from "On" back to "Off." Understandably, this change will then have further ripple effects throughout the system of beliefs.

Ideally, we should personally investigate the truth claim of every single cell in the entire spreadsheet of knowledge. Yet since there are an infinite number of truth claims, this exercise is humanly impossible. We simply do not have the time, ability, or experience to analyze the vast majority of the possible truth claims.

So what are we to do? Well, we humans tend to investigate the ones that are interesting to us, and then accept or reject the rest based on the input of others. To use Einstein again, I don't have the time, ability, or necessary knowledge to analyze the truth claim that $E=MC^2$, but I still believe that this statement is true. Why do I believe it if I haven't really investigated it for myself? I believe it because I believe in Einstein (and other physicists who also believe it). I believe they have studied this truth claim, have understood it, and have agreed that it is true. Therefore, because I trust their judgment on this matter, I believe that $E=MC^2$.

The same exact thing happens with the majority of the cells in our

Excel Spreadsheet of beliefs. Most of the things we believe, we believe because someone else told us to believe them. Some of these claims we later investigate for ourselves, and either confirm or correct them, but the vast majority we simply accept based on the reliability and trustworthiness of the one who initially taught them to us. God, of course, is the most reliable teacher of truth, and so anything He says can be believed. So we should always be open to God showing up in our life to challenge some of what we believe, even if it is the beliefs that we hold dear.

Nevertheless, the potential back-and-forth tidal wave of shifting beliefs can cause some fear and frustration in the minds of those who experience it. It can indeed feel like a house of cards tumbling down around you. This is terrifying for those who thought their "house of cards" was really a true house. When someone thinks that their beliefs are the foundation to all that is true and right, and then this foundation starts to shake and crumble, it can be very disconcerting. Some people will retreat from all questions and investigations just so that they can avoid this feeling.

But I hope that as you come to understand how faith works, you can learn to enjoy and anticipate this feeling of having the rug pulled out from beneath you. If you can view this experience as the most exhilarating ride of life, rather than as the destruction of everything you have worked so hard to build, then the rippling changes of beliefs will not be something to fear, but to enjoy.

For those are terrified of changing their beliefs, or believing something wrong, I would say that the one belief which provides peace of mind and stability of spirit throughout all these shifting tides is the belief that Jesus will never let you go. If you do not know that you are safe and secure in the arms of Jesus for all eternity, then yes, the potential ramifications of changing your beliefs will be terrifying. But do not be terrified. Instead, seek to learn that God loves you perfectly, and perfect love casts out fear. He will never stop loving you, nor will He ever let you go.[19] This belief is a foundational and core belief for life as a Christian. Without it, I do not see how you can safely investigate your faith or navigate this life.

But when you are able to stand firm on the solid rock of Jesus Christ, then no amount of shifting beliefs can shake you. Instead, you can howl into the wind and laugh at the driving rain as you stand side-by-side with Jesus. Embrace the change, for that is where the thrill of the Christian life truly resides.

CONCLUSION

As a result of this chapter, it is possible that you have changed your belief about belief. That is, you now likely believe something different about how faith works than you previously believed. If your understanding of faith has indeed changed, and you now believe something different about faith than you previously believed, this means that several other "cells" in your spreadsheet of beliefs have also likely changed (or are in the process of changing). You have likely stopped believing several false (but popular) misconceptions about faith. The next chapter considers several of these.

---

[19] I invite you to read my book, *The Gospel According to Scripture* (Dallas, OR: Redeeming Press, 2018), so that you might be persuaded and convinced (believe) that Jesus will never let you go.

CHAPTER 3

SIX MISCONCEPTIONS ABOUT FAITH

There are many things that faith is not. Robert Wilkin summarizes some of these when he writes that faith is not "promising to serve God, praying, walking an aisle, being sorry for your sins, turning from your sins, inviting Jesus into your heart ... doing good works, or having heart faith."[1] Strangely, it is exactly these sorts of misconceptions that are quite popular in many streams of modern, evangelical Christianity.

When I teach others that "eternal life is freely given to anyone who simply believes in Jesus for it," it is not uncommon for someone in the room to object by saying, "So you believe that anyone who raises a hand or walks an aisle can be saved?" This sort of question often leads into a short discussion about the nature of faith and the definition of the word "saved."[2] I try to point out that faith is not the same thing as raising a hand, signing a card, walking an aisle, or saying a prayer. All such actions are works, and faith is not a work.

Similarly, the concept of faith is often portrayed with faulty illustrations.[3] This book began with the illustration of the wheelbarrow over Niagara Falls, but there are numerous other popular (and misleading) illustrations as well. Some people talk about faith as a chair in which you must sit if you are going to demonstrate your faith that the chair can

---

[1] Wilkin, *Confident in Christ*, 9.
[2] See my book, *The Gospel Dictionary* (Dallas, OR: Redeeming Press, Forthcoming).
[3] Bob Wilkin, "Evangelistic Illustrations: The Good, The Bad, and the Ugly," GES Annual Conference Audio CD, 2003.

hold you up. I have heard others teach that faith is like a rope off the side of a cliff to which you must cling for dear life. If you stop believing and let go of the rope you will plummet to your death on the rocks below. Then there is the illustrations of the airplane that needs two wings, both faith and works, before it can properly fly.

We could go on and on with many similar faulty illustrations. But let us just note for now that illustrations are not proofs of a concept. Rather, they are nothing more than pictures that the speaker or author uses to help others understand a concept. If the concept is inherently wrong, then the illustrations will also be wrong. And since many people falsely conflate the concepts of faith and works, thinking that the terms are identical, synonymous, or that faith always results in good works, this means that many illustrations of faith also include an element of works. They say "You have to hold on to the rope … you have to sit in the chair." But when we understand faith as it has been presented in this book, we are able to see that many of these illustrations about faith are wrong, and so also are the concept of faith that rest behind these illustrations.

So in this chapter we are going to consider several misconceptions about faith. Many of these misconceptions are quite popular and have led many Christians into bad theology and poor thinking about how we gain, keep, or prove that we have eternal life, as well as how to live the Christian life. Since faith is central to both types of life, we must rid ourselves of any misconceptions about faith we have if we are to live life as God wants and desires. The following chapter accomplishes this by looking at six misconceptions about faith.

FAITH IS NOT A BLIND LEAP

Every time I hear someone talk about faith as a blind leap, I think of the scene from "Indiana Jones and the Last Crusade" where the treasure map tells him to leap over a gaping crevice to get to the other side. But it is too far to jump. However, just before he turns back, he hears his dying father cry out, "Just believe!" So Indiana takes a deep breath, closes his eyes, clenches his hand over his chest to calm his beating heart, and then steps out into the void. Upon doing so, however, he discovers that there was a hidden bridge across the crevice, which had been painted to look exactly like the far side of the crevice. Now that he was on the bridge, his perspective had changed, and so he could see the bridge perfectly. He walks across and continues toward the treasure.

For many people this is how faith works. They think of faith as stepping out into the void and hoping that something catches them. This is why it is referred to as "blind faith" or "taking a leap of faith." Some even refer to this type of faith as "faith like a child," which apparently means that they don't need reason or logic to believe something, but instead "just believe it." The faith like a child passage (Matt 17:20) will be discussed in a later chapter, but for now, simply note that "faith like a child" is not an ignorant, uncomprehending leap into the great unknown. Similarly, there is no such thing as "blind faith" or a "leap of faith." By definition, it is impossible to accept unproven facts or to believe something you don't (at least partially) understand.

While it is true that different people require different levels of persuasion to believe certain truths, and while some people can believe things with very little evidence to support their belief, there is no such thing a completely blind leap of faith. When we believe something "blindly" we are actually basing that belief on a whole set of additional beliefs in the background. You might believe in the reliability of the person who told you what to believe, and since you believe in them, you believe what they say. Similarly, a person might not recognize how their network of beliefs are related and interconnected, so their "blind leap of faith" appears to be an unconscious logical step of faith, when in reality, it is based on what is already believed.

Furthermore, nowhere does the Bible talk about anything related to blind faith or a leap of faith. Quite to the contrary, the Bible invites us to use our minds, and to engage in reasonable questioning with God about life and faith (Isa 1:18). Jesus doesn't chide Thomas for not believing that He is risen, but instead, provides the evidence Thomas needed to believe that Jesus has risen from the dead (John 20:27). The Bereans are praised for questioning what Paul taught and reasoning from the Scriptures to see if they should believe what he said (Acts 17:11). Paul even encourages the doubting Corinthians to corroborate his story of the resurrected Christ with other living eye-witnesses (1 Cor 15). In all such cases (and everywhere else in the Bible), no one is commanded or invited to take a leap of faith, but instead to think, learn, question, study, discuss, and reason things out so that they might believe.

Consider the scene once again from "Indiana Jones and the Last Crusade." While it is true that he did not know about the hidden bridge, he did know that the treasure map in his hands had never led him astray. He also saw the very clear picture in the treasure map of what he was supposed to do, namely, step straight out into the apparent void. Also, he knew that the word of his father could be trusted. So for Indiana Jones, in this situation, these foundational beliefs logically led him to believe that if he stepped out into the chasm, he would somehow get across. He didn't know *how* he would get across, but he had enough reason to know (or believe) that it would work.

So the concept of blind faith is nothing more than a modern invention. And since it does not fit with any biblical perspective of faith, nor does it fit with how faith actually works, we must eradicate all thoughts about blind faith from our thinking and theology. Blind faith does not exist, and we must stop telling people to "Stop thinking and just believe!" Similarly, we must never say, "You're asking too many questions; you just have to experience God!" Such phrases and ideas cause non-believers to think that Christianity is little more than a fairy-tale to entertain people with weak minds. We must instead invite people to think, question, and doubt. We must tell them that if Christianity is true, then it can stand up to any and all questions.

And indeed it can. There are rational reasons to believe in Jesus, and rational arguments for the existence of God. While a person is not required or expected to know *all* of these explanations and arguments for anything they believe, they do need to know enough to be persuaded or convinced in their own mind of what they believe. If they do not know, then they do not believe. So-called "blind faith" is not faith at all, but is little more than wishful thinking, and does not have any place in Christian theology.

FAITH IS NOT "ALL OR NOTHING"

This misconception about faith was partly addressed in the previous chapter, but it is worth considering here as well. Some people think that when it comes to "believing in Christianity" you have to believe all of it or none of it. This is the "all or nothing" approach to faith. My Grandmother was a person who thought like this. Before she passed away, my Grandmother thought that since she could not believe that Methuselah lived to be 969 years old, this meant that she could not believe anything in the entire Bible.

Greg Boyd's "house of cards" analogy also fits within this misconception of faith. As he rightly pointed out, if someone thinks that the entire Christian faith stands or falls together, then whenever one particular facet of faith is challenged or changed, the entire house of cards comes tumbling down. This is a terrifying prospect for the Christians who hold the "All or Nothing" approach to faith, which is why so few Christians ask hard questions or investigate any ideas that might challenge their beliefs.

So the proper approach to faith is to recognize that while the various beliefs we can hold are all interconnected and related to each other in a vast network, they do not all stand or fall together. Faith is not a house of cards. Yes, changing one belief can cause a cascading change to ripple through numerous other beliefs, but the end result of this process is a stronger set of beliefs that can now stand up against further questions and stronger storms of life. And while it can be disconcerting and scary the first few times these largescale changes occur, if you remember that Jesus will never let you go, then you will start to enjoy the thrill of the rollercoaster ride of faith, rather than dread any new change that comes along.

If I were able to have a conversation with my Grandmother today, I would praise her for questioning the idea that Methuselah lived to be 969. After all, all questions are good questions. I would even tell her that it is completely okay if she never believed this particular historical claim. But I would then encourage her to move past this difficult idea from Scripture, and consider some of the more central truth claims from the Bible, such as some of the claims about Jesus as found in the Gospels. And if she wasn't yet able to believe most of these either, that also would be okay. We would keep reading, discussing, questioning, and learning, as we built upon whatever truths she could believe. Faith is not "all or nothing" but is an adventure in which you move from what you know into the great unknown, so that some of the other hidden gems of God and treasures of truth might be discovered and enjoyed.

FAITH IS NOT HOPE

Often, when people use the word "believe," they use it in a way that confuses it with hope. Though someone might say they believe the Bears will win the Super Bowl this year, they know, as does everyone else, that their belief is little more than hope. You even sometimes hear people say "I believe I will win the lottery!" In this case, the word "believe" doesn't even rise to the level of hope, but is nothing more than fanciful thinking. Yet people might also say "I hope the Bears win the Super Bowl" or "I hope I win the lottery" and mean essentially the same thing as when the word "believe" was used. Since "believe" and "hope" can be used interchangeably to refer to a wish or desire, it makes sense that English speakers confuse the two concepts.

Yet in Scripture, faith and hope are distinctly different. In 1 Corinthians 13:13, for example, Paul writes, "And now abide faith, hope, and love ... but the greatest of these is love." If faith and hope were the same, then Paul's statement would be nonsense. A similar idea is taught in Hebrews 11:1, which says, "Now faith is the substance of things hoped for ..." Again, if faith and hope are the same, then the author is saying that belief is the substance of things believed for. This makes no sense. So while it is true that faith and hope are intimately connected in Scripture, they are not synonymous terms.

In biblical usage, what do the two words mean and how are they connected? We have already seen that faith is the confidence, persuasion, or conviction that something is true. Faith is (as will be discussed further below) the mental assent to a factual statement. Biblical hope is built upon the foundation of faith. Unlike modern usage where hope is wishful thinking, biblical hope is the eager expectation of the future realization of a promise of God. Hope occurs when we believe what God has said about some future event, and then we look forward to it with earnest anticipation.

While faith is the knowledge that something is true, and this knowledge can involve past, present, or future events, hope is primarily concerned with the future. Hope involves that which has yet to happen, while faith can involve things in the past and present as well, including ideas and truths that have no reference to time at all. Hope, however, is always used in reference to a future event. Paul writes in Romans 8:24 that "hope that is seen is not hope; for why does one still hope for what he sees?" People do not hope for things they have already obtained or seen; hope is for things that will yet come to pass.

Since we believe what Jesus has said, and since we believe that Jesus will come again, we look forward to His return. That is, the return of Jesus is our blessed hope (Titus 1:2; 2:13; cf. John 14:3). Similarly, because we believe in Jesus and what He has said, all the promises of Scripture about our future life and blessings in eternity can be hoped for with an eager expectation (cf. 1 Tim 1:1). Hope, therefore, is a natural outcome of faith.

The relationship between faith and hope is illustrated by a young child who is told by her parents that they will be going to Disney Land later that year. Since she believes what her parents say, and since she believes that they can fulfill their promises to her, she looks forward to the trip to Disney Land. She hopes for it with eager anticipation. Her faith in her parents and what they say leads the child to hope.

So while faith and hope are complementary, they are not the same thing. We could say that while faith is grounded in facts and the reality of the past and present, hope is grounded in faith and expectations for the future. Faith leads to and gives birth to hope. This relationship between faith and hope also helps us understand the relationship between faith and trust.

FAITH IS NOT TRUST

Just as many people confuse and conflate faith and hope, so also, many people confuse and conflate faith and trust. In English, the two words are often used interchangeably. Banks remind their customers that their deposits have the "full faith and credit" of the United States Government. This means that the customer can trust the bank to keep and protect their money, and even if the bank closes down or declares bankruptcy, the US Government will make sure the customers get their money back. So just as "faith" and trust" are nearly identical in financial terminology, so also, the two words are nearly identical in the minds of many Christians. Most people do not see any real difference between the two statements "I trust Jesus" and "I believe Jesus."

Recall once again the example of the tightrope walker with the wheelbarrow. The tightrope walker asked the crowd if they believed he could walk across Niagara Falls while pushing somebody in a wheelbarrow. While they all enthusiastically shouted their support, when it came to actually trusting him with their own life, nobody wanted to get into the wheelbarrow. This illustration is sometimes presented as evidence that faith is not truly faith unless it includes trust.

But what this illustration *actually* proves is that there is a great difference between faith and trust. The people truly believed he could walk across Niagara Falls on a tightrope while pushing someone in a wheelbarrow. In fact, it is also quite likely that many people also believed he could do it with them in the wheelbarrow. But they did not believe he could do it *every single time.* They did not trust him to be 100% without mistake or error, nor did they trust themselves to be able to sit still while in wheelbarrow. So while they did believe, they did not fully trust. This lack of trust does not show a lack of belief, but instead reveals a key distinction between faith and trust.

Since faith is a mental assent in a proposition or a conviction and persuasion that something is true, trust is a particular *type* of belief. Trust is a belief in the strength, reliability, or dependability of someone or something. Not all beliefs are trusts, but all trusts are beliefs. Furthermore, while there are no degrees to faith (you cannot 99% believe something), there can be degrees of trust. I know that this can be confusing, for I just stated that trust is a form of belief, but a look back at the illustration of a giant Excel spreadsheet of beliefs helps clarify the difference between trust and belief.

On everybody's spreadsheet of beliefs are many thousands of statements about trust. For example, one cell says "I trust everything my parents taught me." Probably nobody (except very young children) would agree with that truth claim. For most people, this cell is turned "Off." Therefore, almost nobody believes this statement. However, there is another cell that says, "I trust a lot of what my parents taught me." More people are likely to agree with this, and so for them, this cell is turned

"On." Some people, however, had terrible parents, and so they don't have either one of these two previous cells turned "On." Instead, they have a cell turned "On" which says, "I trust almost nothing my parents taught me."

So each statement resides in a separate cell on the spreadsheet of beliefs, but each cell contains a statement about the level of trust, or amount of trust, that someone has in another person. And depending on which cell is turned "On," this helps determine which other cells are turned "On" as well. Those who have more trust in their parents will therefore believe more of the truth claims they learned from their parents. Those who have less trust in their parents will believe less of what their parents taught. In this way, while belief in a particular factual statement is either "On" or "Off," the factual statement itself can have varying degrees of actuality.

To take this analogy a bit further, there is another cell on everyone's spreadsheet which says, "I 100% trust God to tell the truth." If a person believes this, then they know that God's words can always be trusted, and therefore, believed. A bit of careful thinking, however, reveals that while God can be trusted to always tell the truth, we humans cannot be trusted to always accurately understand what God has said. There is a vast difference between the statement "I 100% trust God to tell the truth" and "I 100% trust me to understand what God has said." Personally, I believe the first but not the second.

This distinction is similar to what we saw with the wheelbarrow story. While the crowed believed that the man *could* take someone across in the wheelbarrow, they did not believe that he *always* would. Instead, they believed with certainty that eventually, something would happen which would cause the man and a person in the wheelbarrow to plummet to their death below. Maybe it would be the person in the wheelbarrow who causes this fatal mistake. Nobody wanted to be in the wheelbarrow when that happened. So did they believe that he could do it? Yes. Did they fully 100% trust that he always would? No.

All of this reveals something critically important about the trust claims on our spreadsheet of beliefs. We have seen that while not every cell on the spreadsheet of beliefs is a trust claim, it is nevertheless true that every cell on the spreadsheet of beliefs is dependent or built upon several foundational trust claims. In other words, trust claims are foundational beliefs to nearly all of the cells on the spreadsheet. Early on in life, children trust their parents, and so their beliefs develop in accordance to what their parents teach them. As this trust in their parents grows or diminishes over time, the child's beliefs will also change.

All of this helps make better sense of what Scripture teaches about the relationship between trust and faith. The Greek word for trust is *peithō* and means "to have confidence" (cf. Matt 27:43; Mark 10:24; Luke 11:22; 18:9; 2 Cor 1:9; 10:7; Php 2:24; 3:4). This shows the connection between faith and trust, in that both are a form of confidence. Trust, however, is the confidence in the strength, reliability, or dependability of someone or something. The two concepts are related, but not identical.

For example, while Scripture everywhere calls us to believe in Jesus for eternal life (John 3:16; 5:24; 6:47; etc.), Scripture does not call us anywhere to trust in Jesus for eternal life.[4] Instead, since we trust what God has said, and Jesus is the perfect revelation of God, then we know we can believe everything Jesus says. Therefore, when Jesus offers eternal life to those who believe in Him for it, we know He is speaking the truth. The same thing is true for all the other teachings of Jesus. Since we trust Him, we can therefore believe in what He says. To put it another way, because we trust the character and truthfulness of Jesus, we are able to believe what He says. Belief in what Jesus says is based on the prior belief in the reliability and trustworthiness of Jesus.

If we think that belief and trust are identical, then statements like, "I believe what He says because I trust Him" would simply mean "I believe

[4] Bob Wilkin, "The Subtle Redefinition of Faith via Trust," https://faithalone.org/blog/the-subtle-redefinition-of-faith-via-trust/ Last Accessed March 17, 2018.

what He says because I believe Him," which is no reason at all. If we believe someone simply because we believe them, then our belief has no firm foundation and no basis on which to stand. We can, however, believe what someone says because we have previously understood that the person is reliable and trustworthy. When we believe that someone is reliable and knowledgeable in what they teach, then this trust leads us to also believe what they say.

This distinction between faith and trust is further seen by the fact that while we can trust a person, we cannot really "believe a person." We can believe *what a person says*, or believe factual statements *about a person*, but you can no more "believe a person" than you can weigh a color or smell a number.[5] So although we do often say that we "believe Jesus," this is just a shorthand way of saying that we "believe various factual propositions about Jesus as well as truth statements from Jesus."

In the end, the relationship between faith and trust can be summarized this way: Though trust is a type of faith, it is not synonymous with faith. Though all trust claims can be believed or not, not all faith claims are trust claims. Instead, what and who we trust is a major determining factor in what or who we believe. Trust, therefore, is a precondition, or foundational element, to many aspects of faith. Just as faith leads to hope, so also, trust leads to faith. Quite often, we believe what we believe because we trust the person who taught these beliefs to us.

One of the reasons it is important to clarify the connection between faith and trust is because in the minds of many, trust involves action. When people equate faith and trust by saying that the two terms are synonymous, they will usually also say that eternal life is not simply by faith *alone*, but also involves some sort of action on our part, such as submitting to the Lordship of Jesus, persevering in obedience, or committing our life to Christ. We are told that these sorts of actions are indicative of true trust.

This leads to serious problems. When faith is equated with trust, and

---

[5] See Shawn Lazar, "Is Faith Trust in a Person?" https://faithalone.org/blog/is-faith-trust-in-a-person/ Last Accessed March 17, 2018.

then trust is defined to include works and human activity, then works become a condition for receiving eternal life. This is why it is essential to maintain the distinction between faith and trust as explained above, and also to remember that faith is not a work. Faith is never something we *do*, or that requires us to *do* something in order to prove that we truly have faith. It is to this concept we now turn.

FAITH IS NOT AN ACTION

Almost nobody in evangelical Christianity argues that faith is a good work that we *do* to receive eternal life. Rather, most argue that if a person truly believes, then they will have the good works to back up their belief, or to prove that they have *really* believed. They argue that true faith always results in good works. Logically, therefore, if a person does not have the necessary good works, then they do not have faith. I argue against this entire line of thought in my book, *The Gospel According to Scripture*, and so what appears below is little more than a summary of the arguments presented in that other volume.

Note that if true faith always leads to good works, then this logically means that good works are a necessary requirement to spend eternity with God. Imagine two people who both claim to have faith in Jesus for eternal life. According to the "faith always results in works idea," if only one of them has the good works which provides the evidence for faith, then only the one with the good works will spend eternity with God. Since the only difference between them is the presence of good works, this means that good works were the deciding factor on whether or not a person spends eternity with God. In this way of thinking, faith alone in Jesus Christ is not sufficient for an eternal relationship with God. Instead, good works decide a person's eternal destiny.

When this point is brought up, one common objection is that even "faith alone in Jesus Christ" involves works, because we invite people to believe in Jesus. If believing in Jesus is something people *do*, or if faith is a human action, then even the call to "believe in Jesus" is a call to good works. Some argue, therefore, that whether it is the "good work" of faith, or the good works of obedience, eternal life is always gained through some form of good works. If this is true, we should all stop arguing about the role of faith and works in gaining eternal life for the believer, and instead call all people to a life of faith and good works toward God.

But eternal life is not based on human good works or effort in any way, shape, or form. It can be shown from Scripture, logic, and experience that faith does not necessarily lead to works, nor is faith itself a work. Let us consider both ideas in turn.

Despite the claims of many, true and genuine beliefs do not always lead to behaviors that match these beliefs. Quite to the contrary, people often behave in ways that do not match their beliefs. A smoker may rightly believe that smoking is bad for them, but due to a nicotine addiction, they continue to smoke. Does their ongoing habit prove that they don't *actually* believe that smoking is bad? Of course not. Other factors are in play so that such a person genuinely believes one thing, but acts in a way that is contrary to their belief. Numerous other examples could be provided. One could almost argue that as a general rule, humans act in ways that are contrary to their beliefs. Therefore, while our actions do *sometimes* indicate what we believe, actions are never an infallible guide for determining what a person believes or does not believe. Faith does not necessarily lead to works that match a person's beliefs, nor do the presence (or absence) of works indicate what a person believes.

What then can be said about this idea that faith is a good work? While it is definitely good to believe the truth, this is quite different than saying that belief is a good *work*. As seen earlier in this book, faith is something that happens to us when we are persuaded or convinced by the truth. While faith is mental assent to a stated proposition (see the section below), faith is not an act of the will that we set out to achieve or accomplish. We cannot "choose" to believe, "make a decision" to believe, or force ourselves to believe. Instead, as we discover the truth about a particular topic, or as that topic is taught to us, we are persuaded to believe, sometimes against our will. Therefore, if we do not choose to believe something, then it cannot be said that faith is an action or a work that we *do*. Faith is passive. It is something that happens to us when we are presented with the evidence for or against a particular idea.

It is critically important to recognize that faith is not a work or an action that we humans perform, for if it was a work, or a human action, then humans would be working for or earning their eternal life. In other words, since eternal life is received through faith, then if faith is a work we would have to conclude that eternal life is received through human work and action. But Scripture everywhere teaches exactly the opposite. Indeed, Paul clearly states in Romans 4:5 that God's righteousness is given to those who *do not work,* but believe. If faith was a work, then Paul would be saying that God justifies those who do not work, but work.

Grant Hawley, in his book *The Guts of Grace,* writes this:

> Phrases like, "For by grace you have been saved through faith … not of works …" (Eph 2:8-9), and, "to him who does not work but believes" (Rom 4:5), are complete nonsense, if works are part of the definition of the words faith and believe. If a woman at a wedding reception said, "The one who does not move, but dances, enjoys the reception," you would wonder if she had had too much to drink because moving is part of the definition of the word dances.[6]

It is impossible and contradictory to say that salvation is by grace through faith apart from works (Rom 4:4-5; Eph 2:8-9), but through a faith that includes works. There are no works in faith. The two are diametrically opposed. Faith is not a special sort of human work, nor is it a divine work in the heart of the unbeliever. Faith is not a work at all; it is the opposite of works. Just as we do not receive eternal life by faith *and*

---

[6] Hawley, *The Guts of Grace,* 124.

works, so also, we do not receive eternal life by faith *that is* a work. Just as faith cannot be part of the definition of works, so also, works cannot be part of the definition of faith. The two are not related in any way, but are polar opposites. Both faith and works, by definition, are mutually exclusive.

So the idea that faith is a work is "a theological fiction which cannot be supported from Scripture."[7] Eternal life is the free gift of God to anyone who believes in Jesus for it. Eternal life is not received by works of any kind. Faith is being persuaded or convinced that what God says is true. God gives eternal life to anyone who believes in Jesus for it. Because of all that God has done in history, through various forms of revelation, and by His Holy Spirit, people are able to believe in Jesus for eternal life. Though all are invited and called to believe in Jesus for eternal life, this faith does not mean we are working for eternal life or in any way earning eternal life from God.

FAITH IS NOT A GIFT

Even though we have just seen that faith is not a work, some teach that faith *is* a work, but that it is a work of God. They say that faith is a work of God performed in the heart or mind of a person. Another way of saying this is that faith is a gift from God to the heart of human beings. Those who hold to this view say that God gives faith to those whom He has chosen for eternal life. There are three reasons that some people teach that faith is a gift of God.

First, some believe that since unregenerate people are "dead in trespasses and sins" (Eph 2:1), and have had their minds darkened or blinded (cf. (Eph 4:18; 2 Cor 3:14),[8] they cannot do anything good, including believing in Jesus for eternal life. Those who hold to this view teach that

---

[7] Kevin Butcher, "A Critique of The Gospel According to Jesus," *JOTGES* 2 (Spring 1989), 38.

[8] Yes, I agree with what all of these passages are saying. I just do not agree with how some Christians understand and explain them.

if a person is going to believe in Jesus for eternal life (or even believe anything good and pleasing about God at all), they can only believe if God sovereignly bestowed up them the gift of faith.

Various texts are often referenced in defense of this idea (cf. Acts 5:31; 11:18; 13:48; 16:14; Rom 12:3; 1 Cor 12:8-9; Eph 2:8-9; Php 1:29; 2 Tim 2:25; 2 Pet 1:1). But in several of these, faith is not even mentioned (e.g., Acts 5:31; 11:18; 2 Tim 2:25), and the others can all be reasonably explained in the context. A few will be explained below, with several others in a later chapter.

Note, however, that this entire line of thought stems from thinking that faith is a good work. In other words, the idea that faith is a gift derives from the false idea that faith is somehow meritorious. After all, if faith is a work, then we *must* say that faith is a gift from God, for we cannot teach that humans are able to work for eternal life.

But as we learned above, faith is not a work; it is not meritorious. Faith is the opposite of works (Rom 4:4-5). Faith does not earn, achieve, or gain good standing with God in any way. Therefore, faith does not *need* to be a gift from God. People are persuaded about all sorts of things, and no such persuasion is ever considered to be a good work or a meritorious action, or a gift from God. So the faith to believe in Jesus is also *not* a gift from God.

The second reason that some people believe and teach that faith is a gift of God is because they confuse this idea with the biblical teaching about the "spiritual gift" of faith. Even though Paul does write about the gift of faith in 1 Corinthians 12:9, this is the spiritual gift of faith, and is not the same thing as the so-called "gift of faith" which some teach God gives to people before they can believe in Jesus for eternal life. Furthermore, Paul is quite clear that we all have different spiritual gifts (Rom 12:6). If everyone had to receive the "gift of faith" from God in order to receive eternal life (John 3:16; 5:24; 6:47), then this would mean that all Christians have the spiritual gift of faith, which Paul says we do not.

So what is the *spiritual gift* of faith? As I wrote in my book on the spiritual gifts, a person has the spiritual gift of faith when they firmly persuaded of God's power and promises to accomplish His will and purpose and to display such a confidence in Him that circumstances and obstacles do not shake that conviction (1 Cor 12:8-10; cf. Heb 11).[9] They know what they believe and why they believe it, and are able to inspire action in others based on their beliefs. Those with the gift of faith are often called upon to encourage others to step out in faith and follow God to accomplish seemingly impossible tasks. As with all the spiritual gifts, the spiritual gift of faith is for the edification and encouragement of others in this world.

Often, those with the spiritual gift of faith are able to lead others in the direction God wants them all to go, even when the others do not believe. In a way, the spiritual gift of faith can serve as "proxy" faith for those who do not have it. There was a time in my life where I doubted almost everything I had formerly believed about God, church, and the Bible. I knew that God existed, but I doubted that He was good and loving. I doubted the power of God to work in our lives. I doubted that Jesus cared very much for me. I doubted that God heard our prayers or answered them. For a period of a few years, I entered into a deep depression, and believed that God had abandoned me, forsaken me, and His only interest in me was to play games with my life. I felt like a pawn on a divine chessboard of life.

But during this time, my wife, Wendy, never stopped believing in the goodness and love of God. And while I was unable to believe, I saw her faith and was inspired by it to not completely give up on God. Though I did not believe that God was good, I saw that she believed this, and her faith served as a guiding light for my faltering faith. Though I had trouble believing much of anything good about God, I did believe in my wife, and what she knew to be true about God. Her unwavering faith eventually brought me back to faith as well. Of course, my beliefs were

---

[9] J. D. Myers, *What are the Spiritual Gifts?* (Dallas, OR: Redeeming Press, 2018).

significantly altered and changed during this time of questions and doubt, but ultimately, my wife's spiritual gift of faith led me back to faith as well.

This is how the spiritual gift of faith works. It is not about God mystically opening up a person's mind to believe certain things that others cannot. Nor is it about some people believing more firmly, or more strongly, than others, for once again, there are no degrees to faith. Such a person might believe a larger number of difficult truths than others, which means they would have "great faith," but God did not "flip a switch" in their mind so that they believed these things.[10] Yes, God might present various truths to a particular person at a particular time, knowing that the presentation of these truths *at that time* will lead a person to believe, but this is not the same thing as God giving the gift of faith to this person. The timing and presentation of truths to a person might be a sovereign act of God, but the giving of faith *itself* is not.

So people believe difficult truths in the same way that anybody is persuaded to believe: the truths are taught to them and they are persuaded to believe based on the evidence presented to them. When they believe these difficult truths, they have "great faith." But that itself is not the spiritual gift of faith. The spiritual gift of faith is when God enables a person who already has "great faith" to lead and inspire others to accomplish great tasks, and to encourage others who are struggling with their faith.

Therefore, in light of all this, we can see that the spiritual gift of faith to some Christians for the edification of others is not the same thing as God giving faith to all Christians so that they can believe in Jesus for eternal life. So biblical passages about the spiritual gift of faith cannot be used to support the idea that God gives faith to unregenerate people so they can believe.

---

[10] Some do teach that the spiritual gift of faith is the divinely-bestowed ability to easily believe some of the more difficult truths about God, Jesus, and Scripture, but I have difficulty finding evidence for this idea in Scripture.

The third reason that some people think faith is a gift from God is because of what Paul seems to say in Ephesians 2:8. He writes, "For by grace you have been saved through faith, and that not of yourselves, it is the gift of God." Some people see the phrase "and *that* not of yourselves, *it* is the gift of God" as referring back to the word "faith." They read Ephesians 2:8 this way: "For by grace you have been saved through faith, and faith is not of yourselves, faith is the gift of God."

There are numerous problems with this approach to Ephesians 2:8, the greatest being that it reveals a complete disregard for the Greek text. Greek words have gender: masculine, feminine, and neuter. When relative pronouns (such as "that" and "it") are used to refer back to a noun, they always agree with the gender of the noun. The word "faith" in Greek is feminine. Therefore, if Paul was intending to say that faith is not of ourselves, but faith is a gift of God, he would have used a feminine relative pronoun for the word "that" (the word "it" is not actually in the Greek).

But the word "that" is not feminine; it is neuter. Therefore, it is impossible for Paul to be thinking about "faith" when he wrote "and that is not of yourselves, it is the gift of God." So what was Paul referring to, if not to faith? Scholars have proposed various solutions, but the best solution is to see that the gift of God is the entire "salvation package" that Paul is writing about in Ephesians 2:1-22. Paul is teaching that humanity suffered under the problem of sin which we could not solve on our own, and so God stepped in to reveal the problem to us and show us the way out. This is the gift of God. If we believe in what God has shown, and live in light of it, we will be saved from the problem that has plagued humanity since the foundation of the world.[11] So Ephesians 2:8 does not teach that faith is the gift of God.

So we have seen the three main reasons that people think that faith is

---

[11] Note that in this context, "salvation" is not about going to heaven when we die, but is instead about living like Jesus in this life. In Ephesians 2, "salvation" is deliverance from the enmity that existed between humans so that we can live in in peace and unity with others instead.

a gift from God. Let us now briefly consider six reasons we know that faith is *not* a gift from God. Many of these are drawn from an excellent article titled "Is Faith a Gift from God or a Human Exercise?" by René Lopez.[12]

First, Lopez points out that the idea that faith is a gift from God confuses the gift of eternal life from God with the instrumentality of faith, by which that gift is received. In other words, God does indeed give a gift to humans, but this gift is eternal life; not faith. Human receive the gift of eternal life through faith. To say that God gives the gift of faith as well is to confuse the gift itself with the receiving of the gift.

Second, Lopez says that "If God divinely imparts faith, then human responsibility is nullified."[13] In other words, if God is the one who sovereignly bestows faith upon a person, then no person can be held responsible by God for their lack of faith. If we receive eternal life by faith in Jesus, but nobody is able to believe unless God gives them the gift of faith, then God also cannot hold people responsible for not believing. If faith is a gift of God, then only God is responsible for people not having faith, and therefore, God has no basis on which to judge people for failing to believe.

Third, although the Bible calls people to believe in Jesus for eternal life, Lopez points out that if faith is a gift, then people should not be called to believe in Jesus (for they cannot). Instead, they should be called to pray and plead with God that He might regenerate them and give them the gift of faith. Strangely, these indeed *are works,* and so if a person cannot believe on their own, but can only pray and plead with God to give them faith so that they might receive eternal life, we have now brought human works and effort back into the equation. Eternal life is no longer by faith alone, but is gained by praying and pleading with God

---

[12] René Lopez, "Is Faith a Gift from God or a Human Exercise?" *Bibliotheca Sacra 164* (July–September 2007): 266-274. http://www.dts.edu/download/publications/bibliotheca/BibSac-Lopez-IsFaithAGiftfromGodoraHumanExercise.pdf

[13] Lopez, "Is Faith a Gift From God or a Human Exercise?" 275.

for the gift of faith.

Thankfully, God does not call anyone to pray and plead that He might give them faith so that they might receive eternal life. To the contrary, God invites and calls all people to simply believe in Jesus. Although there are numerous calls throughout Scripture for people to believe in Jesus for eternal life (John 3:16, 36; 5:24; 6:47; etc.), there is not only place in Scripture where people are invited to hope and pray to God for regeneration (John 3:16; 5:24; 6:47). And when people believe, this faith is ascribed to humans, not to God (Matt 9:2, 22, 28-29; 10:52; Luke 7:50; 8:50; 17:19; 18:42; etc.)[14]

The fourth reason faith is not a gift from God is related to sanctification. If faith is the automatic gift of God to those whom He sovereignly regenerates, then it only makes sense that God also automatically and sovereignly guarantees that such people are sanctified in holiness and obedience. Indeed, this is what some theologians actually teach. But such a belief cannot be defended from Scripture, reason, or experience. The Bible is written, not to tell us to just sit back and wait for God to sovereignly sanctify us, but so that we might change our beliefs and behaviors to bring them into conformity to the person and work of Jesus Christ.

> If faith is a gift, then many commands in Scripture that exhort, command, prompt, and warn believers to live obediently become superfluous because the ultimate end of infused faith guarantees the sanctification of believers without their involvement.[15]

The fifth reason that faith cannot be a gift from God is that such an idea raises too many questions from Scripture. For example, if faith is a gift from God, how could demonic activity restrict the faith of some (Luke 8:12; 2 Cor 4:4)? Why is it harder for some people to believe than others (cf. Titus 1:12-13)? What would be the point of the drawing work of the Holy Spirit (John 6:44; 12:32), or of evangelism and missions?

---

[14] C. Gordon Olson, *Beyond Calvinism and Arminianism: An Inductive Mediate Theology of Salvation* (Cedar Knolls, N.J.: Global Gospel Publishers, 2002), 225.

[15] Lopez, "Is Faith a Gift From God or a Human Exercise?" 275.

Why was Jesus sometimes amazed at people's lack of faith (Matt 8:26; 14:31; 16:8)? None of these questions have good answers if faith is a gift of God.

Finally, if faith is a sovereign gift of God, God Himself appears to engage in favoritism. If God bestows faith on those whom He wants, why are there so many Christians in Europe and America, and so few in North Africa and the Middle East? Does God have something against the people in those neglected regions? On this last question, missiologist C. Gordon Olson writes that if faith is a gift of God, then "one is forced to the conclusion that God is partial and loves Americans more than others."[16]

So we must conclude that faith is not a gift from God. There is no good reason to hold this idea. Therefore, since faith is not a gift from God, this means that anybody can believe in Jesus for eternal life. Even a little child. Of course, usually the more religious a person becomes, the harder it is for them to believe that God freely gives eternal life to anyone who simply and only believes in Him for it. This is why we can say that while faith in Jesus is simple, it is not easy. Most humans, especially those who are religious, want to add some of their own works and effort into the mix so that they can somehow earn eternal life from God. But they can't. Eternal life is a free gift, given to those who believe in Jesus for it. And some find this too hard to believe.

But once we break through the concepts of works-based righteousness and legalistic religion, faith in Jesus is quite simple. Anybody can believe in Him. God does not give some people the ability to believe in Jesus while denying this faith to others. No, faith is open and available to all. It is not a gift of God.[17] Each person is persuaded by the facts and ideas presented to them. And how is a person persuaded? If faith is not a gift, how does a person come to believe? It all begins with hearing the truth.

---

[16] Olson, *Beyond Calvinism and Arminianism*, 227.
[17] Cf. Wilkin, *The Ten Most Misunderstood Words*, 18-19.

CONCLUSION

Since there are numerous ways that faith is presented in churches and Christian books, it is important to understand what faith is and is not. This chapter sought to clear up six of the more popular misconceptions about faith. Hopefully you now believe something new about belief! Hopefully you are becoming persuaded and convinced about how faith works and what faith is. But to further aid your thinking in this matter, the next chapter looks at five additional clarifications about faith. By understanding these five clarifications, you will come to further understand the nature of faith and how to know that you believe.

CHAPTER 4

FIVE CLARIFICATIONS ABOUT FAITH

I still remember when I got my first pair of glasses. Prior to getting glasses, I didn't know I was half blind. I just figured that the world was perpetually blurry for everyone. I discovered this was not the case in my early teens when I started taking Driver's Education. As we were driving around, the instructor told me to take a left on Davis Street. So as I approached the next intersection, I slowed way down and squinted at the little green sign so I could read what it said. It was Elm Street. So I sped up a bit until I reached the next intersection, and slowed down again to read the sign. It also was not Davis. Finally, I found Davis Street at the third intersection and made a left.

But the instructor noticed what I had done, and pointed to a big sign a couple hundred yards down the road. He said, "As we get near that sign, tell me when you can read it." We got nearer and nearer to the sign, and finally, when I was about fifty feet away, I read the sign to him. In reply, he said, "Pull over!" Then he explained that I was half blind, and he would not let me drive again until I got some glasses.

I went home and told my parents, and the next day I had an exam with the eye doctor. A few days later we went to pick up my new glasses. When I walked out of the doctor's office, I was amazed at what I saw. Trees were no longer green blobs; I could actually see individual leaves fluttering in the wind! I could actually see birds flying through the sky! A whole new world had opened up to me. It was the same world I had always lived in, but now I could actually see it. Rather than the world being filled with colorful blobs, I now saw things clearly and with precision.

The same exact thing can happen with faith. Many people grow up with fuzzy thinking about faith, and so they are never quite sure whether or not they actually believe. Many of them are trying to drive around without being able to clearly see the signs on the road. This is dangerous to them, and to others. It is important to know *what* you believe, *why* you believe it, and also *that* you believe. This chapter provides five clarifications about faith which will help you in all these areas. The five truths considered below will clear up your faith vision so that you can better see to understand Scripture and follow Jesus.

FAITH COMES BY HEARING

The first clarification is how we come to believe anything in the first place, and more specifically, how we come to believe in Jesus for eternal life. There are a large variety of factors behind every individual belief. Our beliefs are influenced by life experiences, education level (more is not always better), and how much trust we give to the authority figures who teach us. But in all cases, before we can believe something, we must first hear the idea or fact that we are invited to believe. We cannot believe something if we have never heard it.

This is why Paul writes in Romans 10:17 that "faith comes by hearing." This is true of all beliefs. You cannot believe that 2+2=4 until you first hear this mathematical fact. But hearing a fact is not the same thing as believing it. To believe it, we also need to understand the idea presented and agree that it is true. We come to agree with a fact when we are persuaded or convinced by the evidence presented in favor of it. A math teacher might show that two black marbles and two white marbles can come together to make four marbles. This sort of evidence helps children believe, agree, and become convinced that 2+2=4.

It is the same with spiritual beliefs. We cannot believe something about God or some spiritual truth about ourselves, until and unless we first hear the truth presented to us, along with various arguments and ideas that might help us believe this truth. According to Paul, the Word of God is a primary source of hearing these truths (Rom 10:17), but we must also not forget about the illuminating work of the Holy Spirit, or the influence of other people who pass on to us what they themselves believe. So before a person can believe in Jesus for eternal life, they must first hear the truth about eternal life in Jesus Christ, and also come to be persuaded or convinced about the truth of this offer by the evidence provided to them.

Nevertheless, some people criticize the idea that people are called and invited to believe in Jesus for eternal life. They say that this requires humans to take the first step toward God before He takes a step toward them. But nothing could be further from the truth. God has always taken the first step toward us. Indeed, God has taken the first trillion steps. He provided revelation through creation, conscience, Scripture, dreams, visions, and angelic messengers.

Furthermore, He sent prophets, missionaries, pastors, teachers, and evangelists to share the Gospel. He sent Jesus to fully reveal the true character and nature of God to humanity (John 14:9; Col 1:15; Heb 1:3). He sent the Holy Spirit to convict the world of sin, righteousness, and judgment, and uses the Holy Spirit to draw all people to Himself (John 6:44; 12: 32; 16:7-11; Acts 16:14, 29-30; 24:25). He created us with reason, intellect, emotions, and will. He constantly sends forth His grace and mercy upon all people (John 1:9; Titus 2:11). He forgives all sin, and is patient, loving, and kind to all.

These steps, and countless more specific steps in the life of each and every person, are the sorts of things God has done on our behalf to call each of us to believe in Jesus for eternal life. Human faith, then, is not the first step, or even the millionth step, in the process of coming to God or believing in Jesus for eternal life.

When it comes to the question of who has taken the first step, the answer is clearly God. In fact, there is no step that God could take which He has not already taken or will not take. If God *can* take a step to help us believe in Jesus; He will take it. But the one step which God cannot take is the step of forcing us to believe. God does not force Himself on anybody. Instead, people are able to believe in Jesus for eternal life because God has first done absolutely everything that is within His power, made everything available to us by His grace, and flung open the door to eternal life by His will. It is only because of this multitude of "first steps" by God toward us that anyone and everyone who wants to receive God's offer of eternal life may do so by simply and only believing in Jesus Christ for it.

This leads to the second clarification about faith. Since faith comes by hearing and reasonably considering the truth presented to us, this means that faith occurs within the human mind. In other words, faith is mental assent.

FAITH IS MENTAL ASSENT

Have you ever been accused of having "false faith" or "dead faith" because some person says that you only have an "intellectual faith"? I have. Now I agree (as my wife attests) that I have a tendency to overthink and overanalyze almost everything. This book might be a perfect example. Few people have attempted to dissect and analyze how faith works as I have done in this book. When I talked to my wife about the content of this book, she told me, "In an attempt to understand faith, it's like you're dissecting a cat to understand it. But you will enjoy and understand a cat much more if you simply pet it while it sits on your lap and purrs."

She has a point. But at the same time, all animal lovers need to be thankful for the animal analyzers who study and research animals, and even dissect them, for this is the only reason we have veterinarians and medicines that help keep our beloved pets alive. It is the same with faith.

We must have people who think, analyze, study, read, research, and learn about what faith is and how faith works, for without such people, we would be tossed to and fro and carried about with every wind of doctrine (Eph 4:14).

And what we have so far seen about faith in this book is that faith truly does involve the mind. Faith uses the intellect; it *is* intellectual. Whether we realize it or not, all of our beliefs are based on reason, thinking, and analysis. Some people require more analysis than others, but nobody believes anything without first engaging in some sort of thought process about it. I challenge you to think of a single belief you have that you have not thought about in some way. You will not be able to find one, for you cannot believe anything without thinking about it intellectually to some degree or another.

Nevertheless, for some odd reason, people often discredit a "thinking" faith. Some argue that if you have to think about it, then it's not real faith. They say that people can miss heaven by 18 inches because they have a "head faith" instead of "heart faith." But no such terms or ideas are found in the Bible.[1] Others accuse people of having an "intellectual faith" which is only based on a "mental assent" to facts.

But isn't this exactly what faith *is*? Again, since faith occurs when we are convinced or persuaded that something is true, then this persuasion involves the mind. In other words, it is not wrong at all to say that faith is an intellectual assent to an idea or proposition, for that is exactly what faith *is*. Faith is being convinced or persuaded that a proposition is true. This is faith, and there is no other kind of faith. Faith is mental assent. Faith is intellectual.

In his book, *Beyond Doubt,* Shawn Lazar has an excellent summary of the types of things that can be believed.[2] He points out that you cannot believe physical objects, numbers, colors, or emotions, but you can believe in *statements* about such items. You can believe that a stone is heavy,

---
[1] Cf. Ibid., 11.
[2] Lazar, *Beyond Doubt*, 111-119.

but you cannot believe in the stone. You can believe that green is a combination of blue and yellow, but you cannot believe in green and yellow themselves. I believe that it makes me happy to drink coffee, but I do not believe in happiness itself. Furthermore, we can always believe (or not believe) promises and truth claims. If I promised to give you a $1 million, I hope you would not believe me. But since we know that Jesus never lies, we can believe anything and everything He says.

What this means is that beliefs are always based on propositions of things that might or might not be true. If we agree that a proposition is true, then we believe it. If we believe that a proposition is not true, then we do not believe it. If we are unsure about the truth of a proposition, then once again, we do not believe it. This means, therefore, that faith is propositional.[3] Sometimes people criticize others for having a "propositional faith" but in reality, there is no other kind. Faith is propositional. Faith is intellectual. Faith is mental assent.[4]

In fact, the word "assent" comes from the Latin word *assensus*, which can be translated as "assent, agree, approve, believe, or admit the truth of something." So mental assent is to admit or agree that something is true, which is exactly the definition of "faith" that has been defended throughout this book. And of course, such "assent" takes place in your mind, which means that "mental assent" is a good synonym for faith.

> Believing is not something you do with your body, but with your mind. Someone tells you that "Canada is north of Mexico" and you *think* about what the proposition means. You weigh the evidence for and against it, you consider other possibilities, and ultimately, you come to a conclusion about whether it is true or false. You're either persuaded in your mind that the proposition is true, or you aren't. That's what faith is.[5]

The reason this is so important is because some people criticize the idea of "faith alone in Jesus Christ alone for eternal life" as a teaching

---

[3] Ibid., 117.
[4] Cf. Wilkin, *The Ten Most Misunderstood Words*, 10-11.
[5] Lazar, *Beyond Doubt*, 119.

that requires nothing more than "mental or intellectual assent" to some facts about Jesus." When I hear this, I am glad, for they have properly understood that faith is nothing more than mental assent. No works, trust, actions, or effort is involved. In order to believe something, you must understand what is being said, and you must agree, or assent, to the stated proposition.[6] Since belief is a persuasion or conviction that something is true based on the evidence provided, to "believe something" is another way of saying you "mentally assent" to it, that is, you understand and agree with it. So the next time someone accuses you of "just teaching mental assent" agree with them, for this is exactly right.

This is why the Bible includes so many facts and persuasive arguments about these facts. These historical facts and arguments are included so that we might be persuaded and convinced in our minds that what we read is true. God, through Scripture, wants us to give mental assent to what we read. When the biblical authors set out to teach what God wanted us to know, they did not simply lay out the facts and say "Just believe it!" Instead, along with the ideas we are to believe, they presented evidence.

Luke, for example, wrote that he was presenting a history of Jesus Christ (Luke 1:1-4) so that the reader could investigate these ideas and know with certainty that they were true. Similarly, when Paul set out to teach the Corinthian believers about the resurrection of Jesus, he didn't simply tell them to believe it, but instead presented rational arguments and eye-witness testimony about the resurrection so that they might be persuaded and convinced of what he wrote.

All the biblical authors (and therefore God Himself as the One who inspired the authors) wrote in a way that encourages people to think and reason about the ideas presented, so that they come to understand and agree with what is read. Those who engage with Scripture in this way are praised for doing so (cf. Acts 17:11).

[6] Cf. Ibid., 108.

So faith is mental assent. There is no other kind of faith than an intellectual faith. But if faith involves reason, investigation, and mental assent to the facts, then what does the Bible mean when it refers to childlike faith? This is the next clarification we consider.

FAITH LIKE A CHILD

Some Christians say that they don't need reasons or explanations for what they believe, because they have "faith like a child" or "childlike faith." When they say this, they mean that they don't ask questions about their beliefs, nor do they wonder if what they believe is true. Childlike faith is often described as a faith that does not doubt, question, or seek explanations; it just believes. But this is not childlike faith. So what is?

In seeking to understand what childlike faith *actually* is, let us look at four reasons why the lack of desire to ask questions is not "childlike faith."

First, while it is completely fine if a person does not *want* to ask questions about what they believe or seek answers about *why* they believe what they do, they should not look down upon those who do ask questions. Nor should they prohibit people from doing so. Some who claim to have "childlike faith" wear it as a badge of honor, seeming to indicate to others that their unquestioning faith is superior to those who ask questions and seek explanations.

For this reason, "childlike faith" could actually be called "arrogant faith" for those who claim to have it sometimes look down on those who require reason, logic, and explanations for what they believe. People who have this attitude will often say "I just believe the Bible" or "God says it, I believe it, that settles it." In reality, they don't "just believe the Bible." They believe a particular interpretation or explanation of the Bible, and often claim to "just believe the Bible" when someone comes along and presents a different perspective or explanation.

When faith is thought of as "blind faith" or a "leap into the void" in a way that does not require reason, logic, or explanation, those who are able to maintain this sort of faith sometimes have the tendency to look down on those who require reason, logic, and explanation for their beliefs. Of course, the opposite is also true. People who use reason and logic to support their beliefs often condemn those who don't for having an "ignorant and uneducated faith." This is not good either.

So if a person does not want to ask questions, there is no requirement to do so. Many people do not enjoy the "life of the mind" and should not be expected to engage in such practices. However, this preference should not be equated with childlike faith. Those who do not seek to dive deep into theology and seek answers to questions should not look down on those who do seek such answers as having a "lesser faith" (and *vice versa*). We will see below that both types of people can have childlike faith. So rather than say that a faith which does not question is "childlike faith" it might be better to simply call it an unquestioning faith.

This is the second reason that childlike faith cannot be equated with the lack of desire to ask questions. Childlike faith is not about the avoidance of questions, for children ask many, many questions. As any parent will tell you, the unrelenting barrage of questions from a two-year old can become quite exhausting. Therefore, it could easily be argued that true "childlike faith" is actually a faith that asks *lots* of questions. So the desire (or lack of desire) to ask questions has nothing to do with whether or not a person has childlike faith.

The third reason that a faith which does not ask question or seek explanations cannot be called "childlike faith" is because there are explanations and reasons for what a child believes … even if they themselves are not aware of what those reasons are. In other words, children do not believe anything without reason. The most common reason that children believe what they believe is because someone they trust told them what to believe. Children often simply believe whatever their parents and teachers tell them. This is not an unthinking faith, for the authority of the person who teaches is a factor that faith takes into consideration.

Something similar occurs whenever a person has a so-called "unquestioning faith." They do not believe without reason; they simply have not thought through what the reasons and explanations for their beliefs might be. They believe what a pastor or teacher taught them, or what seems to be the "plain reading" of Scripture (though careful, contextual studies of the text often reveal that the "plain reading" is not the best reading). There is nothing wrong with not knowing exactly *why* you have the beliefs you have, but a lack of understanding about *why* should not be confused with a lack of explanation. There *are* explanations for why you believe what you believe, even if you don't know what these explanations are.

And that's okay. Nobody has a complete explanation and understanding for why they believe what they believe. But everybody, over time, naturally and normally grows in their understanding and gains explanations for their beliefs. While initially, a belief might be gained because "I learned it in Kindergarten," this belief will either remain unquestioned and unchallenged throughout life, or it will be challenged and questioned. If it is challenged and questioned, the belief will either be supported and affirmed, or disproven and denied. But nobody's beliefs all stay the same throughout all of life. Instead, everybody matures and grows in what they think and believe. This is normal, natural, and just as God intended. Just as children grow and mature, so also does faith. This is the way God made humans, and this is the way God made faith.

Which brings up the fourth and final reason that unquestioning faith cannot be equated with childlike faith. And it is this: "childlike faith" is not found in the Bible. There is no such thing as biblical "childlike faith." When people refer to "childlike faith" or "faith like a child," they have in mind the sorts of things Jesus says in Matthew 18:3, Mark 10:14, and Luke 18:17, where He teaches that the kingdom of heaven belongs to little children. But in these passages, Jesus isn't talking about faith. In fact, He doesn't mention "faith" at all. Instead, Jesus is talking about entering the kingdom of heaven, and He encourages His listeners to humble themselves like a child and receive Him like a child (Matt 18:4-5; Mark 10:14) if they want to see the kingdom of heaven. In other words, there is something essential about the childlike perspective for the person who wants to see the kingdom of heaven.

But what is Jesus talking about? What is this childlike perspective that Jesus has in mind?

To begin with, it is critical to recognize that the kingdom of heaven is not eternal life. The phrase "see the kingdom of heaven" does not mean "go to heaven when you die." "Seeing the kingdom of heaven" is not the same thing as "going to heaven." These two concepts are not equivalent in the Bible. It is important that we recognize this, because Jesus says that seeing the kingdom of heaven requires humility. If seeing the kingdom of heaven was the same as going to heaven, then the good work of personal humility would be required for entrance into heaven after death. But eternal life is received by faith alone in Jesus Christ alone (John 3:16; 5:24; 6:47); not by living humbly before God. Good works are not required to gain entrance into heaven.

What then is the kingdom of heaven? In the Gospels, the phrase "kingdom of heaven" or "kingdom of God" refers to the rule and reign of God in our lives *now* on earth. It is about God's will being done on earth, as it is done in heaven (Matt 6:10). All the kingdom imagery and terminology in the Gospels is not about "leaving earth and going to heaven when we die" but about "heaven coming down to earth while we live." Seeing the kingdom of heaven is not about life after death, but about living and experiencing God's life in *this life* here and now.

This is what Jesus has in mind when He teaches about becoming like a little child. Experiencing the life of God in this life requires humility like a little child. In what way? Not by remaining ignorant, for God gave us Scripture so that we might learn, grow, mature, reason (Isa 1:18), and become students, disciples, and followers of Jesus Christ (Matt 28:19-20;

2 Tim 2:2). Instead, becoming like a little child means that we maintain the wonderful and beautiful characteristics and qualities of children that life in this sinful world tends to beat out of us.

Like what?

Like tenderness of conscience. Openness about emotions and feelings. Creativity and imagination.[7] Wonder and awe. Joy. Eternal hope. Playfulness and humor. Trust. Easy forgiveness. Undying love. Boundless exuberance and energy. Always thinking the best about life and other people. Being willing to learn and grow. These are the sort of qualities that tend to define children, but which get stripped out of people as they encounter the sin and brokenness of this world.

As adults, we get bored with flowers, bugs, and sunsets. We lose delight in talking with others about nothing. We become jaded and disinterested. Adults hold grudges, harbor fears, and stay angry. Adults refuse to forgive. Adults remember slights. Adults lose hope because their hopes have been dashed and destroyed so many time. Adults do things "because they've always been done that way" and have trouble imagining anything different.

But children do not behave in any of these ways. Nor did Jesus. One of the things that attracted people to Jesus is that He was "childlike." Does this mean He lacked wisdom and understanding? Far from it. Jesus was "childlike" because He was full of the wonder of life, the hope for humanity, and the beauty of creation. Jesus lived in awe of life, awe of God, and awe of humanity.

And this awe was contagious. People who saw how Jesus lived began to see how life should be lived. Jesus revealed how God intended life to be lived. In other words, those who begin to live life like Jesus are those who begin to see heaven come down to earth. They begin to see the rule and reign of God unfold in their own life with all its beauty, majesty, glory, and creativity. This is what Jesus Himself lived, and this is what Jesus invited others to live also. He taught that if you want to experience

---

[7] Cf. Gregory Boyd, *Seeing is Believing* (Grand Rapids: Baker, 2004) and Walter Brueggemann, *The Prophetic Imagination* (Minneapolis: Augsburg Fortress, 2001).

God's life in this life (the kingdom of heaven), then you need to become like a little child once again.

So yes, ask questions. Lots of questions. But also have fun. Laugh. Play. Imagine. Sing. Dance. Hope. Dream. Forgive. Create. Trust. Live life to the full. Be excited. Be adventuresome. Be tender of heart. And most of all, love. When you live this way, you will become like a little child, and will see the kingdom of heaven rise again in your life.

FAITH AND "THE FAITH"

The fourth clarification about faith is the difference between "faith" and "the faith." There are various texts in the New Testament which include the definite article "the" before the noun "faith" (called the *articular* use). Most often in the Greek New Testament, the word "faith" appears without the definite article (called the *anarthrous* use). When the word "faith" does not have the article "the" in front of it, the word can be understood as defined and explained in this book.

However, there are several texts in the New Testament which include the definite article before the noun. Most English Bibles translate this phrase as "the faith" (cf. Acts 6:7; 13:8; 14:22; 16:5; Rom 1:5; 1 Cor 16:13; 2 Cor 13:5; Gal 1:23; 3:23; 6:10; Eph 4:13; Php 1:25-27; Col 1:23; 1 Tim 3:9-4:6; 5:8; 6:10, 21; 2 Tim 2:18; 3:8; 4:7; Titus 1:13; Jude 3). If we try to understand these texts as referring to "a persuasion or conviction that something is true" many of them will not make sense. In a few places, the New Testament even seems to contrast "faith" with "the faith" by sometimes including various good works and acts of obedience with "the faith" (e.g., Acts 6:7; 14:22; Rom 1:5; 1 Cor 16:13; 2 Cor 13:5).

It is better, therefore, to recognize that the articular use of faith in the Greek New Testament does not refer to "faith" or "belief" itself, but to the belief *system* of Christianity. In other words, while "faith" refers to the conviction that a particular statement is true, "the faith" refers to all the beliefs and behaviors which comprise basic Christianity. So "the faith" is a shorthand way for New Testament writers to speak about "the Christian faith." This is similar to how we might talk and write about "the Buddhist faith," or "the Muslim faith." All such terms are shorthand ways of referring to the traditions, beliefs, practices, and behaviors that are included within those individual "religions."[8]

So while "faith" can be defined as a persuasion or conviction that something is true, the articular term "the faith" refers more comprehensively to all the fundamental Christian teachings and practices that separate followers of Jesus from followers of some other teacher or world religion. "'The faith' is the body of truth that has been delivered to us from God."[9] Therefore, "the faith" is a phrase used to describe the comprehensive system of basic Christian creed and conduct. It refers to what Christians teach in regard to both beliefs and behaviors. This understanding helps make sense of most of the New Testament texts which refer to "the faith." A few of these texts will be examined more closely in the following chapter.

FAITH AND FAITHFULNESS

The final clarification about faith that needs to be made is how it differs from the word faithfulness. The reason this is important is because there are numerous authors and teachers today who argue that the biblical concept of "faith" is better understood as "faithfulness," and therefore, it does not primarily refer to what a person knows to be true in their minds, but instead to how a person lives over the course of their life. As a result, these authors argue that the term "faith" in the Bible more rightly

---

[8] I don't consider Christianity *a religion*, but there was no better term to describe it in comparison to the various other world religions.

[9] Robert N. Wilkin, *Secure and Sure: Grasping the Promises of God* (Irving, TX: Grace Evangelical Society, 2005), 101.

refers to loyalty, allegiance, or ongoing obedience.[10] In light of this idea, such authors teach that we receive eternal life from God, not by believing in Jesus for it, but by living a life of faithfulness, allegiance, and obedience to Jesus.

For numerous reasons, it does not seem best to understand the word "faith" (Gk., *pistis*) as "faithfulness." While there does initially seem to be some evidence for this understanding in various biblical and extrabiblical contexts, such a view opens the door for a works-based approach to gaining, proving, or keeping our eternal life, and so should be rejected. After all, if *pistis* can sometimes refer to allegiance, loyalty, or ongoing obedience, then there is nothing to stop someone from saying that most references to faith in the New Testament carry this idea, and therefore, eternal life is not gained by simply believing in Jesus for it, but instead by living loyally and obediently to Him. This is indeed what some argue.[11]

Yet once we properly understand that faith is a conviction or persuasion that something is true, we are then positioned to better understand the various texts in English Bibles which translate *pistis* as faithfulness. When studied in their contexts, we see that these controversial passages do not require for *pistis* to refer to loyalty, allegiance, or ongoing obedience, but could instead refer to a persistent and ongoing faith (Matt 23:23; Rom 3:3; Gal 5:22; Titus 2:10). Remember, faith is like a light switch. When it comes to the various truths we can believe, faith is either "On" or "Off." If it stays "On" for a long time, then it is persistent faith.

Not all beliefs stay "On" all the time. We often change our beliefs due to new evidence that is presented to us. Sometimes we change our beliefs as we learn more about God through Scripture and in fellowship with other believers. In such instances, we turn away from falsehood and embrace the truth, so that our network of beliefs comes to more closely match what is actually true. We can also stray from the truth and fall into

---

[10] See, for example, Michael W. Bates, *Salvation by Allegiance Alone: Rethinking Faith, Works, and the Gospel of Jesus the King* (Grand Rapids: Baker, 2017).

[11] Ibid.

dangerous and unhealthy teachings. It is not uncommon for true believers to fall prey to false teaching so that they come to deny the truth and turn instead toward lies and deceptive ideas. But as long as a Christian maintains a belief in what is actually true, their belief is persistent. This persistent faith is which Scripture invites us to strive and long for. Therefore, the texts that seem to require a translation of "faithfulness" are not referring to allegiance and obedience, but to this ongoing and persistent faith.[12] It is a faith that remains.

This is even true when the Bible refers to the faith of God or the faith of Jesus. It is not necessary to understand these texts as referring to the faithfulness of God or the faithfulness of Jesus. Since faith is the knowledge, conviction, or persuasion that something is true, then it is obvious that both God and Jesus can have faith. Indeed, the Trinitarian God is the only being in the universe who has perfect faith. All other beings in the universe do not have perfect knowledge of all things, and therefore, do not believe or know all things. Only God's faith is eternally perfect and persistent. Since faith or belief is the conviction that something is true, God knows everything that is true, and therefore, believes it and will always believe it.

Furthermore, He even has faith toward us. He knows what is true about us, even when we do not (Rom 3:3-4). He also knows what *will be* true about us, and He speaks these things to us so that we might be inspired by His testimony toward us to believe these things as well. God wants us to live as He sees us; not as we see ourselves. God believes in us and invites us to believe in Him so that together, our belief will bring God's vision of the future into reality.

This understanding helps clarify some of the tricky texts which seem to require "faithfulness" as a translation of *pistis*. Such texts do not refer to allegiance or ongoing obedience, but to an ongoing and persistent belief. And this belief can lead to other beliefs as well. For example, once we

---

[12] Besides, when various biblical authors *do* want to refer to loyalty or allegiance, there are perfectly fine Greek words which they can (and do) use to refer to these concepts. We must let faith remain faith and stop trying to add works into it.

have believed in Jesus for eternal life, this does not mean that faith has no more place in the life of the believer. Just as we have received Jesus Christ, so also we must continue to walk with Him (Col 2:6). And how is it that we received Jesus? By faith. So we are to continue our life with Him by faith as well.

This is not only true because ongoing faith gives us the best life possible with Jesus, but also because other truths we can believe depend on continuing to believe previous truths. Remember that all of our beliefs are interconnected like a vast Excel spreadsheet. Many of the more advanced truths and ideas on this spreadsheet will not be discovered and cannot be believed unless we maintain our belief in some of the earlier, foundational truths. In other words, future faith builds upon our former faith. Believing simple and elementary things allows us to later believe more difficult and hard things. This is what Paul means when it talks about going from "faith to faith" (cf. Rom 1:17) and when he refers to faith as a fruit of the Spirit (Gal 5:22). As we walk with God in faith and by the Spirit, we grow in our faith and come to believe things that draw us closer to God and make us more like Jesus.

So regardless of which stage of faith we are talking about, faith does not involve ongoing obedience. Faith does not begin with simple belief and then end with allegiance and loyalty. There are no works in faith, for faith is the opposite of works. While faith can lead to works, the presence or absence of works do not necessarily indicate anything one way or another about a person's faith. In all cases, faith is simply being persuaded and convinced about what we have been told. When we believe in Jesus for eternal life, we are persuaded that Jesus, as the author and finisher of our faith, loves us, forgives us, and freely grants eternal life to us, not because of anything we have done but simply and only because of God's grace toward us. No commitment to allegiance or ongoing obedience are required. Therefore, the word *pistis* is not ever properly translated as "faithfulness."[13]

CONCLUSION

With these five clarifications about faith, we have now put on our faith glasses and can see life and Scripture more clearly. We can be less fuzzy in our thinking about faith and can see the individual leaves on the trees of various verses. Many of the passages which previously caused confusion and consternation about whether we have the right faith or enough faith are now easily understood. This is what the next chapter reveals as we turn to consider several key biblical texts about faith.

---

[13] I might be fine with "faithfulness" if it was understood to refer to an ongoing or persistent faith. But since few think of "faithfulness" this way, it is best to not translate *pistis* as faithfulness.

CHAPTER 5

UNDERSTANDING SCRIPTURES ON FAITH

Now that we understand what faith is and is not, and have considered several misconceptions and clarifications about faith, we are now in a position to better understand many tricky biblical texts that refer to faith. Some of these texts have created numerous problems in church history and have caused many Christians great amounts of consternation and fear. If this is true of you, then this final chapter will be helpful. When your understanding about faith is cleared up by the ideas found in this book, your fear about faith is also cleared away. You will understand what the Bible teaches about faith and that your faith rests on a firm foundation.

This chapter does not contain a comprehensive examination of all the verses in the Bible that mention faith. Instead, the Scriptures considered below are representative of the types of passages the Bible contains about faith. By using what we have learned about faith in this book and by seeing how this understanding better helps us grasp the meaning of various biblical texts which mention faith, you will be able to comprehend any other passage about faith as well. Let us begin by looking at Abraham, the "Father of Faith."

GENESIS 12 AND 15

And he believed in the LORD, and He accounted it to him
for righteousness
(Gen 15:6).

Genesis 12 and 15 reveal truths about faith by presenting the faith of Abraham.[1] And since Abraham is "the Father of Faith" (or maybe "the Father of Our Faith") these two chapters in Genesis are foundational for understanding faith. Since the faith of Abraham is so important in Scripture, it is no surprise that Abraham's faith is mentioned in so many contexts. Stephen praises Abraham's faith in Acts 7:2-8. Paul praises the faith of Abraham in Romans 4 and Galatians 3. The author of Hebrews places great emphasis on the faith of Abraham in Hebrews 11, the "Hall of Faith." And James connects Abraham's faith with Abraham's obedience in James 2:21-24 (a passage that will be considered below). Therefore, since Abraham provides the premier example of faith in the Bible, it is important to understand what he believed and how his faith worked.

It is important to begin where the faith of Abraham began. Many people believe that Abraham was just minding his own business when God showed up and told him to go to Canaan, so Abraham got up and went. In light of this, we say "What amazing faith! Abraham didn't know much about God, but God told him to go, so he got up and went! He never doubted; he never questioned; he never looked back." But the truth is that this is not what happened at all. Abraham's faith worked just like ours.

To many, the story of Abraham begins in Genesis 12:1 when God comes to him and says "Get up and go." Most think that when Abraham heard God's instructions at age seventy-five, he believed what God said and immediately departed Haran for Canaan (Gen 12:4). But some careful study of the text reveals something else entirely. There are seven key insights about Abraham's faith we can learn from these chapters.

First of all, Genesis 12 does not make any mention of Abraham's faith. The faith of Abraham is not mentioned until Genesis 15:6. So although Abraham does depart Haran and travel to Canaan in Genesis 12:4, there is nothing from the text that indicates Abraham did this because he believed what God said. We don't know what he believed.

---
[1] For the sake of consistency, I will refer to him as "Abraham" even though his name was not changed until Genesis 17:5.

Second, the call of God in Genesis 12 to get up and go is not the first time God had said this to Abraham. In fact, God initially called Abraham many years before, when he was living in Ur. According to Joshua 24:2, Abraham was an idol-worshiper when he lived in Ur, and Stephen says in Acts 7:2-4 that it was when Abraham lived in Ur that God first told him to leave his country and relatives and go to a new land. And though it appears that Abraham did get up and go, he did not leave his family. Instead, he took his father, Terah, and his nephew, Lot, with him. Furthermore, he didn't go to Canaan. Instead, he only traveled to Haran, which was northwest of Ur.

We do not know how long Abraham lived in Haran before God told him *again* to follow God where He would lead. But the evidence seems to indicate that once again, Abraham did not believe and obey. Though God told Abraham to leave his father and his relatives, Abraham waited in Haran until his father died (Gen 11:31-32; Acts 7:4). I do not think it true obedience to "leave your father" if you wait until your father leaves you by dying. Regardless, when Abraham is seventy-five years old, he finally sets out to see where God is leading him.

Third, when Abraham finally arrives in Canaan, the land where God was leading him, one of the first things he does is leave for Egypt (Gen 12:10-20). He does not seem to believe that God will be able to provide for him in this land, even though God led him here. For all we know, the famine in Canaan which caused Abraham to leave for Egypt might actually have been the means by which Abraham could have gained large sections of Canaan for himself and his family. But since Abraham fled to Egypt, the only land which God ever "gave" to Abraham was a small burial plot which Abraham purchased at great expense as a burial plot for Sarah (Gen 23:15-16).[2]

Fourth, even when Abraham's faith is finally mentioned in Genesis 15:6, Abraham still asks for evidence from God so that he can believe

---

[2] I am not saying, nor does the text, that God sent the famine.

what God has said. Abraham doesn't place blind faith in God, but wants proof. He basically says, "How shall I know that what you are saying is true?" (Gen 15:8). This is not wrong, since faith often depends on evidence, but it is certainly not the blind faith that many attribute to Abraham. Beyond this, Abraham is now around 85 years old (Gen 16:16) and had been journeying with God for over ten years. He had seen how God provided for him and protected him, and yet even now, when he finally believes what God says, he asks for evidence to support and confirm his belief.

Fifth, and maybe most significantly, Abraham's faith did not keep him from frequent doubt and sin. For example, even though his father, Tereh, had sired Abraham when Terah was 130, Abraham wondered if God could let him have a child when he was 100.[3] And when it comes to sin, many of the moral failures Abraham committed before he believed are identical to the moral failures he committed after he believed. Abraham lied about his wife and put her in danger both before and after he believed (Gen 12:10-20; 20:1-18). Furthermore, it is only *after* Abraham believed that he slept with his wife's maidservant, Hagar. People who say that "true and genuine faith leads to a changed life and a perseverance in good works" cannot point to Abraham, the father of faith, as an example. Abraham's faith did not necessarily lead to better actions and morality.

Of course, there is one action that is said to reveal Abraham's faith most clearly, and it is the action he is most known for: the near-sacrifice of Isaac on the altar in Genesis 22. This is the sixth truth we learn about Abraham's faith. We are not exactly sure how old Abraham was when he set out for Mount Moriah, but since Isaac was "a lad" (Gen 22:5) this likely means that Isaac was at least ten years old,[4] making Abraham at least 110 (Gen 21:5). So this great act of faith came 25 years after Abraham initially believed in God and was justified, and at least 35 years after

---

[3] See this article for an explanation of the numbers and what Abraham was possibly thinking: https://www.apologeticspress.org/ apcontent.aspx?category=6&article=665. Last Accessed Mach 31, 2018.

[4] He could not have been older than 36 (Gen 17:17; 21:5; 23:1).

Abraham initially started following God. This is not what we call an immediate, life-changing transformation where a person who was an idol-worshiper one day is a committed and devoted follower of God the next. No, this was a 35-year journey with God, full of false starts, doubts, questions, fears, and moral failures. Just like our life.

The father of faith in the Bible reveals that faith is not monumental, all-inclusive, once-for-all conviction to follow and obey God no matter what. To the contrary, faith is about taking one little step at a time with God, and often in a way that includes backward steps as well. Faith requires time to build and grow. Faith requires evidence and experience. Faith allows for the setbacks of sin and moral failure. This is just like our faith as well. Abraham is the father of faith, not because he had such amazing faith, but because he shows us what faith looks like and how faith works.[5]

Seventh, note something else about Abraham's faith. We are told in Genesis 15 that Abraham believed God and God credited him with righteousness (Gen 15:6). But Abraham doesn't look or act much like a righteous believer for the next several chapters. Therefore, some argue that the "proof" or "evidence" of Abraham's justification is found in Genesis 22 where he nearly sacrifices his son, Isaac, on an altar. Those who hold this view often use James 2:21-24 as support.

James 2 will be discussed in more detail later in this chapter, but note for now that no action of Abraham in Genesis 22 gives proof or evidence that he was in fact declared righteous by God, or that he had believed in God 25 years earlier. To the contrary, Hebrews 11:17-19 reveals that when Abraham offered his son Isaac on the altar, he did this because he believed that God could raise Isaac from the dead. This is a completely different belief than the belief of Abraham in Genesis 15.

In Genesis 15, Abraham believed that God would give him descendants that outnumber the stars, whereas in Genesis 22, Abraham believed

---

[5] We can also say that Abraham is the father of faith in that he is the father of "the faith." In other words, he is the founder of the Jewish faith.

that God could raise Isaac from the dead. On the Excel spreadsheet of belief, these are two completely different cells. Certainly, the second is connected to, or depends upon, the first.ABraham knew that before he could have a multitude of descendants, he first had to have one descendant. And while he initially tried to obtain this first descendant through Hagar, this was not part of God's initial plan, and so Abraham eventually had Isaac as well.

So when Abraham was told to sacrifice Isaac, Abraham's new belief—that God would raise Isaac from the dead—was based upon his previous belief, that God would give Abraham many descendants. The two beliefs are connected, but they are not the same beliefs. This reveals that even with Abraham, there was an interconnected network of beliefs that changed and grew as Abraham matured in his relationship with God.

But since this is true, what exactly did Abraham believe in Genesis 15? People sometimes wonder how Abraham could have been justified by God when it appears that all he believed was that he would have descendants that outnumbered the stars. According to the New Testament, however, people are justified, or receive eternal life, when they believe in Jesus for it. Abraham clearly could not have believed in Jesus (for the birth of Jesus was still 2000 years in the future), but it also does not appear that Abraham believed that a future Messiah was coming. In other words, there is no indication in the text that Abraham believed what God said *about a Messiah who would give eternal life*. Instead, Abraham believed what God said, namely, that he would have many descendants. How is this justifying faith? Can someone be justified by believing any random truth from God, whether or not it has anything to do with righteousness received through faith in Jesus?

The answer to this question is that Abraham knew more than we think and more than the Bible records. We know this because Jesus Himself says that "Abraham rejoiced to see My day; he saw it and was glad" (John 8:56). What did Jesus mean by this? We don't really know, and neither did the Jews in His day (John 8:57). Some speculate that when the text says that the LORD appeared to Abraham (Gen 12:7), it was actually Jesus who appeared to him. Others posit that Melchizedek was actually a pre-incarnate Jesus (cf. Gen 14:18-24; Heb 7:1-4). Others think that one of the three men who visited Abraham might have been Jesus (Gen 18:1-33). The truth, however, is we don't really know what Jesus meant when He said that Abraham had seen His day. It does reveal to us, however, that Abraham knew more than the biblical text records, and that somehow, Abraham truly did know Jesus.

I also believe that Abraham would have been familiar with the story of Adam and Eve, especially since the original Eden was likely in the same region as Ur. Therefore, Abraham would have known about the promised seed of the woman who would crush the head of the serpent and restore humanity to our rightful place within this world (Gen 3:15). It is quite possible that Abraham saw his calling by God as the next step in the fulfilment of this prophecy. Therefore, whatever Abraham believed about a coming Messiah, or however it was that he saw the day of Jesus, it is quite likely that Abraham believed that God was somehow going to fix the problems of this world through the child that would come from him and Sarah. He might not have known exactly how, but he believed what God said, and as a result, God credited him with righteousness.

Since Abraham is the father of faith, with all of his struggles, failures, doubts, and yes, successes, it is no surprise to see a similar blending of faith and doubt, success and failure, all the way throughout the stories of Scripture. So when you see similar struggles in your own life, this does not mean that your faith is weak or that you have false faith. Quite to the contrary, it means that your faith is perfectly normal, and that God is patiently walking by your side, just as He did with Abraham, calling you to take one more step with Him. Don't give up on Him, because He has not given up on you. Believe in Him and what He says, because He believes in you.

These same themes of faith are found throughout the rest of the Hebrew Scriptures, and so rather than look at several other similar examples, let us turn instead to the New Testament to see what we can learn about faith from the teachings of Jesus and the writings of the apostles.

MATTHEW 6:30

Now if God so clothes the grass of the field, which today is, and tomorrow is thrown into the oven, will He not much more clothe you, O you of little faith?

Matthew 6:30 causes some people to fear that they do not have enough faith or the right kind of faith in order to please God. The reason for this fear is that Jesus talks about those who have "little faith." The theme of "great faith" versus "little faith" is compared and contrasted throughout the Gospel of Matthew (8:10 vs. 8:26; 9:22-24; 14:31 vs. 15:28; 16:8; 17:20; 21:21) and so it is important to understand what is meant by this term "little faith."[6]

The concepts of little faith and great faith were discussed in a previous chapter, but a short summary will be helpful here.

Little faith and great faith is not about having more or less faith, or a higher percentage or degree of faith. Faith does not work like that. We can either believe something or not believe it. When it comes to an individual statement or proposition, we either believe it or not. In our Excel spreadsheet of beliefs, the cell is either "On" or "Off." Yet some of the statements in these cells are easy to believe, while others are more difficult. The propositions of quantum physics are much harder to understand and believe than the basic mathematical fact that 2+2=4.

This applies to theology as well. On the scale of difficult theological truths, it is easier to believe that "I exist" than it is to believe that "God exists." It is easier to believe that "A man named Jesus existed" than it is

---

[6] For an excellent explanation of the difference between great faith and little faith, see Bob Wilkin, "Should We Rethink the Idea of Degrees of Faith?" *JOTGES* (Fall, 20016), https://faithalone.org/ journal/2006ii/01%20Wilkin%20-%20great%20faith.pdf Last Accessed April 2, 2008.

to believe that "This Jesus is God." As you can see, each theological proposition has a relative level of difficulty. It is this relative level of difficulty that Jesus is referring to when He talks about little faith and great faith. Those who have little faith do not believe some of the relatively simple truths, whereas those who have great faith believe things that are more difficult to believe and which almost nobody believes. This is what we see from Matthew 6:30.

To begin with, it is important to note that Jesus is not teaching about how to receive eternal life, or any related concept. He is teaching about God's protection and provision for His disciples. As evidence of this provision, Jesus points to God's tender care for sparrows and flowers (Matt 6:25-30). Since God feeds the birds and clothes the lilies, will not also God feed and clothe the disciples? In other words, the evidence is all around the disciples that God will feed and clothe them. They are not asked to believe such a thing in spite of the evidence, but in light of it. Yet the disciples do not believe this, and so Jesus chides them for having "little faith." Instead of believing, they worry about tomorrow and wonder if God will provide.

If we are honest, nearly all of us have "little faith" in this regard. After all, we have plenty of evidence to support our lack of faith. If we really look at the birds of the air and lilies of the field as Jesus instructs, the picture is not as rosy as He presents it. Millions of birds suffer and die each and every day around the world. They are killed by cats, slaughtered for food, broken by storms, hit by cars, fly into closed windows, and drop dead from disease. It's worse with plants. Innumerable plants and flowers die every day from fire, harvest, disease, drought, and human carelessness.

So while there truly is much evidence that God cares for these parts of His creation, this does not mean that all birds and plants live happy, healthy, carefree, and pain-free lives. God's creation is "red in tooth and claw"[7] and often gets damaged through famine and fire. Therefore, it is understandable that we humans often doubt God's ability or desire to care for us. Indeed, when we look at billions of people starving all over the world, and millions of people dying from war and famine, the evidence against Jesus' words seems to be stronger than the evidence in favor.

I was once conducting a Bible study with some non-Christian friends when we came to this passage. I had previously told them that they did not need to believe what they were reading, but should only consider what the Bible was saying, and react honestly to it. Several of the people in this group had experienced great pain and difficulties in life, and had abandoned or rejected God as a result. So when they read these words of Jesus, one of them said, "This is bull$#!t. Look at all the people dying overseas. Look at the girls being sold into sex slavery. Look at the people starving in Africa or even here in our own country. If I had been there listening to Jesus when He said this, I would have called Him out on it."

My friend had a good point and I told him so. Most Christians are too afraid to honestly say what they think about some of what they read in the Bible (or even to think honestly about the Bible). This is why it is so refreshing to study the Bible with non-Christians. If you ever get the chance to attend a Bible study with atheists, I highly recommend it. They feel the freedom to speak their mind and object to what they read. By allowing their unbiased eyes to see what our biased eyes cannot, you gain great insight into some of the difficult texts of Scripture.

I wish an atheist had been around when Jesus spoke the words of Matthew 6:30. I wish someone listening to Jesus had objected to what He said. Of all the questions the disciples asked Jesus, why didn't one of them ask Jesus for some clarification about this statement? The idea that God will care for us as He cares for birds and plants is just not very reassuring. Jesus says we have "little faith" if we don't believe God will provide for us, and yet the evidence Jesus presents seems to pretty clearly

---

[7] See the poem "In Memoriam" by Alfred, Lord Tennyson.

show that God will not always protect and provide for us. Why didn't the disciples push back? Why didn't Peter raise his hand and say, "Eh … Jesus … you may want to rethink your analogy. Remember what we saw on our way here this morning? There was that nest of dead baby birds on the ground. Did God take care of them? Then there was that donkey eating all those flowers. What about them?"

But nobody asked, and so no clarification was offered.

Yet there was a later follower of Jesus who does seem to have asked this question. Better yet, he seems to have an answer to this question as well, and he wrote about it in Scripture. But before we look at who this was and what he learned, let us first see what we can learn from Jesus.

We must begin by recognizing that since Jesus so clearly *seems* to be wrong about God's care and provision, this can only mean that *we* are wrong in how we have understood Him. Jesus is never wrong; but we often are wrong in how we understand His words. So we must assume that in this instance, we have misunderstood what Jesus is teaching about the protection and provision of God. Let us consider three insights from the text that will help us better understand the words of Jesus.

First, much of the Sermon on the Mount falls into the biblical genre of "Wisdom Literature." Wisdom Literature never provides universal rules for how life *always* works. It instead presents general principles and themes that help us navigate through life. Much like the book of Proverbs, this sermon by Jesus provides broad overarching principles about how life works in the kingdom of God. So the teaching about God's provision and protection is a general principle, not a universal rule.

Second, note that this protection and provision is only in reference to food and clothing. It is not about long life, health, or freedom from pain or sickness. It is about daily sustenance only. So even though Jesus is only providing a general guideline, it doesn't apply to all of life or to all aspects of life, but only to God's daily provision for food and clothing.

The third thing to note is that Jesus provides this teaching within the context of seeking the kingdom of God (Matt 6:33). It appears that these promises are primarily directed toward those who seek first the kingdom. In other words, the promised provision and protection of God is not a blanket promise for all people everywhere. It is instead a promise for disciples of Jesus who seek to spread the kingdom of God through their life and actions. Since Jesus teaches this truth about God's provision within the context of His "Discipleship Manual" (Matt 5–7), it is no surprise that the promises He makes for provision apply primarily to those who are His disciples and who are carrying out the work of the kingdom.

This third insight is specifically applied by Jesus to His disciples when He later instructs them to carry the message of the kingdom of God into the surrounding countryside (Luke 9:1-6; 10:1-12). He says that as they carry out the work of the kingdom, they should not take food, money, or extra clothing with them, but should expect that their daily needs of food and shelter would be met by the people to whom they ministered.

This brings us back around to the person in Scripture who might have wondered how this promise of God's provision really worked and what he said about it. Who was this person? It was James, the brother of Jesus. James didn't always follow Jesus, but after Jesus died and rose again, James became one of the leaders in the early church (Acts 15:13, 19; Gal 2:9). And many sections of the letter that bears his name serve as a commentary on how to apply various portions of the Sermon on the Mount.

So when James writes that "If a brother or sister is naked and destitute of daily food ..." (Jas 2:15), we are to immediately remember what Jesus said in Matthew 6 about God providing clothing and daily food to His followers. James has noted that some people in God's church truly do go without clothing and daily food. Doesn't this contradict what Jesus taught, that God will provide food and clothing for His people? In James 2:15-16, James solves this dilemma by basically saying, "If you see someone who doesn't have clothing and food, don't quote Matthew 6:30 at them, saying that God will provide for their needs. And don't pray for them either. What good is that? Prayer and Bible verses will not put clothing on their back or food in their belly. Instead, give them something to wear and something to eat."

So when Jesus says, "God will provide for your daily needs," James clarifies by saying, "Yes, and how does God do this? Through one another as we take care of each other." Therefore, when someone's needs are *not* being met, it is not that God has failed, but that the church has failed to obey God. When people are starving and homeless and we cry out to God, "Why don't you do something?" God cries out to us, "Why don't *you* do something?"

This clarification by James helps us understand the words of Jesus in Matthew 6:30. Those who seek the kingdom of God will never be in want for daily food and clothing because we will always be providing food and clothing for others who need it, and they will be providing it for us.

So Jesus was right all along. He was primarily teaching a truth to His disciples about how their needs for food and clothing would be met as they followed His instructions to carry the message of the gospel to the surrounding region. These needs would be met through the provision of the people to whom they ministered. The disciples should have known that God would provide for them in exactly this way, for as they lived and walked with Jesus, they had seen time and time again that all of their needs for food and clothing had been met by other human beings who gave it to them.

This is why Jesus chides His disciples for having "little faith." The Greek word Jesus uses for "little faith" is *oligōpistos*. This word is not found anywhere else outside of Scripture, and within Scripture, only Jesus uses this term. Some postulate that Jesus coined this phrase.[8] It is also important to recognize that Jesus only uses this word in reference to the faith of His disciples. He never chides anyone else other than His disci-

---

[8] Wilkin, "Should We Rethink the Idea of Degrees of Faith?", 8.

ples for having "little faith." Apparently, since the disciples were following Jesus around, listening to His teachings, and observing His miracles, there were many instances where they should have known better than the average person and more readily believed some of what He taught. Because of their proximity to Jesus, more was expected of them than He would expect of others.

If you don't believe what Jesus says here, it is not necessarily because you have little faith. Instead, it is because you have not yet had the benefit that the disciples had. You have not yet walked with Jesus long enough to see Him miraculously provide time and time again. The disciples had seen this, but they still did not believe. However, if you are seeking first the kingdom of God, and as you have gone about God's work in this way, have seen Jesus provide for you time and time again, but you are still not sure He will provide for your basic needs of today, then yes, you might qualify for having "little faith."

But if you are a non-Christian or a new Christian, or if you are living for yourself rather than for the kingdom of God, or if you have not seen God provide food and clothing for you time and time again just when you need it, then you have no reason to believe that God will meet your basic needs today. You have little evidence to support this promise and little experience in seeing that it is true. If this is your situation, then even if you do not believe what Jesus says, you do not have "little faith." Why not? Because without any evidence or experience, the truth that God will provide for your daily food and clothing is quite difficult to believe.

The disciples, on the other hand, were expected to believe this because of what they had seen, heard, and experienced with Jesus. This is why Jesus gently chides them for not believing it. After everything they had seen and done with Jesus, it should have been a simple thing for them to believe that God would provide for their basic needs of food and clothing as they went about their work of expanding the kingdom of God. But they did not believe this, and so Jesus said they had "little faith." They did not believe something that should have been obvious and easy for them to believe, even though it is not obvious and easy for all of us.

Jesus' other references to "little faith" in the Gospels can be understood in a similar way (Matt 8:26; 14:31; 16:8; Luke 12:28). This term does not mean that the disciples of Jesus needed a higher degree or greater percentage of faith. Again, faith does not work like that. There are no degrees of faith. Rather, it means is that the disciples did not believe something that they should have easily believed. Though they did believe many truths, there are some truths they did not believe which Jesus expected them to easily believe, based on the evidence provided to them through His life, ministry, teachings, and example. Since they didn't believe these truths, He chided them for having "little faith."

If you have trouble believing some of the things Jesus chided His disciples for not believing, do not beat yourself up. It is unlikely that He is chiding you for having "little faith." Why not? Because we do not have many of the same benefits and blessings that the disciples had through their close proximity to Jesus. We do not have the evidence and experience that they had. Therefore, some of the things that He expected them to easily believe, might be very difficult for us to believe. But we might come to believe some of these things as He walks with us and teaches us new truths each and every day.

In fact, if you do come to believe some of the truths which should have been simple for the disciples to believe, Jesus might actually praise you for having great faith. The simplicity or difficulty of believing a particular truth depends entirely on how much evidence and experience a person has. Those with "little faith" do not believe truths that they should believe in light of how much they know and have seen. On the other hand, those with "great faith" are those who do believe truths that most people would not believe with the same level of knowledge and experience. This is what we see from Matthew 8:10 where Jesus praises a man for having great faith.

MATTHEW 8:10 (MATT 15:28; LUKE 7:9)

When Jesus heard it, He marveled, and said to those who followed, "Assuredly, I say to you, I have not found such great faith, not even in Israel!"

There are two kinds of faith that amazed Jesus: great faith and little faith. As seen above, there were times when Jesus marveled at the little faith of His disciples (cf. Matt 6:30; 8:26; 14:31; 16:8; Luke 4:14-30; 12:28). But in Matthew 8:10, Jesus was impressed by the great faith of a Gentile. The Gentile was a Roman Centurion who had a sick servant at home, and he requested that Jesus heal his servant. After a brief conversation, Jesus said, "I have not found such great faith, not even in Israel!"[9] Why did Jesus say this man had great faith?

Since we have properly understood that "little faith" occurs when a person does not believe easy truths, or truths that they clearly should believe based on the knowledge and evidence presented to them, then this means that "great faith" is the exact opposite. Great faith believes difficult truths, or truths for which there is little evidence. Those with great faith believe truths that few other people believe. "Great faith is not some higher level of conviction. It is believing something that is harder to believe, something that is contrary to what most people believe."[10] So "great faith" and "little faith" have nothing to do with the size, amount, or degree of a person's faith. Instead, these terms describe the relative level of difficulty of the truths that are believed.

So in Matthew 8:10, Jesus praises a Roman Centurion for having great faith. What did the Centurion believe that few others believe? He believed two advanced truths that are quite rare for people to believe (even today). First, he believed in his own lack of merit. Though he was courteous, humble, and a good man, though he loved the Jewish people

---

[9] You can read my sermon on Luke 7:1-10 by visiting https://redeminggod.com/sermons/luke/luke_7_1-10/. Last Accessed December 19, 2018.

[10] Wilkin, "Should We Rethink the Idea of Degrees of Faith?", 10.

and built a synagogue for them, he knew he didn't deserve anything from God, or from Jesus Christ. Despite his high standing and all he had done, he knew he was unworthy to meet with Jesus (Matt 8:8). Most people do not believe this. Most people think they do deserve favors from God. Most people think they are pretty good people and that God owes them something. It is much harder to believe that all we have and all we are given is simply and only by the grace of God. But the centurion believed this, and told Jesus that he was not worthy to have Jesus visit his house.

The second thing the Centurion believed was that healing could be done at a distance. He believed in the divine authority of Jesus, even over sickness and disease through space and time. He likened Jesus to a military commander who simply had to give orders for them to be followed (Matt 8:9). He knew that whatever Jesus commanded would be done, even if Jesus was not present where the healing was to take place. He knew that the words of Jesus were sufficient to accomplish whatever He said.

Most people do not believe this. Even today, most people believe that if a person is going to be healed, they need to be touched by the person praying for them. They believe that they have to go visit the healer, and have the healer lay hands on them, say special prayers over them, and anoint them with oil. If a person was seeking healing for their friend and they want to one of the "miracle healers" of today for help, and the healer said, "Go home, your friend will be fine," that person would feel like they had been ignored, slighted, or brushed off.

But this Centurion knew differently. The Centurion believed some truths that few others believed. He believed that if Jesus wanted to heal someone, He could do it with a simple word and from a great distance. He told Jesus, "Only speak a word, and my servant will be healed" (Matt 8:8). This truly is great faith, and few believe such an idea, either in the days of Jesus or today. As a result, Jesus marveled at this man's great faith, and healed his servant from a distance, simply by the power of His word.

All of the other "great faith" passages in the Bible can be understood in similar ways. The context always reveals that someone is believing something that is difficult to believe, and which few other people believe. So great faith is not a large amount of faith or a high percentage of faith. Great faith simply believes truths that are difficult to believe.

Before we move on, note that "great faith" for one person might not be "great faith" for someone else. The faith of this Centurion was "great faith" because he had very little experience with Jesus. He likely had not seen many of Jesus' miracles or heard any of his teachings. Yet the disciples had. So if the disciples had actually believed what this Centurion believed, it likely would not have been considered "great faith" for them. It is simply what they should have believed, based on the evidence that had been presented to them up to this point. Since the Centurion had very little of this evidence, and yet arrived at this belief based on what he knew from the Roman military, he was praised for having "great faith."

When people arrive at advanced truths and difficult concepts early in their relationship with God, they can be praised for having great faith. But people who have more knowledge, experience, and understanding of the things of God and how God works are expected to understand and believe some of these more advanced truths. If they still do not believe, based on everything they have seen and heard, then their lack of faith could even be called "little faith."

Nevertheless, regardless of whether a person has great faith or little faith, Jesus is still adamant that even the smallest faith can accomplish great things. This is what He teaches with the image of the mustard seed in Matthew 17:20.

MATTHEW 17:20 (LUKE 17:6)

So Jesus said to them, "Because of your unbelief; for assuredly, I say to you, if you have faith as a mustard seed, you will say to this mountain, 'Move from here to there,' and it will move; and nothing is impossible for you."

The disciples wanted to know why they were unable to cast out a particular demon. Initially, Jesus says it was because of their unbelief, and He goes on to talk about faith like a mustard seed. He says that even faith as small as a mustard seed can move mountains with a simple word. But since nobody has ever moved a mountain by simply telling it to move, many get confused by this teaching of Jesus. What did He mean and how can this teaching be applied?

It seems that there are numerous layers of meaning to these words of Jesus. First, it seems obvious that Jesus was not primarily referring to literal mountains (but see below). Instead, Jesus was symbolically referring to "mountain-sized" obstacles, such as this stubborn demon that would not be cast out. In this case, Jesus isn't *literally* saying that a person could move a mountain by having the proper "mountain-moving" faith. Instead, He is teaching that when we encounter insurmountable problems in our life, we must believe that God can handle them.

Second, this passage must be read in light of Matthew 13:31-32, where Jesus says that although a mustard seed is the smallest of all the seeds, it grows into a large tree so that even birds can nest it its branches. When read in connection with this text, Jesus is reminding His disciples that big things come from small beginnings. The Kingdom of God will eventually cover the entire earth, but it begins and is spread with small, seemingly insignificant ideas and actions.

Indeed, in the context, Jesus goes on to say that this kind of demon "does not go out except by prayer and fasting" (Matt 17:21). What does fasting and prayer have to do with faith that can cast out stubborn demons? It doesn't seem like one would lead to the other. What does fasting have to do with demons? Jesus is saying that as a person roots themselves in small, seemingly insignificant, Kingdom-focused actions such as prayer and fasting, their faith and relationship with God will grow, and they will eventually have the faith to cast out a demon with a word, just as Jesus does (Matt 17:18). Through prayer and fasting, people come to understand and believe new and deeper truths about God and how the spiritual realm works. In this way, small activities like prayer and fasting can lead to the type of faith that is able to cast out demons.

This understanding is aided by the third layer of meaning from this verse. Like many of Jesus' teachings, He was likely using an actual object that was in view of the disciples to serve as the illustration for His teaching. When He spoke of the birds of the air and the lilies of the field in Matthew 6:30, it is likely because there were some of these nearby. Similarly, when Jesus speaks here of a mountain, it seems likely that there was a mountain nearby to which He directed the gaze of His disciples. So to which mountain might Jesus have pointed?

One of my seminary professors believed that Jesus was referring to Herodium, which is a mountain that Herod literally moved from one place to another so that he could build a palace for himself. The place was originally a small hill, but Herod wanted to make it the largest mountain in the region so that he could build his palace on the peak. So he directed his laborers to move a second, nearby mountain and place it on top of the first. If this is the mountain Jesus referred to, then He was saying, "Just as Herod had a vision for the future, and moved an entire mountain, one shovelful at a time, to achieve that vision, so also, if you believe what I have taught about the future Kingdom of God, then it can be inaugurated one prayer and one fast at a time."

This *application* of Jesus' meaning is likely correct, but it seems doubtful that Jesus could have directed the gaze of His disciples to Herodium, for when Jesus spoke this truth about mustard seed faith, He and His disciples were far north in Caesarea Philippi (17:22, 24) while

Herodium was south of Jerusalem, a few miles from Bethlehem. So if a literal mountain is needed to help understand the words of Jesus, it seems that one in the region of Caesarea Philippi is needed.

Some speculate, therefore, that since Jesus and His disciples were likely staying in the area near the foot of Mount Hermon which contained the "Gate of Hades" (cf. Matt 16:18), a deep cave at the foot of the mountain from which the Jordan River flowed.[11] This area of Israel was dedicated to the worship of the god Pan and it was here that many people participated in great parties of feasting and promiscuity. So it is interesting that in the context, Jesus mentions that certain demons can only be cast out with fasting and prayer, which is the exact opposite of what usually happened in this area.

If this is where Jesus and His disciples were located when He spoke these words, it is possible that Jesus motioned toward a nearby hill which we now call "Tel Dan," or "the hill of Dan." Though the significance of this hill may have been lost on the disciples of Jesus, it has not been lost on modern Christians. Tel Dan has become one of the most important excavation sites in Israel. It is on this site that archaeologists have discovered the David Inscription, the Gate of Abraham, and the shrine of Jeroboam.

If this is the hill to which Jesus pointed, then His statement about moving the mountain could be seen as prophetic. He would be saying, "If you believe and start digging away at this mountain, it will be moved and you will discover great pieces of biblical history." But this view also seems unlikely. Jesus does not appear to speaking prophetically, and His words would not have been understood this way by His immediate audi-

---

[11] http://www.bible.ca/archeology/bible-archeology-tel-dan-laish-leshem-micah-Jonathan-jeroboams-king-of-israel-high-place-altar-temple-1340-723bc.htm
http://www.land-of-the-bible.com/Caesarea_Philippi
https://www.teldanexcavations.com/past---present-excavations http://www.land-of-the-bible.com/Mount_Hermon http://www.land-of-the-bible.com/The_Ancient_City_of_Dan

ence, the disciples.

Therefore, it seems that a third mountain might be the best choice. In the immediate context, Jesus has just come down from a high mountain upon which He had been transfigured (17:9). But nobody knows for sure where this mountain is located. It has traditionally been identified as Mount Tabor, southwest of the Sea of Galilee.

But since there was a Roman garrison on the top of Mount Tabor at this time, and since it appears that Jesus and His disciples were about 70 miles north in the region of Caesarea Philippi (16:13), some suggest that the Mount of Transfiguration was actually Mount Hermon, which is the highest mountain in the entire region. It is, of course, conceivable that they traveled from Caesarea Philippi down to Mount Tabor since at least six days passed between the confession of Peter at Caesarea Philippi (Matt 16:13-20) and the Mount of Transfiguration (Matt 17:1-13). There could be additional time between Matthew 16:20 and 16:21.

But if Jesus had been motioning to the Mount of Transfiguration (wherever it was), then what is the significance of directing the gaze of the disciples to this mountain and saying that it could move if they only had faith like a mustard seed? In this case, the move would be symbolic. Jesus had just been transfigured (17:9), and then came to a multitude of people (17:14). These actions are reminiscent of the similar steps of Moses on Mount Sinai when he went up to the mountain to receive the Law, and then came down the mountain with a radiant face to meet the multitudes of people below (Exod 34:29-35).

In this way, Jesus could be saying that the center of faith had now *moved* from the Law of Moses given on Mount Sinai, to the person of Jesus revealed on the Mount of Transfiguration. Jesus is saying, "If you can believe it, the Mountain of God has moved and so has the center of our faith. The Kingdom of God, which grows from a mustard seed, will come through Me; not through the Law of Moses."

Due to the overall significance and message of the ministry and teaching of Jesus, this third option is preferred. But regardless of *which* mountain Jesus was referring to (*if* there even was an actual mountain to which He pointed), the message of Jesus about mustard-seed faith is still clear. The imagery was not intended to teach that faith comes in tiny amounts. Jesus used this image of the mustard seed to show that even simple, easy beliefs can lead a person to gain great beliefs if we follow through to where they lead (Matt 13:31; 17:20; Mark 4:31; Luke 13:19; 17:6).

In other words, just as a small mustard seed can develop into a large plant, so also, small faith can grow into great faith. A small mustard seed can grow into a large tree, we can move a mountain one shovel-full at a time, and even the center of our faith can shift and change as we allow God to lead and guide us. In all cases, we simply need to believe.

So if you think your faith is small, you do not have to "muster" up more. It's not about how much faith you have, but about Who your faith is in and what your faith believes. When your faith is in God and you follow Him wherever He leads, you will be led on the greatest adventure ever imagined to accomplish the greatest deeds ever done. But all these adventures are traveled one step at a time, just as mountains are moved one shovel-full at a time and entire belief systems are transformed one idea at a time. So do you want to move a mountain? Follow your faith wherever it leads. When you encounter a mountain in your life, mustard seed faith looks at it and says, "With God's help, I can move that." Then it gets to work to see it done.

LUKE 12:42-48 (MATT 24:45-51)

And the Lord said, "Who then is the faithful and wise steward, whom his master will make ruler over his household, to give them their portion of food in due season? ... the master of that servant will come on a day when he is not looking for him, and at an hour when he is not aware, and will cut him in two and appoint him his portion with the unbelievers (Luke 12:42, 48).

Luke 12:42-48 (and the parallel passage in Matthew 24:45-51) has caused many to think that true faith will always lead to good works, so that if a person does not have the good works, this proves they were never a believer in the first place and will therefore be sent to hell for eternal punishment. But several details of the text reveal a completely different understanding.

First, the people in the story are all stewards, or servants, of the master. These terms indicate that the people in view are all Christian disciples of Jesus. Second, the fact that they are Christians is supported by the truth that all the servants are looking for the return of their master (initially, at least), which is the return of Jesus. Only Christians look for the return of Jesus.

Third, it is important to note that the adjective used to describe the servants in Luke 12:42 is exactly the same adjective used in Luke 12:48, except that the second is negated. Many translations have the first as "faithful" and the second as "unbelieving." This leads people to conclude that since some servants stopped thinking that the master was going to return and started mistreating their fellow servants, this means that they didn't really believe in the first place. But if our Bible translations were consistent, they should have translated both adjectives as either faithful/unfaithful or as believing/unbelieving.

If the words were translated as faithful/unfaithful, then this teaching of Jesus would not be about whether or not a person truly believed as evidenced by their works, but whether or not a person remained faithful and obedient to Jesus while awaiting His return. In this case, the text is not about who has eternal life and who does not, but rather about who serves Jesus faithfully during their lives while He is away. The blessings received at His return is not eternal life, but eternal reward.

If, however, the words are translated as believing/unbelieving (which is the translation I prefer), the text is still not about who has eternal life and who does not, for the issue that separates the two types of servants is that some believe that the master will return soon while others do not.

While all of them initially believe that the master will return soon, some stop believing this. This idea fits with the suggestion proposed previously that where the Bible contains the concept of faithfulness, it is best to understand it as "believing and continuing to believe" a particular truth (or set of truths). This is how the words are used in context here.

Furthermore, the belief or unbelief of the servants is not what guides their behavior. Instead, the servants are guided by whether they are wise or foolish. Servants who are wise perform in ways that the master desires, whereas the foolish servants do not.

But what of the consequences at the end of this teaching by Jesus? Does not the imagery of being cut in two and being beaten with many stripes indicate that Jesus does indeed have hell in view? No. From a realistic, practical perspective, it would be physically impossible for a master to cut his servants in half, and then send them to dwell with other unfaithful servants, where they would then all be beaten with many lashes. Cutting someone in half precludes any further disciplinary action. Therefore, it is clearly hyperbole for the sake of making a point.

The picture of cutting them in two is similar to the idea of being "cut to the heart" (Acts 2:37) or the idea found in Hebrews 4:12 where we learn that the Word of God penetrates to divide soul and spirit, joints and marrow, judging the thoughts and attitudes of the heart. This is not a literal cutting, but a divine judgment upon the thoughts, actions, and attitudes of the heart. The same is true of being beaten with many lashes. This is a symbolic way of speaking about the mental, emotional, psychological, and spiritual anguish and shame that a servant of Jesus will feel at His return when they realize how much unbelief they had and how poorly they behaved. The phrase is paired in Matthew 24:51 with "weeping and gnashing of teeth" which is an identical concept. It refers to great shame and regret before Jesus; not to punishment and torture forever in hell.[12]

So Luke 12:42-48 uses the adjective believing/unbelieving to show the importance of ongoing faith that Jesus will return soon. Yes, this ongoing faith helps guide and direct a person's behavior, but their behavior is primarily guided by whether or not they have obtained wisdom. Either way, it is critically important to note that even when a servant stops believing right truths or behaving in wise ways, they still remain a servant. To be the servant God wants and desires, we are expected to continue to believe and to behave in ways that match who we are in Him.

JOHN 3:16

For God so loved the world that He gave His only begotten Son, that whoever believes in Him should not perish but have everlasting life.

John 3:16 is the most famous verse in the Bible. There is good reason for this, since it contains the central invitation of the Gospel, that whoever believes in Jesus receives everlasting life. This is the clear and simple offer of the Gospel, and is what Jesus Himself consistently promised when He spoke about eternal life to others. Eternal life is freely given by God to anyone and everyone who simply and only believes in Jesus for it (cf. John 5:24; 6:47).

Yet although the promise of eternal life to all who believe in Jesus is simple to understand, it is not easy to believe. This is why the term "easy believism" is a misnomer. Yes, eternal life is freely given to those who believe in Jesus, but relatively few actually believe this! Even many who operate under the banner of "Christianity" deny that eternal life is by "faith alone in Jesus Christ alone." They argue instead that eternal life and entrance into heaven is earned through submission to the Lordship of Jesus Christ, perseverance in good works, and a life of ongoing obedi-

---

[12] For a more detailed explanation, see my book, *Am I Going to Hell?* (Dallas, OR: Redeeming Press, 2019).

ence to the commands of God. Most people, even many Christians, find it hard to believe that eternal life is absolutely free to all who believe in Jesus for it.

But there are numerous, easier beliefs that can help persuade and convince us to believe in Jesus Christ *alone* for eternal life. The more we learn about God, ourselves, Scripture, and Jesus, the more we come to understand why eternal life must be a free gift from God. If eternal life was anything other than a free gift from God, no human would be able to earn or achieve it. So the more truths we come to believe from Scripture, the easier it becomes to believe in Jesus for eternal life.[13]

Faith is a bit like a snowball. It builds as it rolls. The more we believe about Jesus, the more we end up believing about Jesus. And somewhere along the way, a person comes to discover that Jesus promises eternal life to anyone who believes in Him for it. When this truth is presented, a person either believes it, or they don't. If they believe it, then they have eternal life. Jesus guarantees it. If they don't believe it, then all is not lost. They simply need to keep moving forward, learning more about Jesus, until they come to the place where they know that Jesus fulfills what He promises. When they believe this, they will also come to believe that they have eternal life through Jesus.

Do you believe in Jesus for eternal life? If so, then eternal life is yours. If not, what is holding you back?

JOHN 6:28-29

Then they said to Him, "What shall we do, that we may work the works of God?" Jesus answered and said to them, "This is the work of God, that you believe in Him who He sent."

---

[13] In my book, *The Gospel According to Scripture*, I discuss several "Preparation Truths" which help convince a person to believe in Jesus Christ for eternal life. This book is forthcoming.

This text has been used in various ways. Some point to this text to show that faith is indeed a work. Some of the people who were following Jesus asked what they could do to do the work of God, and Jesus tell them that the work of God is to believe in Him. This seems to imply that faith is a work, and therefore, eternal life would be gained by a work, namely, the work of faith.

Others use this verse to teach that faith is a gift from God in the mind of the believer. They teach that faith is not something that comes from the mind of a person, but is rather given by God to the person so that they might believe. John MacArthur, for example, wrongly assuming that faith is a work, says that faith cannot be "merely a human work, but a gracious work of God in us."[14]

But a careful look at the text reveals that Jesus was teaching something else entirely. In the immediately preceding context, Jesus told some of His followers that they should "not labor for the food which perishes, but for the food which endures to everlasting life" (John 6:27). Hearing Jesus talk about labor, some of the Jewish people asked what works they can do for God. Notice that they change the wording a bit, and ask Jesus about *works*, plural. As good Jewish people, they are thinking about pleasing God through the works of the law.[15] Jesus, however, changed it back to how He meant it, and refers to the singular *work*, and then explains what this work is. Jesus basically explains that the "work, or action, that God desires, is believing in His Son, the Lord Jesus Christ."[16]

But this does not mean that faith is a work which God performs on our behalf. Though Jesus did use the image of laboring for God, He elsewhere uses the images of *drinking* living water and *eating* the bread of life (John 4:13-14; 6:51). But nobody wonders what we should drink

---

[14] John MacArthur, *The Gospel According to Jesus: What Does Jesus Mean When He Says "Follow Me"?*, Rev. and exp. ed. (Grand Rapids: Zondervan, 1994), 33.

[15] Most Jewish teachers did not believe that eternal life could be earned through works. But they did believe that the works of the law were pleasing to God.

[16] Bob Wilkin, "The Free Grace Position Should Rightfully Hold Claim to the Title Lordship Salvation," *Grace in Focus Newsletter* (2010). https://faithalone.org/magazine/y2010/10F1.html Last Accessed April 8, 2018.

and eat in order to gain eternal life. Instead, people recognize that these are images Jesus used to illustrate His point about believing in Him. It is exactly the same with His image of laboring for food which endures (John 6:27). Jesus is not teaching that people have to labor for eternal life any more than He is saying that people have to drink and eat for eternal life And just as it makes no sense to say that "God eats and drinks for us because we cannot eat and drink on our own," so also, we cannot say that "God works for us because we cannot do the work of God on our own." All of these pictures are ways of speaking about receiving Jesus Christ and eternal life by faith alone.

So Jesus is not saying that faith is a work, or even that faith is a work of God performed in the human heart. Instead, by saying that the work God wants is for people to believe in Him. Jesus was saying that the work that God desires is not work at all, but is the opposite of works, which is faith (cf. Rom 4:4-5; Eph 2:8-9). God does not want us to "do" anything for Him, for He has already done everything for us. He simply wants people to believe in Jesus for eternal life, thereby recognizing that everything which needs to be done has been done in Jesus.

JOHN 11:25-26

Jesus said to her, "I am the resurrection and the life. He who believes in Me, though he may die, he shall live. And whoever lives and believes in Me shall never die. Do you believe this?"

John 11:20-27 contains an excellent example of the spreadsheet of faith analogy that was used previously in this book to illustrate how faith works. Lazarus has just died, and Jesus goes to Bethany to grieve with Mary and Martha. When Jesus arrives, Martha comes out to meet Him on the road and says, "Lord, if you had been here, my brother would not have died" (John 11:21).

Jesus responded by saying, "Your brother will rise again" (John 11:23).

So Mary says, "I know that he will rise again in the resurrection at the last day" (John 11:24).

Each of these statements is a factual statement that exists on Martha's spreadsheet of beliefs. She believes that if Jesus had been present, Lazarus would not have died. Remember, they sent word to Jesus when Lazarus was sick, but He delayed in going to them until after Lazarus had died. So Martha is chiding Jesus a bit. She believes that Lazarus died because Jesus didn't show up when she wanted Him to.

But then Jesus makes another factual statement. He says, "Your brother will rise again." Now, does Martha believe this? She does. For she goes on to say, "Yes, I know, I believe, I agree that he will rise again ... but on the future day of resurrection."

Based on these beliefs, Jesus goes on to teach her some new ideas about Himself. He makes some factual statements to see if they are turned "On" or "Off" in her spreadsheet of beliefs. Jesus says, "I am the resurrection and the life. He who believes in Me, though he may die, he shall live. And whoever lives and believes in Me shall never die" (John 11:25-26).

In these verses, Jesus makes three factual statements. Each one is a truth claim about Jesus, and each one is dependent upon the other two and dependent upon what Martha has already stated about the resurrection. Jesus is inviting her to build upon her previous beliefs and add some new beliefs to them. Jesus claims that (1) Resurrection and life reside in Him, (2) that those who die in Him will also live in Him, and (3) that who live and believe in Him will never die.

After Jesus makes these three factual statements, He says, "Do you believe this?"

Notice how Martha responds. She doesn't say, "Yes, Lord, I believe these three things. I believe that (1) Resurrection and life reside in You, (2) that those who die in You will also live in You, and (3) that who live and believe in You will never die." She does not restate the beliefs and affirm her agreement with them. Instead, she says something that has confused a lot of people over the years. She says, "Yes, Lord, I believe that You are the Christ, the Son of God, who is to come into the world."

Lots of people read these words and get confused. They see Martha state her agreement with Jesus, but then she seems to say something back to Him that is not a restatement of what Jesus just said. In other words, though she agrees, she doesn't state her agreement by summarizing what Jesus just said; instead, she states her agreement by stating her belief in something else entirely. So some people read these words from Martha and say, "Maybe to believe that Jesus is the resurrection and the life is the exact same as believing that Jesus is the Christ, the Son of God."

And while we could say that the two concepts are related, the two concepts are not identical beliefs. That is, to say that Jesus is the Christ is not the same thing as saying that Jesus is the resurrection and the life. We know this for a variety of reasons. There are lots of people in the days of Jesus who believed that He was the Christ, but did not believe that He could raise people from the dead, or even that He Himself would be raised from the dead. Furthermore, there were many people throughout biblical history who were considered to be "Messiahs" or "Christs" (that is, Deliverers, Saviors), but nobody ever thought that these people could raise others from death.

So since believing that Jesus is the Christ is not the same thing as believing that Jesus is the resurrection and the life, why does Martha answer the way she does? She answers the way she does because she is saying that *because* she believes that Jesus is the Christ, she trusts and accepts whatever else Jesus says, including these recent three statements about the resurrection.

To put it another way, Jesus makes three truth claims about Himself and then asks Martha if she believes what He has said. These are new ideas to her, and she has never been told these ideas before. So she can either accept, acknowledge, and agree with what Jesus has just said, thereby believing His words, or she can disagree with Him, thereby not believing.

But since Martha already knows and believes something else on her spreadsheet of faith, namely, that Jesus is the Christ, the Messiah, the son of God, this therefore causes Martha to realize that everything Jesus says can be trusted and accepted. Therefore, because of her belief in Jesus as the Christ, Martha also believes these new statements about Jesus, that He is the resurrection and the life, that those who die in Him will live again, and that those who live in Him will never die.

This is the Excel spreadsheet of faith at work. A cell on her spreadsheet of faith which said "Jesus is the Christ" was turned "On." As a result of this cell, another cell on her spreadsheet of faith which said, "Everything Jesus says is true" was also turned "On." So when Jesus comes along and says something she has never heard or thought of before, and then Jesus asks her if she believes these new ideas, it does not take her long to turn these cells on as well. She didn't fully understand the ramifications of what Jesus was saying, but she did know that Jesus was saying it, and that because He was the Christ, His words could always be trusted and believed. So she believed Him.

Then, of course, to provide further support and proof that her belief in Him was well-founded, Jesus went and raised Lazarus from death.

This is just one example of how the network of beliefs that exists on our spreadsheet of faith works together to consider new ideas and incorporate new beliefs. We see it work very quickly with Martha, but it doesn't always move this fast. Sometimes the process is much slower. But regardless, this example of faith in Martha helps us understand how faith works, and how we consider and accept the various truth claims that bombard us each and every day.

Each belief is built upon others that we might or might not have on our network of faith. Faith is a vast network of individual beliefs that are constantly moving, shifting, changing, and developing over time. It is not something to be afraid of, but can be enjoyed and anticipated as we continue to follow Jesus wherever He leads.

JOHN 20:31

> ... but these are written that you may believe that Jesus is the Christ, the Son of God, and that believing you may have life in His name.

Near the end of his Gospel account, the Apostle John provides the purpose statement for his book. He says that while he could have included many other additional signs and teachings of Jesus in the account, he specifically chose the ones he wrote down because they would help a person believe in Jesus, so that those who believed would have eternal life.

This truth from John fits perfectly with what we have learned about faith. Faith occurs when we are persuaded that something is true. Humans are persuaded by a wide variety of factors, one of which is reading about historical events of the past (cf. Luke 1:1-4). The signs in the Gospel of John are provided to persuade people about the truth regarding Jesus. Specifically, the signs cause people to believe in Jesus for eternal life.[17] Therefore, the Gospel of John is a perfect place to see that faith is persuasion. The concluding purpose of the book, recorded in John 20:30-31, brings this out quite clearly. The signs were written so that those who read them might believe (be persuaded) that Jesus is the Christ, and that through such belief (or persuasion), they might have life in His name.

Once again, we see how believing one thing can lead to believing other related truths. The Apostle John specifically chose to record several historical and miraculous signs which provide proof that Jesus was the Messiah. When we believe this, we will then come to believe that Jesus was telling the truth whenever He spoke. And if we believe this, then we

---

[17] John H. Niemelä, "The Cross in John's Gospel" *JOTGES* (Spring 2003), 27.

can know the truth of what He taught, that anyone who believed in Him would have everlasting life. Believing in what John has written about Jesus leads a person to believe that Jesus was the Messiah, which leads a person to believe what Jesus taught, and therefore, believe in Jesus for eternal life.

ACTS 6:7

Then the word of God spread, and the number of the disciples multiplied greatly in Jerusalem, and a great many of the priests were obedient to the faith.

Acts 6:7 has sometimes been used to defend the idea that faith is a work, or that true faith leads to a life of ongoing obedience and works. But Acts 6:7 includes the article "the" in front of the word faith, indicating that "the Christian faith" is in view rather than "faith" itself. In context, "the Christian faith" is set in contrast to "the Jewish faith" which the priests had formerly believed and practiced.

This articular use of faith does not primarily refer to believing a particular truth, but instead refers to the entire set of beliefs and behaviors that distinguish one "religion" from another. So while these priests had formerly been part of the Jewish faith, they had now converted to the Christian faith. So while "the faith" does include an element of conduct or behavior, and thus it can be spoken of as "obedience," this does not mean that "faith" itself involves works of any kind. Faith is not a work and does not necessarily lead to works.

There are numerous other passages in the New Testament which speak of "the faith" and all of them can be understood in a similar fashion (cf. Acts 13:8; 14:22; 16:5; Rom 1:5; 1 Cor 16:13; 2 Cor 13:5; Gal 1:23; 3:23; 6:10; Eph 4:13; Php 1:25-27; Col 1:23; 1 Tim 3:9-4:6; 5:8; 6:10, 21; 2 Tim 2:18; 3:8; 4:7; Titus 1:13; Jude 3).

ACTS 13:48

Now when the Gentiles heard this, they were glad and glorified the word of the Lord. And as many as had been appointed to eternal life believed.

Some use Acts 13:48 to teach that God chooses who will receive eternal life, and then gives faith to those whom He has chosen. So while this verse is often used in defense of the Reformed teaching on election and predestination, those teachings are intricately connected with the idea that faith is a gift from God. Acts 13:48 is used to defend both ideas.

However, this entire understanding depends on a dubious interpretation of the Greek word *tetagmenoi,* which is sometimes translated as "had been appointed." This word is a perfect participle, which can be understood in either the middle or passive voice. The phrase "had been appointed" reveals the passive interpretation. In this interpretation, the Gentiles are passive recipients of faith. But the Greek participle could also be understood in the middle voice, in which case, the Greek word could be translated as "marshalled themselves, prepared themselves, or disposed themselves."[18] If this is the preferred translation, the Gentiles were not passive in receiving faith, but prepared themselves to believe.

But how can we decide which translation is preferable? The answer, as always, is to look at the context. In the immediate context, those who end up believing Paul and Barnabas had attended the synagogue on the Sabbath, heard the preaching of Paul, and then joined with the Jews in inviting Paul to speak a second Sabbath. The reason these Gentiles joined the Jews is because they were God-fearing proselytes (cf. Acts 13:42-43). After hearing Paul on this second Sabbath, many of these Gentiles be-

---

[18] Henry Alford, *The Greek New Testament and Exegetical and Critical Commentary* (Cambridge: Deighton, Bell, 1976), II:153; Robert Shank, *Elect in the Son; A Study of the Doctrine of Election* (Springfield, MO: Westcott, 1970), 87. Cf. J. Gresham Machen, *New Testament Greek for Beginners* (Upper Saddle River, NJ: Prentice Hall, 1923), 186; Richard Rackham, *The Acts of the Apostles: An Exposition* (Eugene, OR: Wipf & Stock, 2003), 221.

lieved what they heard.

The implication in Acts 13:48 is that these Gentile proselytes had been thinking and mulling over what Paul had said for an entire week, and after hearing him a second time, became convinced of the truth of his words. Their belief was no passive working of God on their hearts and minds, but was their week-long consideration and response to what God was doing in their midst. By the time they heard the gospel on the second Sabbath, they had disposed or prepared themselves to believe the message.

This understanding also fits with the broader context in several ways. First, "Acts 13 is a study in contrasts in how different people *prepare themselves* to hear the gospel."[19] In the beginning of the chapter, the contrast is between Bar-Jesus and Sergius Paulus. One man was open to the truth while the other was full of deceit (cf. Acts 13:7, 10). Then when Luke writes about Paul preaching in Pisidian Antioch, he shows how the Gentiles accept what is preached while the Jews oppose it. This event in Acts 13 marks the beginning of the theme in Acts where the Gentiles often respond favorably to the gospel while the Jews do not.[20]

The reason for this transition, Luke indicates, is not because God has now "chosen" the Gentiles instead of His other "chosen" people, the Jews, but because the Gentiles were more open to hearing, considering, examining, and accepting the things Paul preached to them, while the Jews were more set in their traditional ways and beliefs and so were less willing to consider that they might be wrong. Furthermore, the text uses the middle voice for the word "reject" (Gk., *apōtheō*) in Acts 13:46, showing that the Jewish people *themselves* rejected the message of Paul. This too was not a passive rejection foreordained or predetermined by God. Therefore, if the Jewish rejection was not passive, then neither was the Gentile acceptance.

---

[19] Shawn Lazar, "Election for Baptists," *Grace in Focus Newsletter* (September-October 2014), 6.

[20] Cf. comments by Laurence M. Vance, *The Other Side of Calvinism* (Pensacola, FL: Vance Publications, 1999), 346-348.

Finally, this understanding of *tetagmenoi* as "disposed" fits best with other uses of the same term in Acts. Aside from Acts 13:48, the word is also used in Acts 15:2, 22:10, and 28:23. In Acts 15:2 and 28:23, the word is clearly referring to the actions, attitudes, and decisions of people, rather than to some divinely-ordained predisposition to the gospel which was unconditionally granted by God. Outside of the book of Acts, Luke (who also wrote Acts) uses the word in Luke 7:8 to refer to human authority and control. Paul follows a similar track when he uses this word in 1 Corinthians 16:15 to write about Christians who have devoted themselves to a particular ministry.

So although it is absolutely true that God may arrange historical events which allow a person to hear the message of the gospel, and while God definitely gives eternal life upon those who believe, God does not give the gift of faith to passive recipients. Faith is not a gift or a work. But we can be disposed, or prepared, to believe by what we learn, study, and think.

ROMANS 3:21-26

> *But now the righteousness of God apart from the law is revealed, being witnessed by the Law and the Prophets, even the righteousness of God, through faith in Jesus Christ, to all and on all who believe. For there is no difference; for all have sinned and fallen short of the glory of God, being justified freely by His grace through the redemption that is in Christ Jesus, whom God set forth as a propitiation by His blood, through faith, to demonstrate His righteousness, because in His forebearance God had passed over the sins that were previously committed, to demonstrate at the present time His righteousness, that He might be just and the justifier of the one who has faith in Jesus.*

This text is one of the many from Paul which reveals the similar message we learned from Jesus, that eternal life is by faith alone in Jesus Christ alone. However, Paul doesn't mention "eternal life" but rather the "righteousness of God." The two concepts are related. Since eternal life is God's life, and since we gain God's righteousness when we share His life, the terms "eternal life" and "righteousness of God" are close synonyms in Scripture. While Jesus speaks of eternal life, Paul writes of justification and the righteousness of God (and while Jesus speaks of the Kingdom of God, Paul tends to write about salvation). So while Jesus teaches that God gives eternal life to those who believe in Jesus for it, Paul similarly teaches that God gives His righteousness to all who believe in Jesus. This is what he teaches three times in these verses.

It is also crucial to recognize what Paul says about the death of Jesus in this passage. Paul writes that in previous eras, God passed over the sins that people committed. Why? According to Paul, the violent death of Jesus on the cross reveals that just as God freely forgave us by His grace for committing the greatest sin of all, which was the sin of accusing and killing His Own Son, so also, God freely forgave the sins that were previously committed. God freely forgives because God is a gracious God. God clearly and irrefutably demonstrated this by extending forgiveness to us for the crucifixion of Jesus.

So from this text we see many of the truths about faith come together. Paul uses reason and logic to show why his readers should believe in Jesus for God's righteousness. He points to the teachings of the Law and the Prophets as containing persuasive evidence that God has always invited people to receive His righteousness by faith. Paul points out that anyone and everyone is able to believe, and that faith is not a work because we are justified freely by God's grace. And these verses are really only introductory for the themes that Paul goes on to discuss in the following chapters. In Romans 4–6, Paul provides many historical, biblical, and logical proofs for why his readers should believe in Jesus for God's righteousness. These chapters, and the proofs they contain, show that in Paul's thinking, belief occurs when we are persuaded by the evidence provided.

ROMANS 4:4-5

Now to him who works, the wages are not counted as grace but as debt. But to him who does not work but believes on Him who justifies the ungodly, his faith is accounted for righteousness.

Romans 4:4-5 clearly refutes the idea that faith is a work. After all, if faith was a work (even a work of God), or included any form of human effort or merit, then Romans 4:4-5 would be gibberish. If faith was a work, or included works of some sort, Paul would be saying that God gives His righteousness "to him who does not work but who has the work of faith." This makes no sense. Paul is clearly contrasting faith and works, showing that one has nothing to do with the other.

Paul proceeds in the following context to show that this has always been true throughout time, so that even Abraham, the father of faith, received the righteousness of God by faith before he ever obeyed God's laws or was even circumcised (Rom 4:9-25). Good works performed *before* a person believes do not help a person achieve God's righteousness, and good works performed *after* a person believes do not help them keep God's righteousness. We must not make good works a condition for receiving eternal life, keeping eternal life, or proving that we have eternal life, for the righteousness of God is gained by faith alone in Jesus Christ alone from first to last.

ROMANS 10:17

So then faith comes by hearing, and hearing by the word of God.

Romans 10:17 shows that faith is persuasion. Paul writes that faith comes by hearing, and hearing by the Word of God. The word for *hearing* refers not just to understanding what is read or taught from Scripture, but to understanding, thinking, knowing, reasoning, and assenting to what Scripture says. As people read, study, and hear the Word of God, it works upon their hearts and minds to persuade them of the truth (cf. Gal 3:2). This is why it is so important to use Scripture when sharing the gospel. It is the Word of God that is living and active (Heb 4:12) and through which the Holy Spirit works to draw all people to Jesus Christ.

So faith is not a human work, and neither is it a work of God in the human heart. Faith rises in the human mind as a person hears, understands, and agrees with what Scripture says. Some people may need to understand more and some less, but there can be no faith without hearing and understanding.

2 CORINTHIANS 13:5

> *Examine yourselves as to whether you are in the faith. Test yourselves. Do you not know yourselves, that Jesus Christ is in you?—unless indeed you are disqualified.*

Second Corinthians 13:5 is often used by those who teach that if a Christian does not have the proper type or amount of beliefs and behaviors, then there is a good chance that this person is not actually a Christian. Those who hold this view call on others to examine themselves to see whether or not they are actually a Christian. They call on others to test themselves to see whether or not they have actually believed and whether or not they have the requisite amount of good works to prove that they are a "true" Christian. If not, then such a person should try harder, work longer, and obey more so that they can prove the reality of their faith and genuineness of their conversion.

But since faith is not a work and does not include works, what does this verse mean? This is once again an "articular" use of "the faith." Paul is not telling the Corinthians to question whether or not they have really believed, but is telling them to question whether or not their beliefs and behaviors line up with "the Christian faith" and what Paul himself taught and practiced when he was among them. Paul is not saying, "Make sure you are really a Christian," but is instead saying, "*Since* you are a Christian, make sure your beliefs and behaviors match how Christians should believe and behave."

Paul is *not* saying that if the beliefs and behaviors of the Corinthian Christians do not line up with the proper beliefs and behaviors of "the Christian faith" then this means that they are not really Christians. No, it just means that their life and theology does not line up with who they really are.

Paul repeatedly and consistently throughout his letter affirms that the Corinthians are believers and have the righteousness of God. As a result, based on this certain reality, Paul calls them to live in light of who they actually are (cf. 1:24; 3:3; 6:14-15; 7:1; 8:9; 13:11). This is also what Paul means in 13:5. He affirms that they are his brethren in Christ, and on the basis of this affirmation, invites them to check their beliefs and behaviors to see whether or not they conform to "the [Christian] faith" (cf. the nearly identical use of "the faith" in Col 1:23).

The reference to being "disapproved" also has nothing to do with eternal life or going to heaven, but is instead about Paul's apostolic ministry. Some in Corinth were claiming that Paul's ministry was invalid. Paul brilliantly counters this argument by saying that if his ministry is disqualified, then everyone in Corinth is also disqualified for ministry, because they only became Christians through his ministry among them. But if their ministry is valid, then this proves that his is valid as well (cf. 13:3-7; 1 Cor 9:2).

EPHESIANS 2:8-9

For by grace you have been saved through faith, and that not of yourselves; it is the gift of God, not of works, lest anyone should boast.

Ephesians 2:8-9 is one of the key passages which is sometimes used to defend the idea that faith is a gift from God. For example, R. C. Sproul, in his book, *What is Faith?* writes this:

> What is meant by "not your own doing"? Is it grace or is it faith? According to all the rules of Greek grammar, there is only one possible answer to that question. In the grammatical structure of the text, the antecedent of the word *this* is the word *faith*. [21]

Strangely, Sproul provides no grammatical evidence for his assertion, and indeed, the Greek grammar of Ephesians 2:8-9 reveals exactly the opposite of what Sproul writes.[22]

In the preceding context, Paul is referring to what God has done for humans in Jesus Christ (Eph 2:1-7). After writing that while we were dead in trespasses (Eph 2:1-4), God made us alive together with Jesus Christ (2:5; which is a preview of 2:11-22), Paul states the main theme: "by grace you have been saved" (2:5). Paul repeats this theme in Ephesians 2:8 while adding to it the element of faith. It is in 2:8 that he also writes that "it is the gift of God."

But what is the gift of God? To what does the phrase "and *that* not of yourselves, *it* is the gift of God" refer? In other words, what is it that did not come from us humans, but came from God as a gift? Some argue that "it" is faith. And indeed, from the English, this would make sense as pronouns usually refer to their nearest antecedent. If I say, "The monkey ate the apple, and it was a gift from the zookeeper," the rules of English

---

[21] R. C. Sproul, *What is Faith?* (Orlando: Reformation Trust, 2010), 53.

[22] For a detailed analysis of the Greek Grammar, see René Lopez, "Is Faith a Gift from God or a Human Exercise?" *Bibliotheca Sacra 164* (July–September 2007): 266-274. http://www.dts.edu/download/publications/bibliotheca/BibSac-Lopez-IsFaithAGiftfromGodoraHumanExercise.pdf Last Accessed July 13, 2014.

grammar dictate that the word "it" refers to the apple rather than the monkey. But this is not the case with Greek.

All Greek words have gender: masculine, feminine, and neuter. When a relative pronoun is used, it always agrees with the gender of the noun to which it refers. The word "faith" in Greek is feminine, and so if Paul wanted to write that faith was not of ourselves but was a gift of God, he would have used a feminine relative pronoun for the word "that" (the word "it" is not actually in the Greek). But Paul did not use the feminine version of the word "that." Instead, he used a neuter (neutral) pronoun. Therefore, it is grammatically impossible for the word "that" to refer to "faith."

The problem is that there is no neuter noun in the preceding context. So what was Paul referring to, if not to faith? It is not faith itself, but the entire "salvation package" that Paul is writing about in Ephesians 2. The description of Paul about what God has provided to us in Jesus contains a mixture of masculine and feminine nouns. So Paul uses a neuter pronoun to refer to the entire "salvation package." If God did not reveal the truth to us about human sin, we never would have realized it on our own (Eph 2:1-4). But God did reveal the truth to us, through the work of Jesus Christ, and especially the death of Jesus Christ on the cross (Eph 2:13). As a result of this revelation in Jesus, we can live free from the sin that separates us from each other, and live in love and unity instead (Eph 2:11-22). All of this is the gift of God. If, therefore, we believe what has been revealed to us through Jesus, then we will be saved from the problem of sin that has enslaved humanity since the foundation of the world.

In light of this overall context, we discover that Paul is not writing in Ephesians 2 about how people can receive eternal life or go to heaven when they die. The word "saved" in Ephesians 2:8-9 does not refer to eternal life or our eternal destiny. Instead, Paul's overall point in Ephesians 2 is about how God solved the problem of human division and strife that is caused by racial, religious, and political differences (Eph 2:1-

4). Paul shows how God revealed the problem and the solution through the crucifixion of Jesus (Eph 2:5-10) so that we can all live in peace and unity with one another in this life (Eph 2:11-22), as God has always wanted and desired.

So faith is not the gift of God. The gift of God is His revelation to humanity and the salvation which comes to us by His grace. When we see, understand, and believe what God has revealed to us and done for us through the life, death, resurrection, and exaltation of Jesus, it is then that the peace of God starts to become a reality in our life here and now. It is then that all who were formerly at enmity with each other are fitted together to grow into the holy temple in the Lord, as a dwelling place of God in the Spirit (Eph 2:21-22). This is the mystery of the church, which Paul goes on to explain in Ephesians 3–4. All of this is the gift of God, and when we receive it by faith, we begin to experience this new reality in this life and on this earth.

COLOSSIANS 1:23

> *… if indeed you continue in the faith, grounded and steadfast, and are not moved away from the hope of the gospel which you heard, which was preached to every creature under heaven, of which I, Paul, became a minister.*

Although Colossians 1:23 is frequently cited by some teachers as proof that a failure to persevere in faith will cause someone to lose their eternal life or will prove that we were never justified in the first place, this is once again a text that can be clarified by recognizing that "*the* faith" is in view, rather than "faith." As with all the other references to "the faith" in the New Testament, the terms points to "the beliefs and behaviors that constitute Christianity" rather than to faith in Jesus for eternal life.

It is entirely possible for a person to receive eternal life through faith in Jesus, but then to later fall away from "the faith" and abandon Christianity. Such a person still has eternal life, but they no longer believe and behave the way they should. What happens to such a person? In the context, Paul explains that those who continue in "the faith" will receive a better presentation before Jesus Christ than those who do not.[23]

A time is coming when all Christians will stand before the Judgment Seat of Christ to answer for the things done in the body (2 Cor 5:10). Those who faithfully followed and served Jesus will receive additional blessing and honor from Him (cf. 1 Cor 3:12-17). When we stand before the Judgment Seat of Christ, this does not determine our eternal destiny, but only our eternal reward. So Paul encourages the Colossian Christians to continue in the beliefs and behaviors of "the faith" which he had declared to them so that they might be presented as holy, blameless, and above reproach in His sight at the Judgment Seat of Christ.[24]

1 TIMOTHY 5:8

But if anyone does not provide for his own, and especially for those of his household, he has denied the faith and is worse than an unbeliever.

This passage is easily understood when it is recognized that Paul is referring "the [Christian] faith" rather than to *belief* itself. And this is important to recognize, for if Paul were writing here about what was necessary to receive eternal life, he would be teaching that eternal life can be lost if a person does not properly take care of their family.

Yet it is indeed possible for a Christian to have eternal life while failing to take care of his or her family. Everybody is aware of families like this. You might even come from one. But when a Christian lives in such a neglectful way, this does not mean that they are not really a Christian,

---

[23] Bob Wilkin succinctly defends this position in "Is Perseverance Required for Holy Presentation?" *Grace in Focus Newsletter* 19:1 (Jan/Feb 2004).

[24] Cf. Bob Wilkin, "Is Continuing in the Faith a Condition of Eternal Life? Colossians 1:21-21" https://faithalone.org/magazine/y1991/91march3.html Last Accessed December 29, 2018.

or don't really believe in Jesus. Instead, their neglectful behavior simply means that they are failing to follow the teachings and traditions of the Christian faith about the importance of loving and providing for our family members. "Part of the Christian faith—the teachings of Christianity—is to honor your parents. To neglect one's widowed mother by not taking care of her would be to deny what Christianity teaches."[25]

Some might argue that Paul's phrase at the end of this verse indicates that he does indeed have eternal destinies in mind. After all, he says that if a person doesn't take care of their family, they are "worse than an unbeliever." But this phrase doesn't mean that those Christians who fail to provide for their families will end up in hell. It means that even most unbelievers take care of their families, and so Christians who don't are behaving in worse ways than non-Christians. While Christians should be leading the way in how to love and provide for our families, when a Christian fails in this regard, their behavior is worse than that of unbelievers (cf. 1 Cor 5:1; Titus 1:13).

JAMES 2:14-26

What does it profit, my brethren, if someone says he has faith but does not have works? Can faith save him? … You believe that there is one God. You do well. Even the demons believe—and tremble! … For as the body without the spirit is dead, so faith without works is dead (Jas 2:14, 19, 26).

James 2:14-26 has needlessly caused much angst and strife throughout the years. It has been used to teach that true faith will always result in a life of good works, so that if a person does not have the required amount of good works, this means they don't really have faith. "True faith is an active faith," people will say. "While we are saved by faith alone, we are not saved by a faith that is alone. We are not saved by faith plus works, but by a faith that works. If you claim to have faith, but don't have

---

[25] Ken Yates, "Denying the Faith?" *Grace in Focus Newsletter* (Jan/Feb 2018), 8.

works, then you have dead faith, which is a spurious, false, non-existent faith." Similarly, when someone teaches or writes that eternal life is by faith alone in Jesus Christ alone, there will nearly always be someone who objects by saying that "even the demons believe."

But James 2:14-26 teaches *none* of these ideas. James 2 does not disagree with Jesus or with Paul that eternal life is by grace alone through faith alone in Jesus Christ alone. When we take everything we have learned about faith in this book and apply it to James 2, we discover the beautiful truths of this text and how the message of James fits perfectly with the message of Jesus and Paul. Three key insights about this text reveal what James is teaching.

First, eternal life is not in view. James is not writing his letter to tell people how to receive eternal life, or even how to know they have eternal life. Instead, James is writing this letter to deal with some practical issues that have arisen in the church and to tell Christians how to handle them in a Christlike and loving way. This is a practical letter full of discipleship truths for Christians.

In many ways, this letter is quite similar to the Discipleship Manual of Jesus as found in the Sermon on the Mount (Matt 5–7). James knows his readers are Christians and wants them to live in light of their identity. He knows they are brethren and he knows they have faith (Jas 1:2-3). So this letter contains practical teaching for Christians on how to live as the family of God in this world.

James 2:14-26 must be read in light of this overall theme of the letter. James does not want his readers to question whether or not they have eternal life, or whether or not their faith is "real." Instead, James has noticed a practical and relational issue in the church and is seeking to address it. What is this issue? It is that some Christians had daily, physical needs for food and clothing (2:15), and other Christians were responding to these needs by saying, "I believe God will provide for you" (2:16). James mocks this response by saying, "What good is that?" (2:16-17).

Not even the word "save" in James 2:14 indicates that James is writing about eternal life. The word "save" always means "deliverance" and only context can determine what kind of deliverance is in view. Here, James is writing about how a person can help save his Christian brethren from hunger and nakedness (2:15). Good works can also save our relationships with other Christians (1:19-20), and save our lives from premature physical death (1:21; 5:20). Good works can save women and orphans from being mistreated and abused (cf. Jas 1:27). So good works are critically important, and good works do "save" us, but they have no place in helping us gain and keep our eternal life, or prove that we have it.

So James is saying that when someone is hungry, naked, sick, lonely, or poor, faith, by itself, is worthless. James says, "Do not tell others that God will provide for their needs ... *you* provide for their needs. Do not tell them that you will pray for them ... *do something* for them. Do not speak a word of faith that they will be clothed and fed ... *you* clothe and feed them." James is saying that faith, by itself, does not fill bellies or provide warmth. Food and clothes do that. So it is good if you believe God can provide for the needs of others. But God wants to provide for their needs through you. This is what James is teaching.

James is saying that if you want to affect change in this world, don't stop at belief; you need to *do something*. While mental, emotional, spiritual, and psychological change can occur through changing our beliefs, bringing about physical change in this world and in the lives of others requires a change in behavior. Believing and praying that God will stop war, end poverty, and rescue children from slavery does nothing to actually accomplish these tasks. If you want there to be progress in these areas, you need to get out of your prayer closet and actually start working to bring about the change you want to see.

This does not mean that faith and prayer are ineffective. It means that they are ineffective *by themselves* to accomplish change in this world. Faith and prayer are to be the catalysts that help us see the heart of God and discuss with Him how He wants us to get involved in advancing His

Kingdom on earth. Faith and prayer provide the vision for how to get involved in the action of bringing heaven down to earth.

All of this is in relation to physical, worldly needs and issues. James does not have in view the spiritual need of eternal life, nor is he writing about this topic. James would agree that when it comes to the spiritual need of every person for eternal life from God, faith alone is enough, for faith is all that is needed. No amount of good works or human effort can ever achieve the righteousness of God (Jas 2:10). Eternal life is a spiritual need, and is therefore received through spiritual faith, and nothing else. James does not disagree with or modify this truth at all.

So James is not challenging whether or not people *really* believe, or whether or not their faith is *genuine*. He is just saying that when it comes to practical, physical needs of other people, faith, by itself, accomplishes nothing.

This leads to the second critical point that helps us understand what James is saying in these verses. Many people believe that James is teaching that true faith will lead to visible actions, so that if a person doesn't have the visible actions, this means they don't have true faith. But James is actually teaching the exact opposite truth. The point of James throughout these verses is that no one can ever *see* faith in someone else. James is teaching that faith is invisible, that it cannot be seen at all. James points this out in various ways throughout this section that actions and behaviors tell us almost nothing about what a person believes.

We see this first in James 2:14 where he writes, "If someone says he has faith." He does not write, "If someone has faith." Why not? Because we cannot see whether or not a person has faith. The only indication we have that someone else has a particular belief is if they tell us they have it. There is no other way to know what beliefs another person has. The NIV translation of this phrase as "if a man *claims* to have faith" is somewhat misleading, as it gives the impression that the man doesn't actually have the faith which he claims to have. But there is no other way to know what a person believes than by them telling us what they believe. So if they tell us they have a certain belief, since it is impossible to see into their mind if they truly do have this belief, we must give them the benefit of the doubt, and believe that they know what it is that they believe.

When people hear that it is impossible to see faith, someone always objects that behaviors truly do reveal beliefs. James is aware of this objection, and gives voice to it in 2:18-19. It is obvious from the phrase "But someone will say ..." that James has introduced the objection. What is not so obvious is where the objection ends. The NKJV puts it half-way through verse 18: "You have faith, and I have works." But the NASB puts the end-quote at the end of verse 18, so that the entire verse is included in the objection. Since Greek did not have quote marks, how can we know where the quote of the objector ends?

The answer is to understand the grammatical rules of "Epistolary Diatribe." Since ancient letter-writers did not have quote marks at their disposal, they used other methods in writing their letters (epistles) to indicate when they are dialoguing with someone who disagrees (diatribe). There were three basic rules (which are not universally applied in every instance). First, the words of the objector are introduced with the verb "say" or "said" (e.g., "You have heard it said," Or "But someone will say,"). Second, when the letter-writer wants to begin his refutation of this objection, he begins by inserting an adversative conjunction (e.g., "But" or "Of course not!"). Finally, to indicate his disagreement, the letter-writer includes a gentle mocking, or name-calling, of the person being refuted (e.g., "Who are you, Oh man?" or "Oh foolish man!"). Clear examples of this "Epistolary Diatribe" can be found in Romans 9:19-20 and 1 Corinthians 15:35-36.

James 2:18-20 is also a clear example of "Epistolary Diatribe." James introduces the objector with the words, "But someone will say." And where do we see an adversative conjunction followed by a gentle name-calling? Not in the middle of verse 18, or at the beginning of verse 19, but at the beginning of verse 20. James begins his refutation of the objector in verse 20 by saying, "*But* do you want to know, *O foolish man* ..." This means that all of verses 18 and 19 are the words of the objector.[26]

This helps us understand the overall argument and thought flow of James. It is the objector, not James, who argues that works reveal faith. It is the objector, not James, who says that the faith of demons is clearly seen in how demons tremble in fear before God. This means that when people quote James 2:19, "Even the demons believe," they are not quoting James, but somebody who disagrees with James. James does not disagree that demons have faith. Of course demons have faith! All beings believe things, including demons. Demons believe many things about God, themselves, and humanity. And many of their beliefs are correct beliefs. Indeed, in the context here, the objector says that the demons believe that God is one. This is a correct belief. James believes this; I believe it; and I hope you believe it too.

Note that nobody receives eternal life by believing that God is one. God gives eternal life to those humans who believe in Jesus for it. Eternal life has not been offered to demons, and there is no indication anywhere in Scripture that they believe in Jesus for eternal life. So people who use James 2:19 as a way to oppose the biblical gospel teaching that eternal life is by faith alone in Jesus Christ alone are simply revealing that they do not understand the offer of eternal life in the gospel, what it is that James is actually teaching in this passage, or that they are quoting with approval someone who actually disagrees with James.

So in 2:20, when James sets out to refute the objector, his point is to show the opposite of what the objector argued. Since the objector argued that faith *does* reveal itself by actions, James wants to show that it does *not*. And while the objector used the central Jewish statement of faith (God is One) as "Exhibit A," James uses the central Jewish example of faith as his Exhibit A. James uses the example of Abraham, the father of faith.

[26] One Bible translation which recognizes this structure is the *The Weymouth New Testament* (New York: Baker & Taylor, 1903).

In 2:21, James writes that Abraham was "justified by works when he offered Isaac his son on the altar." This is a very challenging verse for some Christians, because we have been taught that we are justified by faith, *not* by works (Rom 4:4-5). Yet James seems to say the exact opposite. The apparent contradiction is solved by noting that whenever Paul writes about Abrahams' justification by faith, he points to Abraham's justification *before God* as recorded in Genesis 15:6. But when James writes about Abraham's justification, he points to Genesis 22 where Abraham offered his son Isaac on the altar.

James is showing that while Abraham *said* he had faith in God (and indeed, Scripture says he did), no one could actually see this faith. In fact, quite often during the 25 (or more) years between his reported faith in Genesis 15 and his near-sacrifice of Isaac in Genesis 22, Abraham's actions seemed to indicate a complete lack of faith. His actions did *not* always match his "claim" to faith. But he did have faith.

So when James writes that Abraham was justified by works when he almost offered his son Isaac on the altar, he is not talking about justification by faith before God, but is talking about justification by works in the sight of men. Since humans cannot see faith, but can see actions, only actions can tell us anything about a person. For decades, Abraham had been saying that he was a friend of God, but it was only after Abraham almost sacrificed his son, and then was stopped from doing so by God, that people were able to see that Abraham truly was a friend of God (Jas 2:23). People saw his righteous actions, and so declared that he truly was righteous. He was justified by his works in the sight of other people.

Following this example, James puts the nail in the coffin of his objector's argument by using a complete opposite example. Since Abraham was the father of the Jewish faith, and was chosen by God, James shows that the same truths apply to Rahab, a female Gentile prostitute (Jas 2:25). She likely told the spies that she believed that God would hand Jericho over to them, but they had no way of seeing her faith. But she was justified by her works in their eyes when she did not hand them over to the authorities, but instead sent them out another way. Once again, faith by itself does nothing, and it cannot be seen by humans or verified by them. To actually help other people, it is works that are needed.

With all of this in mind, we now understand what James means by "dead faith" (Jas 2:19, 26). This is the third and final key which helps the meaning of James 2 become clear. Dead faith is not non-existent faith, spurious faith, fake faith, or false faith. Dead faith is ineffective faith. Dead faith is faith that exists, but doesn't *do* anything meaningful. Just like a dead body. The dead body exists, but it just lays there. It does not do what God intended bodies to do. Does a dead body exist? Yes, it does. A dead body is not a non-existent, spurious, fake, or false body. It is a real body. It simply is not functioning the way God intended or desired.

So also with faith. A dead faith is a real faith. It really exists. It is truly there. It is just unproductive and "unenergized." Just as the spirit energizes the body to help it actually *do* things in this world, so also, works energize faith to help it accomplish things in this world (Jas 2:26). While we cannot see faith, we can see actions, and should encourage people who say they have particular beliefs to energize their faith with their actions.

The person who says they have a particular belief should be praised and encouraged for having this belief. We have no reason to doubt someone when they say they believe something. If someone says they believe something, we should believe them. Since we cannot see into a person's heart or mind, and since actions do not irrefutably reveal what a person believes, if a person says they believe something, we have no good reason to doubt them.

But we have every right, says James, to remind a person that we cannot see their faith. Faith is invisible to the human eye. While faith alone is perfectly fine for receiving eternal life from God, faith by itself does nothing when it comes to interpersonal relationships and meeting human needs. So when a person says they believe that God will provide, meet a need, take care of a situation, heal, comfort, care, feed, clothe, or whatever the case may be, we can say, "It is wonderful that you believe this; but what are you going to *do* about it? I cannot see your faith, but I can see your actions, and in this situation, your actions are more beneficial than your faith."

So James does not contradict anything we have learned about faith in this book. He agrees that faith is not a work and that faith does not necessarily lead to works. He also agrees (and in fact proves) that works do not indicate anything one way or the other about a person's beliefs. Only God can see a person's heart and mind, and therefore, only God can see what a person believes. We humans can, however, see actions. This means that rather than tell people we believe that God will provide for them, or that we are praying for their needs, we should actually do something about their needs. Similarly, we must not make judgments about a person's beliefs (or their eternal destiny) based on their actions. Actions and good works are critically important for the Christian, but they do not help us gain eternal life, keep eternal life, or prove that we have eternal life.

CONCLUSION

There are many dozens of passages about faith that have not been considered in this chapter. But hopefully the sampling of texts discussed above provides a framework for how all the other texts can also be understood. And hopefully, as you have read and studied these texts on your own, you have come to be persuaded by some new ideas about faith. In other words, I hope that the evidence provided in this chapter from Scripture brought you to the place where you changed some of your beliefs about belief. This is, after all, how faith works.

CONCLUSION

This book was written in reverse. Though the first several chapters of this book presented several key truths about faith and then concluded with a chapter that considered several key biblical passages about faith, the initial study and research for this book went in the opposite direction. I originally believed something very different about faith than I do now. But as I set out to study what the Scriptures teach about faith, I uncovered some truths from the various texts that convinced and persuaded me to change my beliefs about belief. Maybe the same thing has happened with you.

But regardless of what you now believe about belief, I would like to end this book with two final exhortations.

First, no matter how you view faith, never let go of the truth that eternal life is received by grace alone through faith alone in Jesus Christ alone. This central gospel truth is a guiding light for all other truths in Scripture. Those who neglect or forsake this truth always end up traveling some strange doctrinal paths. So hold on to this truth and let your study of Scripture continually affirm and support it, for this is one of the central truths of the Bible. As you hold on to this central gospel truth, Jesus will, by His Spirit, uphold and guide you into all truth.

Second, as long as you know that you are safe and secure in the arms of Jesus, you will never need to be afraid of changing or challenging your beliefs. Knowing that you cannot ever be taken out of God's hands will give you the courage to tread where few others dare to go. You will have no fear of doubt or deception, because you know that God will keep you safe and secure. This is the only recipe for moving forward with your faith and taking the next step in your adventure with God.

So have you encountered hard questions? Ask away, knowing that God will show you the answers you seek. Do you have fears? Leap into the great unknown, trusting that God will raise you up. Do you have doubts? Embrace them, for doubt is the first step on the road to truth. Do you wonder where God is taking you? Jump into the wheelbarrow and enjoy the ride.

Faith is an adventure of the mind, and you are now set free to follow the road wherever it goes.

AFTERWORD

"Blessed assurance! Jesus is mine!"
–Fanny Crosby

Christians often will sing what they are too afraid to say. I sincerely believe more doctrinal truth has been transferred from one generation of Christians to the next through the songs that are sung than through the sermons that are heard or the books that are read. Fanny Crosby's famous hymn declares, with boldness and clarity that is not common enough among Christians today, her absolute assurance regarding her standing in Christ. It seems some people are afraid if they allow themselves to seem too confident in their eternal life, or if they give others confidence of their own eternal life, then perhaps Christians will lose their motivation for serving God. Others fear they might become too "dogmatic," rigidly holding to things the rest of the culture knows to be false. Nothing could be further from the truth.

I would encourage you, reader, to go back over the short "Conclusion" section of this book one more time. Assurance of your eternal life, or to use Jeremy's expression (borrowed from another Crosby hymn), knowing you are "safe and secure in the arms of Jesus" is the starting point of spiritual growth. If you are shaky on whether or not God even accepts you, or if you fear that perhaps He might at some point cease to accept you, then all of your attempts at serving Him will be tinged with fear and frustration, rather than growing from the love, joy, and peace that comes from a life lived in the Holy Spirit.

This is where I believe the importance of this book lies. Confidence in your belief can not long endure without some understanding of what it actually means to believe. In a Christian environment where everyone seems to agree that eternal life is by faith alone, the greatest danger to a believer's assurance is a challenge to the definition of the word "faith." Many caution the questioning Christian with statements like "Sure, eternal life is by faith alone, but is what you have *actually* faith?" This book equips the believer to have a strong and satisfying answer.

It is likely, as you continue along your spiritual journey, you will be confronted with the kind of teaching Jeremy described in the early parts of the book. A well-meaning but dangerously misguided teacher will likely try to cause his hearers to avoid particular sins or to be more zealous in their service when he brings up some of the verses Jeremy mentioned in his last chapter. Especially using James 2, such teachers will suggest that perhaps your faith is not actually "real," or perhaps is not strong enough, or maybe it's the wrong "kind" of faith. Likely this will be followed by an admonition to prove the genuineness of your faith, both to others as well as to yourself, by doing certain works or by abstaining from certain sins. This is, of course, getting the cart dangerously ahead of the horse, and will inevitably lead to the frustrating experience described in Romans 7:14-24. Legalism is operating under the principle of Law. "To be acceptable to God you must do ..." Grace is the opposite. Grace says all "doings" are able to be done because of the fact that you are already accepted by God. The opportunity to serve Him, as well as our being equipped to serve, are just more gifts that He is pleased to give.

So now, dear reader, having read this book you have been well-taught and are now well-equipped. When someone tries to cause you to question the validity of your faith, whether it be a human teacher or simply your own weakness of conscience, you need not be deceived. If you think that your only options are to look at your own righteousness scorecard, to look internally to see if you have been sufficiently transformed to merit assurance of a genuine faith, then you would be headed for great turmoil of soul, and likely to ineffectiveness is service.

But since you now know what faith is, you know the better solution. I admonish you, remember what you have learned. Don't look to yourself, to your zeal in service, your avoidance of particular sins, or even to the "degree" of strength of your faith. Do not look to yourself at all. Instead, look always and only to Jesus. Look at His divine power and His infinite love. Look to His finished work on the cross. It is He who is the "perfecter of your faith" (Heb 12:2), and there is no work the Holy Spirit loves to do more than to make much of Him. With your spiritual eyes on the Savior, the Giver of eternal life to all who believe, all worry about yourself fades to nothing. The more you see of Him, the more your heart will say with the apostle Paul (as you've likely sung more times than you can remember):

"I know whom I have believed, and am persuaded that he is able …"[1]

–Kent Young
Contributing author at TheGracelings.com,
ThinkOutsidePolitics.com,
and SeekerOfChrist.org

---

[1] 2 Timothy 1:12, as sung in the hymn "I Know Whom I Have Believed" by D. W. Whittle.

ABOUT J. D. MYERS

J. D. (Jeremy) Myers is a popular author, blogger, podcaster, and Bible teacher who lives in Oregon with his wife and three daughters. He primarily writes at RedeemingGod.com, where he seeks to help liberate people from the shackles of religion. His site also provides an online discipleship group where thousands of like-minded people discuss life and theology and encourage each other to follow Jesus into the world.

If you appreciated the content of this book, would you consider recommending it to your friends and leaving a review online? Thanks!

JOIN JEREMY MYERS AND LEARN MORE

Take Bible and theology courses by joining Jeremy at
RedeemingGod.com/join/
Receive updates about free books, discounted books,
and new books by joining Jeremy at
RedeemingGod.com/read-books/

WHAT IS HELL? THE TRUTH ABOUT HELL AND HOW TO AVOID IT

Have you ever wondered if you are going to hell?

Many people are terrified about going to hell when they die. And for good reason. If hell is a fiery torture chamber where lost souls scream in agony for all eternity, everybody should be worried about meeting such a terrible fate.

But is this really what the Bible teaches about hell?

In *What is Hell?*, author J. D. Myers answers your most pressing questions about hell. After summarizing the three common views about hell, this book presents a fourth view. Myers defends this alternative view by showing how the concept of hell evolved over time, and then considers eight terms from Scripture that have traditionally been equated with hell.

As you read, you will learn the truth about hell. You will discover what hell is, where hell is, how you can avoid going to hell, and how you can rescue people who are in hell.

The book includes an Appendix which explains most of the key biblical texts that have traditionally been used to defend the doctrine of hell.

Read this book to be delivered from both the fear and fire of hell.

REVIEWS

My eyes have been opened and my understanding has changed for the better. I believe this book is a must-read for most Christians. The reason for the death of Jesus has also become so much clearer to me from reading this book. It just makes more sense now. This book will be used by me as a reference in the future so I will read it again. –Pete Nellmapius

This may be Jeremy's best book yet! What is more important than defending God's character? Jeremy shows in a scholarly but readable way that the traditional understanding of Hell does not actually exist. The Great News is that you don't have to defend or imagine God tortures people for beliefs while living for a short time on earth. – Mike Edwards - Writing at: What-God-May-Really-Be-Like

Reading this book was a powerful, transformative experience! With every new chapter of explication, from Genesis to Revelation, I gained a fuller understanding of hell. And, with this Biblical understanding came a deeper sense of God's sovereignty, brilliance, and love. I've already read it twice and each time I find myself enlightened and rejuvenated. It's as thorough as a textbook, yet it's easy to read. Chalk that up to Jeremy's gift for clear writing. I'd say I'm stoked about this book (pun intended). –Elaine O'Connor

I've enjoyed every book of Mr. Myers until this one. But this one i LOVED! The book goes through great lengths in explaining how the Kingdom of Heaven that Jesus came to bring unto our world is opposed to the Kingdom of Hell that rules the Earth. And how Hell has been under siege ever since. –ThePilgrimm

Jeremy Myers does an exceptional job explaining the critical passages of the bible that are typically used to teach that there is a hell waiting for all of us sinners. He always is exceptional in explaining the original text and making it easy to understand. This is a great book if you are trying to understand this topic and I feel you will come away with a much greater understanding. –Jim Maus

NOTHING BUT THE BLOOD OF JESUS: HOW THE SACRIFICE OF JESUS SAVES THE WORLD FROM SIN

Do you have difficulties reconciling God's behavior in the Old Testament with that of Jesus in the New?

Do you find yourself trying to rationalize God's violent demeanor in the Bible to unbelievers or even to yourself?

Does it seem disconcerting that God tells us not to kill others but He then takes part in some of the bloodiest wars and vindictive genocides in history?

The answer to all such questions is found in Jesus on the cross. By focusing your eyes on Jesus Christ and Him crucified, you come to understand that God was never angry at human sinners, and that no blood sacrifice was ever needed to purchase God's love, forgiveness, grace, and mercy.

In *Nothing but the Blood of Jesus*, J. D. Myers shows how the death of Jesus on the cross reveals the truth about the five concepts of sin, law, sacrifice, scapegoating, and bloodshed. After carefully defining each, this book shows how these definitions provide clarity on numerous biblical texts.

REVIEWS

Building on his previous book, "The Atonement of God," the work of René Girard and a solid grounding in the Scriptures, Jeremy Myers shares fresh and challenging insights with us about sin, law, sacrifice, scapegoating and blood. This book reveals to us how truly precious the blood of Jesus is and the way of escaping the cycle of blame, rivalry, scapegoating, sacrifice and violence that has plagued humanity since the time of Cain and Abel. *Nothing but the Blood of Jesus* is an important and timely literary contribution to a world desperately in need of the non-violent message of Jesus. –Wesley Rostoll

My heart was so filled with joy while reading this book. Jeremy you've reminded me once more that as you walk with Jesus and spend time in His presence, He talks to you and reveals Himself through the Scriptures. – Reader

THE ATONEMENT OF GOD: BUILDING YOUR THEOLOGY ON A CRUCIVISION OF GOD

After reading this book, you will never read the Bible the same way again.

By reading this book, you will learn to see God in a whole new light. You will also learn to see yourself in a whole new light, and learn to live life in a whole new way.

The book begins with a short explanation of the various views of the atonement, including an explanation and defense of the "Non-Violent View" of the atonement. This view argues that God did not need or demand the death of Jesus in order to forgive sins. In fact, God has never been angry with us at all, but has always loved and always forgiven.

Following this explanation of the atonement, J. D. Myers takes you on a journey through 10 areas of theology which are radically changed and transformed by the Non-Violent view of the atonement. Read this book, and let your life and theology look more and more like Jesus Christ!

REVIEWS

> Outstanding book! Thank you for helping me understand "Crucivision" and the "Non-Violent Atonement." Together, they help it all make sense and fit so well into my personal thinking about God. I am encouraged to be truly free to love and forgive, because God has always loved and forgiven without condition, because Christ exemplified this grace on the Cross, and because the Holy Spirit is in the midst of all life, continuing to show the way through people like you. –Samuel R. Mayer

> This book gives another view of the doctrines we have been taught all of our lives. And this actually makes more sense than what we have heard. I myself

have had some of these thoughts but couldn't quite make the sense of it all by myself. J.D. Myers helped me answer some questions and settle some confusion for my doctrinal views. This is truly a refreshing read. Jesus really is the demonstration of who God is and God is much easier to understand than being so mean and vindictive in the Old Testament. The tension between the wrath of God and His justice and the love of God are eased when reading this understanding of the atonement. Read with an open mind and enjoy! –Clare N. Bez

THE RE-JUSTIFICATION OF GOD: A STUDY OF ROMANS 9:10-24

Romans 9 has been a theological battleground for centuries. Scholars from all perspectives have debated whether Paul is teaching corporate or individual election, whether or not God truly hates Esau, and how to understand the hardening of Pharaoh's heart. Both sides have accused the other of misrepresenting God.

In this book, J. D. Myers presents a mediating position. Gleaning from both Calvinistic and Arminian insights into Romans 9, J. D. Myers presents a beautiful portrait of God as described by the pen of the Apostle Paul.

Here is a way to read Romans 9 which allows God to remain sovereign and free, but also allows our theology to avoid the deterministic tendencies which have entrapped certain systems of the past.

Read this book and—maybe for the first time—learn to see God the way Paul saw Him.

REVIEWS

Fantastic read! Jeremy Myers has a gift for seeing things from outside of the box and making it easy to understand for the rest of us. The Re - Justification of God provides a fresh and insightful look into Romans 9:10-24 by interpreting it within the context of chapters 9-11 and then fitting it into the framework of Paul's entire epistle as well. Jeremy manages to provide a solid theological exegesis on a widely misunderstood portion of scripture without it sounding to academic. Most importantly, it provides us with a better view and understanding of who God is. If I had a list of ten books

that I thought every Christian should read, this one would be on the list.
–Wesley Rostoll

I loved this book! It made me cry and fall in love with God all over again. Romans is one of my favorite books, but now my eyes have been opened to what Paul was really saying. I knew in my heart that God was the good guy, but J. D. Myers provided the analysis to prove the text. ... I can with great confidence read the difficult chapters of Romans, and my furrowed brow is eased. Thank you, J. D. Myers. I love God, even more and am so grateful that his is so longsuffering in his perfect love! Well done. –Treinhart

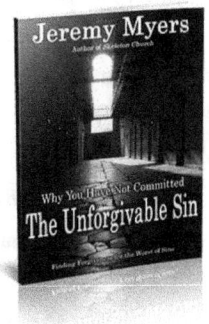

WHY YOU HAVE NOT COM-MITTED THE UNFORGIVABLE SIN: FINDING FORGIVENESS FOR THE WORST OF SINS

Are you afraid that you have committed the unforgivable sin?

In this book, you will learn what this sin is and why you have not committed it. After surveying the various views about blasphemy against the Holy Spirit and examining Matthew 12:31-32, you will learn what the sin is and how it is committed.

As a result of reading this book, you will gain freedom from the fear of committing the worst of all sins, and learn how much God loves you!

REVIEWS

> This book addressed things I have struggled and felt pandered to for years, and helped to bring wholeness to my heart again. –Natalie Fleming

> A great read, on a controversial subject; biblical, historical and contextually treated to give the greatest understanding. May be the best on this subject (and there is very few) ever written. – Tony Vance

> You must read this book. Forgiveness is necessary to see your blessings. So if you purchase this book, [you will have] no regrets. –Virtuous Woman

> Jeremy Myers covers this most difficult topic thoroughly and with great compassion. –J. Holland

> Wonderful explication of the unpardonable sin. God loves you more than you know. May Jesus Christ be with you always. –Robert M Sawin III

> Excellent book! Highly recommend for anyone who has anxiety and fear about having committed the unforgivable sin. –William Tom

As someone who is constantly worried that they have disappointed or offended God, this book was, quite literally, a "Godsend." I thought I had committed this sin as I swore against the Holy Spirit in my mind. It only started after reading the verse about it in the Bible. The swear words against Him came into my mind over and over and I couldn't seem to stop no matter how much I prayed. I was convinced I was going to hell and cried constantly. I was extremely worried and depressed. This book has allowed me to breathe again, to have hope again. Thank you, Jeremy. I will read and reread. I believe this book was definitely God inspired. I only wish I had found it sooner. –Sue

SKELETON CHURCH: A BARE-BONES DEFINITION OF CHURCH (PREFACE TO THE CLOSE YOUR CHURCH FOR GOOD BOOK SERIES)

The church has a skeleton which is identical in all types of churches. Unity and peace can develop in Christianity if we recognize this skeleton as the simple, bare-bones definition of church. But when we focus on the outer trappings—the skin, hair, and eye color, the clothes, the muscle tone, and other outward appearances—division and strife form within the church.

Let us return to the skeleton church and grow in unity once again.

REVIEWS

I worried about buying another book that aimed at reducing things to a simple minimum, but the associations of the author along with the price gave me reason to hope and means to see. I really liked this book. First, because it wasn't identical to what other simple church people are saying. He adds unique elements that are worth reading. Second, the size is small enough to read, think, and pray about without getting lost. –Abel Barba

In *Skeleton Church*, Jeremy Myers makes us rethink church. For Myers, the church isn't a style of worship, a row of pews, or even a building. Instead, the church is the people of God, which provides the basic skeletal structure of the church. The muscles, parts, and flesh of the church are how we carry Jesus' mission into our own neighborhoods in our own unique ways. This eBook will make you see the church differently. –Travis Mamone

This book gets back to the basics of the New Testament church—who we are as Christians and what our perspective should be in the world we live in today. Jeremy cuts away all the institutional layers of a church and gets to the heart of our purpose as Christians in the world we live in and how to affect the people around us with God heart and view in mind. Not a physical church in mind. It was a great book and I have read it twice now. –Vaughn Bender

The Skeleton Church ... Oh. My. Word. Why aren't more people reading this!? It was well-written, explained everything beautifully, and it was one of the best explanations of how God intended for church to be. Not to mention an easy read! The author took it all apart, the church, and showed us how it should be. He made it real. If you are searching to find something or someone to show you what God intended for the church, this is the book you need to read. –Ericka

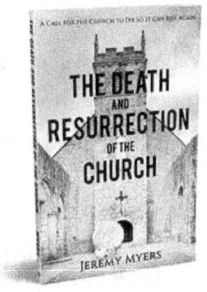

THE DEATH AND RESURRECTION OF THE CHURCH (VOLUME 1 IN THE CLOSE YOUR CHURCH FOR GOOD BOOK SERIES)

In a day when many are looking for ways to revitalize the church, Jeremy Myers argues that the church should die … so that it can rise again.

This is not only because of the universal principle that death precedes resurrection, but also because the church has adopted certain Satanic values and goals and the only way to break free from our enslavement to these values is to die.

But death will not be the end of the church, just as death was not the end of Jesus. If the church follows Jesus into death, and even to the hellish places on earth, it is only then that the church will rise again to new life and vibrancy in the Kingdom of God.

REVIEWS

I have often thought on the church and how its acceptance of corporate methods and assimilation of cultural media mores taints its mission but Jeremy Myers eloquently captures in words the true crux of the matter—that the church is not a social club for do-gooders but to disseminate the good news to all the nooks and crannies in the world and particularly and primarily those bastions in the reign of evil. That the "gates of Hell" Jesus pronounces indicate that the church is in an offensive, not defensive, posture as gates are defensive structures.

I must confess that in reading I was inclined to be in agreement as many of the same thinkers that Myers riffs upon have influenced me also—Walter Wink, Robert Farrar Capon, Greg Boyd, NT Wright, etc. So as I read, I frequently nodded my head in agreement. –GN Trifanaff

The book is well written, easy to understand, organized and consistent thoughts. It rightfully makes the reader at least think about things as ... is "the way we have always done it" necessarily the Biblical or Christ-like way, or is it in fact very sinful?! I would recommend the book for pastors and church officers; those who have the most moving-and-shaking clout to implement changes, or keep things the same. –Joel M. Wilson

Absolutely phenomenal. Unless we let go of everything Adamic in our nature, we cannot embrace anything Christlike. For the church to die, we the individual temples must dig our graves. It is a must read for all who take issues about the body of Christ seriously. –Mordecai Petersburg

PUT SERVICE BACK INTO THE CHURCH SERVICE (VOLUME 2 IN THE CLOSE YOUR CHURCH FOR GOOD BOOK SERIES)

Churches around the world are trying to revitalize their church services. There is almost nothing they will not try. Some embark on multi-million dollar building campaigns while others sell their buildings to plant home churches. Some hire celebrity pastors to attract crowds of people, while others hire no clergy so that there can be open sharing in the service.

Yet despite everything churches have tried, few focus much time, money, or energy on the one thing that churches are supposed to be doing: loving and serving others like Jesus.

Put Service Back into the Church Service challenges readers to follow a few simple principles and put a few ideas into practice which will help churches of all types and sizes make serving others the primary emphasis of a church service.

REVIEWS

Jeremy challenges church addicts, those addicted to an unending parade of church buildings, church services, Bible studies, church programs and more to follow Jesus into our communities, communities filled with lonely, hurting people and BE the church, loving the people in our world with the love of Jesus. Do we need another training program, another seminar, another church building, a remodeled church building, more staff, updated music, or does our world need us, the followers of Jesus, to BE the church in the world? The book is well-written, challenging and a book that really can make a difference not only in our churches, but also and especially in our neighborhoods and communities. –Charles Epworth

I just finished *Put Service Back Into Church Service* by Jeremy Myers, and as with his others books I have read on the church, it was very challenging. For those who love Jesus, but are questioning the function of the traditional brick and mortar church, and their role in it, this is a must read. It may be a bit unsettling to the reader who is still entrenched in traditional "church," but it will make you think, and possibly re-evaluate your role in the church. Get this book, and all others on the church by Jeremy. –Ward Kelly

DYING TO RELIGION AND EMPIRE (VOLUME 3 IN THE CLOSE YOUR CHURCH FOR GOOD BOOK SERIES)

Could Christianity exist without religious rites or legal rights? In *Dying to Religion and Empire*, I not only answer this question with an emphatic "Yes!" but argue that if the church is going to thrive in the coming decades, we must give up our religious rites and legal rights.

Regarding religious rites, I call upon the church to abandon the quasi-magical traditions of water baptism and the Lord's Supper and transform or redeem these practices so that they reflect the symbolic meaning and intent which they had in New Testament times.

Furthermore, the church has become far too dependent upon certain legal rights for our continued existence. Ideas such as the right to life, liberty, and the pursuit of happiness are not conducive to living as the people of God who are called to follow Jesus into servanthood and death. Also, reliance upon the freedom of speech, the freedom of assembly, and other such freedoms as established by the Bill of Rights have made the church a servant of the state rather than a servant of God and the gospel. Such freedoms must be forsaken if we are going to live within the rule and reign of God on earth.

This book not only challenges religious and political liberals but conservatives as well. It is a call to leave behind the comfortable religion we know, and follow Jesus into the uncertain and wild ways of radical discipleship. To rise and live in the reality of God's Kingdom, we must first die to religion and empire.

REVIEWS

Jeremy is one of the freshest, freest authors out there— and you need to hear what he has to say. This book is startling and new in thought and conclusion. Are the "sacraments" inviolate? Why? Do you worship at a secular altar? Conservative? Liberal? Be prepared to open your eyes. Mr. Myers will not let you keep sleeping!

Jeremy Myers is one or the most thought provoking authors that I read, this book has really helped me to look outside the box and start thinking how can I make more sense of my relationship with Christ and how can I show others in a way that impacts them the way that Jesus' disciples impacted their world. Great book, great author. –Brett Hotchkiss

CHURCH IS MORE THAN BODIES, BUCKS, & BRICKS (VOLUME 4 IN THE CLOSE YOUR CHURCH FOR GOOD BOOK SERIES)

Many people define church as a place and time where people gather, a way for ministry money to be given and spent, and a building in which people regularly meet on Sunday mornings.

In this book, author and blogger Jeremy Myers shows that church is more than bodies, bucks, and bricks.

Church is the people of God who follow Jesus into the world, and we can be the church no matter how many people we are with, no matter the size of our church budget, and regardless of whether we have a church building or not.

By abandoning our emphasis on more people, bigger budgets, and newer buildings, we may actually liberate the church to better follow Jesus into the world.

REVIEWS

This book does more than just identify issues that have been bothering me about church as we know it, but it goes into history and explains how we got here. In this way it is similar to Viola's *Pagan Christianity*, but I found it a much more enjoyable read. Jeremy goes into more detail on the three issues he covers as well as giving a lot of practical advice on how to remedy these situations. –Portent

Since I returned from Africa 20 years ago I have struggled with going to church back in the States. This book helped me not feel guilty and has helped me process this struggle. It is challenging and overflows with practical suggestions. He loves the church despite its imperfections and suggests ways to break the bondage we find ourselves in. –Truealian

Jeremy Meyers always writes a challenging book ... It seems the American church (as a whole) is very comfortable with the way things are ... The challenge is to get out of the brick and mortar buildings and stagnant programs and minister to the needy in person with funds in hand to meet their needs especially to the widows and orphans as we are directed in the scriptures. –GGTexas

CRUCIFORM PASTORAL LEADERSHIP (VOLUME 5 IN THE CLOSE YOUR CHURCH FOR GOOD BOOK SERIES)

This book is forthcoming in early 2019.

The final volume in the *Close Your Church for Good* book series look at issues related to pastoral leadership in the church. It discusses topics such as preaching and pastoral pay from the perspective of the cross.

The best way pastors can lead their church is by following Jesus to the cross!

This book will be published in early 2019.

ADVENTURES IN FISHING (FOR MEN)

Adventures in Fishing (for Men) is a satirical look at evangelism and church growth strategies.

Using fictional accounts from his attempts to become a world-famous fisherman, Jeremy Myers shows how many of the evangelism and church growth strategies of today do little to actually reach the world for Jesus Christ.

Adventures in Fishing (for Men) pokes fun at some of the popular evangelistic techniques and strategies endorsed and practiced by many Christians in today's churches. The stories in this book show in humorous detail how little we understand the culture that surrounds us or how to properly reach people with the gospel of Jesus Christ. The story also shows how much time, energy, and money goes into evangelism preparation and training with the end result being that churches rarely accomplish any actual evangelism.

REVIEWS

I found *Adventures in Fishing* (*For Men*) quite funny! Jeremy Myers does a great job shining the light on some of the more common practices in Evangelism today. His allegory gently points to the foolishness that is found within a system that takes the preaching of the gospel and tries to reduce it to a simplified formula. A formula that takes what should be an organic, Spirit led experience and turns it into a gospel that is nutritionally benign.

If you have ever EE'd someone you may find Myers' book offensive, but if you have come to the place where you realize that Evangelism isn't a matter of a script and checklists, then you might benefit from this light-hearted peek at Evangelism today. –Jennifer L. Davis

Adventures in Fishing (for Men) is good book in understanding evangelism to be more than just being a set of methods or to do list to follow. –Ashok Daniel

CHRISTMAS REDEMPTION: WHY CHRISTIANS SHOULD CELEBRATE A PAGAN HOLIDAY

Christmas Redemption looks at some of the symbolism and traditions of Christmas, including gifts, the Christmas tree, and even Santa Claus and shows how all of these can be celebrated and enjoyed by Christians as a true and accurate reflection of the gospel.

Though Christmas used to be a pagan holiday, it has been redeemed by Jesus.

If you have been told that Christmas is a pagan holiday and is based on the Roman festival of Saturnalia, or if you have been told that putting up a Christmas tree is idolatrous, or if you have been told that Santa Claus is Satanic and teaches children to be greedy, then you must read this book! In it, you will learn that all of these Christmas traditions have been redeemed by Jesus and are good and healthy ways of celebrating the truth of the gospel and the grace of Jesus Christ.

REVIEWS

Too many times we as Christians want to condemn nearly everything around us and in so doing become much like the Pharisees and religious leaders that Jesus encountered. I recommend this book to everyone who has concerns of how and why we celebrate Christmas. I recommend it to those who do not have any qualms in celebrating but may not know the history of Christmas. I recommend this book to everyone, no matter who or where you are, no matter your background or beliefs, no matter whether you are young or old. –David H.

Very informative book dealing with the roots of our modern Christmas traditions. The Biblical teaching on redemption is excellent! Highly recommended. –Tamara

This is a wonderful book full of hope and joy. The book explains where Christmas traditions originated and how they have been changed and been adapted over the years. The hope that the grace that is hidden in the celebrations will turn more hearts to the Lord's call is very evident. Jeremy Myers has given us a lovely gift this Christmas. His insights will lift our hearts and remain with us a long time. –Janet Cardoza

I love how the author uses multiple sources to back up his opinions. He doesn't just use bible verses, he goes back into the history of the topics (pagan rituals, Santa, etc.) as well. Great book! –Jenna G.

JOIN JEREMY MYERS AND LEARN MORE

Take Bible and theology courses by joining Jeremy at
RedeemingGod.com/join/

Receive updates about free books, discounted books, and new books by joining Jeremy at
RedeemingGod.com/read-books/

www.ingramcontent.com/pod-product-compliance
Lightning Source LLC
Chambersburg PA
CBHW070105120526
44588CB00032B/901